Easy HTML-DB Oracle Applica

Create Dynamic Web Pages with OAE

Michael Cunningham
Kent Crotty

RAMPANT
TECHPRESS

Two years ago if you would have asked me my net worth, I probably would have taken a guess and given you a number. Today if you were to ask, the answer would simply be "My Family." First of all, my wife, for supporting my goal of writing a book and giving up those cozy evenings together. My daughter, Marisol, who looked over my shoulder and corrected my punctuation (until I asked her to stop making me feel bad), and Tatiana, with her kind heart, who would tell me she was going to bed early so I could work on the book. If the only thing I get out of writing this book is knowing how much support they have given me it will be enough. I'm not sure how I will repay them, but I have no doubt they will come up with something creative.

For those reason's, and so many more.
This is for my family,

Maria, Marisol, and Tatiana

I Love You

Easy HTML-DB Oracle Application Express
Create Dynamic Web Pages with OAE

By Michael Cunningham & Kent Crotty

Copyright © 2006 by Rampant TechPress. All rights reserved.

Printed in the United States of America.

Easy Oracle Series Book #3

Published by: Rampant TechPress, Kittrell, NC, USA

Editors: John Lavender, Janet Burleson, and Robin Haden

Production Editor: Teri Wade

Production Manager: Linda Webb

Cover Design: Bryan Hoff

Illustrations: Mike Reed

Printing History: March 2006 for First Edition

ISBN: 0-9761573-1-4

Library of Congress Control Number: 2005928016

Table of Contents

Using the Online Code Depot

Purchase of this book provides complete access to the online code depot that contains the sample code scripts. All of the code depot scripts in this book are located at the following URL:

rampant.cc/html_db.htm

All of the code scripts in this book are available for download in zip format, ready to load and use. If technical assistance is needed with downloading or accessing the scripts, please contact Rampant TechPress at info@rampant.cc.

Are you WISE?

Get the premier Oracle tuning tool. The Workload Interface Statistical Engine for Oracle provides unparallel capability for time-series Oracle tuning, unavailable nowhere else.

WISE supplements Oracle Enterprise Manager and it can quickly plot and spot performance signatures to allow you to see hidden trends, fast.

WISE interfaces with STATSPACK or AWR to provide unprecedented proactive tuning insights. Best of all, it is only $9.95. Get WISE download Now!

www.wise-oracle.com

Got Scripts?

This is the complete Oracle script collection from Mike Ault and Donald Burleson, the world's best Oracle DBA's.

Packed with over 600 ready-to-use Oracle scripts, this is the definitive collection for every Oracle professional DBA. It would take many years to develop these scripts from scratch, making this download the best value in the Oracle industry.

It's only $49.95 (less than 7 cents per script!). For immediate download go to:

www.oracle-script.com

Conventions Used in this Book

It is critical for any technical publication to follow rigorous standards and employ consistent punctuation conventions to make the text easy to read.

However, this is not an easy task. Within Oracle there are many types of notation that can confuse a reader. Some Oracle utilities such as STATSPACK and TKPROF are always spelled in CAPITAL letters, while Oracle parameters and procedures have varying naming conventions in the Oracle documentation. It is also important to remember that many Oracle commands are case sensitive, and are always left in their original executable form, and never altered with italics or capitalization.

Hence, all Rampant TechPress books follow these conventions:

Parameters - All Oracle parameters will be *lowercase italics*. Exceptions to this rule are parameter arguments that are commonly capitalized (KEEP pool, TKPROF), these will be left in ALL CAPS.

Variables - All PL/SQL program variables and arguments will also remain in *lowercase italics (dbms_job, dbms_utility)*.

Tables & dictionary objects – All data dictionary objects are referenced in *lowercase italics (dba_indexes, v$sql)*. This includes all *v$* and *x$* views (*x$kcbcbh, v$parameter*) and dictionary views (*dba_tables, user_indexes*).

SQL - All SQL is formatted for easy use in the code depot. The main SQL terms (select, from, where, group by, order by, having) will always appear on a separate line.

Programs & Products - All products and programs that are known to the author are capitalized according to the vendor specifications (IBM, DBXray, etc). All names known by Rampant TechPress to be trademark names appear in this text as initial caps. References to UNIX are always made in uppercase.

Acknowledgments

Mary Schilling, our technical editor. There is no way the quality of the book would have been what we feel it is now without Mary's dedication to technical editing. Mary put in several hours of work and we were often emailing back-and-forth until wee hours of the night. And she did all this for us with the small payment of a hug. We couldn't have done it without you Mary.

Kent Crotty, my co-author, played a big part in getting this book to the printer. I am grateful to Kent for joining me in the writing of this book and for becoming a friend in the process.

Robin Haden, our copy editor who would say things like "Don't worry about it – even a little bit." Those statements helped put a first time author's mind at ease and relieve some of the stress of writing.

I would also like to express my gratitude to the production team at Rampant Publishing, especially Ellie Tuck and Linda Webb.

Without the guidance and encouragement of Don & Janet Burleson I would have never been able to complete the task of writing a book. I thank them for having faith in me and giving me this chance.

Thank you to all,

Michael W. Cunningham

Preface

First of all, Kent and I would like to thank you for buying our book. You have in your hands a book written by two guys who believe in this product and who have enjoyed the freedom it offers. All developers need to develop applications in Oracle Application Express is a browser. We've been in situations where we were able to login to a system to fix something remotely with nothing more than a browser. In my case, it was from a beach chair in Half Moon Bay, California. Kent did a little better than I since he was on the beach of a Caribbean Island. Vacation? Maybe, maybe not. It's just where we decided our offices should be for those weeks.

– That's freedom.

HTML DB was officially renamed Oracle Application Express (OAE) on January 30, 2006. Just enough time to kick us into gear and change the cover of the book to reflect the new name; however, there was no time to redo all the references in the book. That will have to wait until next time. On the Oracle forum, OAE is already being affectionately called Apex. In fact, the new URL to obtain a hosted environment for OAE development is http://apex.oracle.com.

Many have wondered about the robustness of OAE, but that can be disputed no more. Metalink, one of Oracles most visible web applications has been re-written in OAE thereby showing Oracle's commitment to the product. Another new product release from Oracle is Oracle Database 10g Express Edition. The management application to administer the Oracle Express database was also written in OAE.

Oracle Express edition is a free version of Oracle that allows you to create databases up to 4GB in size. Other limits exist such as a 1GB of memory max and it will only use 1 CPU. It comes with OAE built in, so you could literally be up and running ready to start building applications with OAE in less than 10 minutes.

Oracle has a hosted site available to you for developing applications in OAE. It cannot be used for anything production, but it is easy to obtain a workspace and start developing applications on a server provided by Oracle. The OAE forum is available for online support and is located at http://forums.oracle.com/forums/forum.jspa?forumID=137. I sincerely encourage you to use this resource. It is one of the most active forums

Oracle has, and you will find the developers of OAE spending time there answering questions. I have received help directly from the developers by recreating a problem on the Oracle hosted site where they were able to see the issue and provide a solution. I do not know of any other product where you can get support like that.

The Code Depot includes the source code mentioned in the book and also includes an application called EASY Samples. During the course of the book, you will build two applications. One serves as a 'Hello World' application in chapter 4 and the other is built during exercises in the remaining chapters. At the end, you will have built an application that you can use for reference when needed. The EASY Samples application provided in the code depot is a copy of the application Kent and I built during the writing of the book, plus some extras. There is one final application provided in the Code Depot called TheRVLot. This is a real application that will be online soon after the production release of Oracle Database 10g Express Edition. You will have the source code for the application, and you will be able to find the real world application at www.thervlot.net. Finally, you have www.easyhtml-db.com which will be filled with tips, a wiki, a forum, and excerpts from our book.

Enjoy the book and enjoy creating web applications in Oracle Application Express.

Michael and Kent

General Installation and Configuration

HTML DB is so EASY, I wrote my own eCommerce application.

Introduction to the Basics

The installation and configuration is probably not going to be the most popular part of any book as most readers would much rather get to the development part of the book. However, for anyone not having access to an installation of HTML DB, this section should get one up and running in about two hours, depending on download speeds. If HTML DB is already installed somewhere, this section can be skipped and used as reference at a later date when it is needed.

An alternative to spending time on the installation is to go to *http://htmldb.oracle.com* and request a workspace. This is an Oracle hosted and maintained development environment for the public.

The instruction in the first three chapters is meant to get you up and running as quickly as possible with some explanation of what is being installed. It is

---

not meant to be an in-depth reference. The Oracle online documentation can be referenced for more information.

Oracle HTTP Server

The requirements for running Oracle HTML DB are: an Oracle HTTP Server; and an Oracle database, version 9.2.0.3 or above, with the HTML DB objects installed into the database. This chapter covers the installation of Oracle HTTP Server on a computer running the Windows operating system. Some notes to help with UNIX/Linux are also included.

What is Oracle HTTP Server?

Oracle HTTP Server is the web server supplied by Oracle which is based on the Apache HTTP Server. It is the process that will receive HTTP requests from client browsers and submit them to the HTML DB components in an Oracle database. Once the HTML DB components fulfill the request, the HTTP Server will return the HTML to be rendered on the client browser.

In order for the HTTP Server and the HTML DB components to communicate, there is an extension module named mod_plsql. An extension module is an additional piece of software which can be added to the HTTP Server to extend its functionality. The mod_plsql module is loaded by the HTTP Server and acts as a middleman for communication between the Oracle HTTP Server and the HTML DB components.

A brief description of the role of Oracle HTTP Server and mod_plsql goes like this, using Figure 1.1 as reference:

1. The client computer issues an HTTP request. *(http://localhost:7777/pls/htmldb/htmldb)*

2. The Oracle HTTP Server receives the request and redirects the request to mod_plsql.

3. mod_plsql communicates the request to the HTML DB components in the Oracle database.

4. HTML DB generates an HTML web page and replies to mod_plsql.

5. mod_plsql passes the HTML page to the Oracle HTTP Server

6. Oracle HTTP Server replies to the client browser with the HTML page.

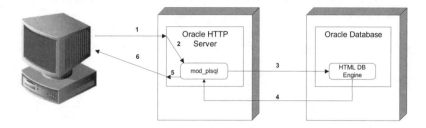

Figure 1.1: *Oracle HTTP Server communication*

Prior to Installation

The following should be verified prior to starting the installation process:

- Meet one of the following Operating System requirements.

    - Windows 2000 Professional or above with service pack 3 or higher

    - Windows XP Professional

    - Windows 2003 for 32 bit systems

    - Linux versions: Red Hat Enterprise version AS/ES 2.1 or above; or SUSE Enterprise Server version SLES-8 or above

- Have available disk space of at least 165 MB

- Be logged into the computer with Administrator privileges for windows or as a member of the oinstall group on UNIX/Linux.

Installing Oracle HTTP Server

The Oracle HTTP Server cannot be installed into an existing Oracle Home. If another Oracle product is installed on the computer, a new Oracle Home name and location for the Oracle HTTP Server Home will have to be chosen.

These instructions also assume access to the Oracle 10g Release 2 Companion CD. The same instructions can applied to the 10g Release 1 Companion CD, but there will be some minor differences. The CD can be obtained from Oracle or downloaded from otn.oracle.com. After downloading it, unzip the files and follow the instructions below. The following link is to the Oracle 10g download site:

```
http://www.oracle.com/technology/software/products/database/oracle10
g/index.html
```

1. Start the Oracle Universal Installer on the Oracle 10gR2 Companion CD.

    ▪ Windows: setup.exe

    ▪ Linux: ./runInstaller

2. At the Welcome screen, click Next.

3. On the Select a Product to Install screen, select the Oracle Database 10g Companion Products 10.2.0.1.0 option and click Next.

4. On the Specify Home Details screen, enter the following for the Destination then click Next.

    ▪ Name: OHS_HOME

    ▪ Path:

        o Windows: C:\oracle\product\10.2.0\ohs

        o UNIX/Linux: /u01/app/oracle/product/10.2.0/ohs

        This may change if a different directory structure is used or if the software is installed to a different hard drive.

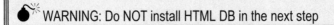

WARNING: Do NOT install HTML DB in the next step

5. On the Available Product Components screen, select only the Apache Standalone 10.1.2.0.0 option. For installation using the 10g release 1 CD, this will be Apache Standalone 9.0.4.0.0. Do not install the HTML DB software at this time. Choosing the HTML DB option would install HTML DB version 1.6 and instructions for installation of version 2.0 are included in the next chapter. After making the proper selections click Next.

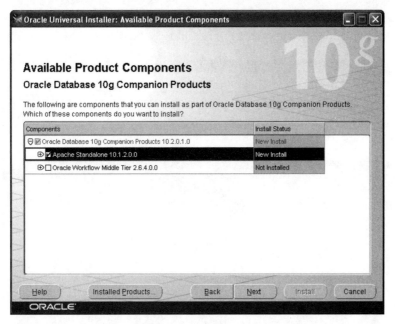

Figure 1.2: *Install Apache, but not HTML DB at this point.*

6. The next screen is the Product-Specific Prerequisite Checks. Verify the status of the items show as Succeeded then click Next.

7. The next screen will be the Summary screen describing all the software to be installed. Click on the Install button. Towards the end of the installation, a screen displays for the Configuration Assistants. Allow that screen to complete.

8. When the installation is complete, there will be an End of Installation screen. It might be handy to print this screen as a reference. At the very least, note the URL shown in the text. It will be similar to: http://localhost:7777. localhost:7777 will be referenced throughout the examples in this book. Whenever a reference to localhost.7777 appears, the user's domain:port should be substituted.

Testing the Oracle HTTP Server Installation

Now that the Oracle HTTP Server has been installed, it should be tested. Start an internet browser session and type the value of the URL from the

End of Installation screen into the URL of the browser. The Oracle HTTP Server should respond with a screen similar to that shown in Figure 1.3.

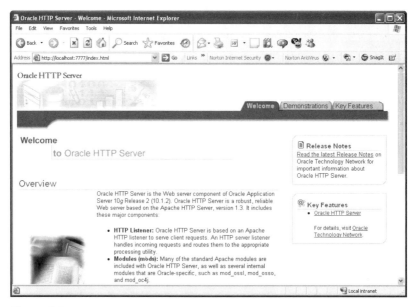

Figure 1.3: *Testing the Oracle HTTP Server*

Post Installation

On Windows, the service created to the run the HTTP Server will be named OracleOHS_HOMEProcessManager. By default, this service should have been set to startup automatically on reboot. If not, it will have to be configured. Changing the service startup type can be done in Administrative Tools → Services.

On UNIX/Linux, for the HTTP Service to restart after a reboot, the following command will need to be run in one of the startup configuration files, such as /etc/rc.local.

```
/u01/app/oracle/product/10.2.0/ohs/opmn/bin/opmnctl restart ias-
component=HTTP_Server
```

Stopping and Restarting the Oracle HTTP Server

The next chapter will walk through installing the HTML DB into an existing database and doing some configuration. After the configuration, it will become necessary to restart the HTTP Server so it can pick up the new setting in the configuration.

For Linux/UNIX, it can be beneficial to create a shell script to restart the HTTP Server. The following is a good example:

```
export ORACLE_HOME=/u01/app/oracle/product/10.2.0/ohs
$ORACLE_HOME/opmn/bin/opmnctl restart ias-component=HTTP_Server
```

Code Depot User ID = reader; Password = easyhtml

On Windows, there is a program group created during installation in Start → Programs → Oracle Application Server - OHS_HOME → Oracle HTTP Server. In this group, there will be two shortcuts to Stop and Start the HTTP Server managed process. I like to create three extra shortcuts that will handle some of the other common Stop/Start tasks that are often performed when making configuration changes. Figure 1.4 shows what the program group will look like after adding the shortcuts.

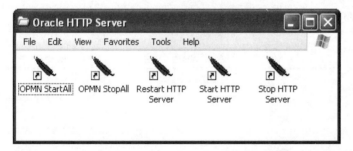

Figure 1.4: *The new and improved Oracle HTTP Server program group*

The shortcuts do the following:

- Start HTTP Server (created by installation): This starts the HTTP Server managed process. For this to succeed, the OPMN service must already be started.

- Stop HTTP Server (created by installation): This stops the HTTP Server managed process and leaves the OPMN service running.

- Restart HTTP Server: This stops and restarts the HTTP Server managed process. This one will have to be created manually, but it comes in handy when making changes to the configuration files. It will also come in handy in the next chapter.

- OPMN StopAll: This stops all managed processes, such as HTTP Server, and also stops the OPMN service. Although it is not necessary to use this in most circumstances, it does become necessary when changing configuration files such as *ORACLE_HOME\opmn\conf\httpd.xml*.

- OPMN StartAll: This starts the OPMN service and all managed processes, such as HTTP Server.

The procedure for setting up the additional shortcut items in the Oracle HTTP Server program group is as follows:

1. Create a copy of any of the shortcuts that currently exist.

2. Rename the shortcut to the text shown in the table below.

3. Open the shortcut properties and change the text in the Target field as shown in the table below.

SHORTCUT NAME	TARGET
Restart HTTP Server	C:\oracle\product\10.2.0\ohs\opmn\bin\opmnctl.exe restartproc ias-component=HTTP_Server
OPMN StopAll	C:\oracle\product\10.2.0\ohs\opmn\bin\opmnctl.exe stopall
OPMN StartAll	C:\oracle\product\10.2.0\ohs\opmn\bin\opmnctl.exe startall

Table 1.1: *Settings for new shortcuts.*

Those following along should replace the underlined portion of the text with the ORACLE_HOME location used during the installation.

That completes the installation of Oracle HTTP Server. The next chapter will cover installing HTML DB into an existing database and performing some configuration. At that point, the configuration files required for Oracle HTTP Server to communicate with HTML DB will be explained. After the configuration, it will be necessary to restart the Oracle HTTP Server so it can pick up the new settings in the configuration.

About OPMN

Before finishing the chapter, the role the Oracle Process Management Notification should be explained with regard to the Oracle HTTP Server. The Oracle Process Management Notification (OPMN) manages Oracle Application Server components. Oracle HTTP Server is a component of the Oracle Application Server and is one of the components managed by the OPMN.

OPMN is a process that runs in the background and checks the health of Oracle Application Server components. If the OPMN recognizes a component has abruptly shut down, it will attempt to restart it. This is referred to as death detection.

OPMN provides a command line interface for controlling the components in Oracle Application Server. Although there are many commands, the ones most applicable to the book are:

- opmnctl.exe stopall

- opmnctl.exe startall

- opmnctl.exe startproc ias-component=HTTP_Server

- opmnctl.exe stopproc ias-component=HTTP_Server

- opmnctl.exe restartproc ias-component=HTTP_Server

Conclusion

This chapter briefly explained the installation of the Oracle HTTP Server (OHS). The OHS is the web server portion receiving requests from a browser and rendering the HTML back to the browser. The examples illustrate how the mod_plsql module plays a role in translating requests to the HTML DB engine to call stored procedures in the database. In the end, they work together to produce the HTML returned to the clients browser.

The next chapter will explain the installation and configuration of the HTML DB engine into an existing Oracle database. Very soon, you will be building HTML DB applications.

Installation and Configuration of HTML DB

Before starting the installation of Oracle HTML DB, it will be necessary to download version 2.0 from the HTML DB web site. The version shipped on the Oracle 10g Release 2 Companion CD is 1.6. Version 1.5 is on the 10g Release 1 CD. The examples in this book will use version 2.0 of HTML DB, which is the current version at the time of publication. When a new release of HTML DB is made generally available from Oracle, any code that does not work with the latest versions of HTML DB will be updated and available in the online code depot.

Preparing for Installation of HTML DB

The Oracle download site for HTML DB can be found at the following URL:

```
http://www.oracle.com/technology/products/database/htmldb/download.html
```

When on the download page for the operating system in use, click the download link for Oracle HTML DB v2.0.

The remainder of this book will refer to a directory named *C:\htmldb_book* for both the directory where the HTML DB download is saved and where the code from the online code depot is stored. Linux users should change the directory according to their naming structure.

The download will provide a file named htmldb_2.0.zip unless a different name is typed in manually. Save this file to the C:\htmldb_book directory. When the files are unzipped, a sub-directory named htmldb will be created. The unzipped files will be in a directory named C:\htmldb_book\htmldb.

Create the HTMLDB20 Tablespace

I like to create a separate tablespace for the HTML DB objects. I recommend this approach because otherwise the objects will likely be created in the SYSAUX tablespace. It is especially helpful when using a DBA to create these objects on a company database. The DBA may be more willing to fulfill the request if he/she knows it can reside in its own tablespace. The following code creates a 100MB tablespace named HTMLDB20.

```
CREATE TABLESPACE htmldb20
DATAFILE 'C:\oradata\hdb20\htmldb20_01.dbf' SIZE 102464K
EXTENT MANAGEMENT LOCAL
UNIFORM SIZE 64K
SEGMENT SPACE MANAGEMENT AUTO;
```

Using a uniform size of 64K will keep the total size of the objects created to approximately 75M. This will leave some room for growth in the 100M tablespace. The use of larger uniform extent sizes will require the size of the htmldb tablespace to be increased accordingly. Be careful using a larger uniform size because there are over 600 objects and disk space requirements will increase dramatically.

Create the HTML DB Database Objects

After the tablespace is created, the HTML DB objects will have to be created. During the installation of HTML DB, there are three schemas created. The names of the schemas and brief descriptions of their purposes are provided in Table 2.1 below:

SCHEMA	DESCRIPTION
FLOWS_020000	This is the owner of all the tables, views, and packages installed for HTML DB. The exception is the table installed in the FLOWS_FILES schema for the storage of files in the database. The FLOWS_020000 account is locked at the end of the installation and cannot be used unless it is first unlocked.
FLOWS_FILES	This schema is created to hold uploaded files. When a file, such as a script, cascading style sheet, document, etc., is uploaded into the HTML DB workspace this is where it is stored. This account is locked at the end of the installation and cannot be used unless it is unlocked first.

SCHEMA	DESCRIPTION
HTMLDB_PUBLIC_USER	This is the schema that is used by Oracle HTTP Server to log into the HTML DB database. It provides HTML DB functionality by using the objects in the other two schemas.

Table 2.1: *HTML DB schemas and their descriptions*

All the necessary HTML DB objects are installed by running the following command in SQLPlus. A description of the command line parameters is provided in Table 2.2.

```
sqlplus "sys/htmldb@hdb20 as sysdba" @htmldbins hdbpwd htmldb20
htmldb20
    temp /i/ hdb20
```

COMMAND LINE PARAMETER	DESCRIPTION
sqlplus "sys/syspwd@hdb20 as sysdba"	starts sqlplus and logs in as sys
@htmldbins	The installation script for HTML DB version 2.0
hdbpwd	The password to be given to the schema owners of the HTML DB objects – FLOWS_020000.
htmldb20	Default tablespace given to the FLOWS_020000 schema owner of the HTML DB objects.
htmldb20	Default tablespace given to the FLOWS_FILES schema owner. The table created in this schema is where any uploaded files are stored. This could be a separate tablespace, but it is easier to just have one.
temp	The name of the default temporary tablespace to be given to all schemas created during installation.
/i/	The name of the virtual directory to be used for images being rendered in HTML DB. The use of this value is recommended
hdb20	This is the connect string for the database where HTML DB is being installed.

Table 2.2: *HTML DB command line parameters and their descriptions*

Installing the HTML DB Images

Now that the HTML DB objects have been created in the database, the necessary images will have to be installed into the directory tree of Oracle HTTP Server. This step not only installs the images, but also installs all the themes, templates, cascading style sheets, java scripts, and other files necessary to support the HTML DB development environment. When using the directory mentioned above, C:\htmldb_book\htmldb, a command similar to the following can be used to install the images.

💣 Before using the command below make sure the target directory referencing the ORACLE_HOME is correct. In the command below, the ORACLE_HOME is expected to be C:\oracle\product\10.2.0\ohs\. This is where the Oracle HTTP Server was installed.

- Windows:

```
xcopy /E /I c:\htmldb_book\htmldb\images
C:\oracle\product\10.2.0\ohs\Apache\Apache\images
```

- UNIX/Linux:

```
cd <htmldb_install_dir>/images cp -r
/u01/app/oracle/product/10.2.0/ohs/Apache/Apache/images
```

Keep note of the directory into which the images are copied. Later in this chapter, a Database Access Descriptor (DAD) will be configured. The DAD is configured to tell the Oracle HTTP Server how to connect to the database, and this directory will be needed during configuration.

Database Access Descriptor

The DAD is a set of instructions for Oracle HTTP Server and the mod_plsql extension module. Together, they will use the information in the DAD for connections to the database.

Please note that the HTML DB documentation refers to a file named marvel.conf in many places. For the purposes of this book, any time the documentation mentions editing the marvel.conf, this reference will apply to the dads.conf file.

The name of the configuration file is dads.conf and is located in the following directory:

- Windows: *ORACLE_HOME\Apache\modplsql\conf*

- Linux: *ORACLE_HOME/Apache/modplsql/conf*

The following is an example of a dads.conf file:

```
Alias /i/ "c:\oracle\product\10.2.0\ohs\Apache\Apache\images/"
<Location /pls/hdb20>
    SetHandler pls_handler
    Order deny,allow
    Allow from all
    AllowOverride                None
    PlsqlDatabaseUsername        HTMLDB_PUBLIC_USER
    PlsqlDatabasePassword        htmldb
    PlsqlDatabaseConnectString   localhost:1522:hdb20
ServiceNameFormat
    PlsqlAuthenticationMode      Basic
    PlsqlDefaultPage             htmldb
    PlsqlDocumentTablename       wwv_flow_file_objects$
    PlsqlDocumentPath            docs
    PlsqlDocumentProcedure
wwv_flow_file_mgr.process_download
    PlsqlNLSLanguage             AMERICAN_AMERICA.AL32UTF8
</Location>
```

When configuring the DAD on Linux, the only change to the DAD in the above example is for the location of the images virtual directory as shown here.

```
Alias /i/ "/u01/app/oracle/product/10.2.0/ohs/Apache/Apache/images/"
```

A few of the items in the DAD configuration are explained in Table 2.3 below, but it is a good idea to read the dads.README file located in the same directory as the dads.conf configuration file. It will explain all the configuration parameters in greater detail.

PARAMETER	DESCRIPTION
Alias	This is set to /i/ and references the location where you installed the images earlier in this chapter. When HTML is rendered to your browser this is the virtual directory for the location of images, cascading style sheets, java scripts, etc.
<Location /pls/hdb20>	This is the name of the virtual path that will be used to access your HTML DB web application.
PlsqlDatabaseConnectString	This is in the format of server.domain:port:sid. Here we used the name httpserver, but if you have a local database you can use localhost for the server.domain part. Then provide the port number the database is listening on and service name (sid). If your database is on a server you may need your DBA to provide you with the necessary information.

PARAMETER	DESCRIPTION
PlsqlDatabaseUsername	This is the username that will be used by the mod_plsql extension module for connecting to the database. Every connection, regardless of the login id and password provided will be connected to the database with this username.
PlsqlDatabasePassword	This should be set to the same password as was provided during the installation of HTML DB. It is the password given to the schema owners of the HTML DB objects and HTMLDB_PUBLIC_USER.

Table 2.3: *Example DAD configuration parameters and their descriptions*

REMEMBER: After configuring the DAD, the HTTP Server process must be restarted as described in Chapter 1.

Encrypting the dads.conf Passwords

The dads.conf file shows that the password is in plain text, which is not the best option for purposes of security. Oracle provides an obfuscation utility to encrypt the password. The dadtool.pl perl script will make a copy of the dads.conf file and modify the PlsqlDatabasePassword configuration parameter to an encrypted format. This will prevent anyone from being able to read the password from the dads.conf file. To run the obfuscation tool, navigate to the *ORACLE_HOME\Apache\modplsql\conf* directory in a DOS prompt and run the following command:

```
perl dadTool.pl -o
```

This may require setting some environment variables. To make it easy, I create a batch file to run the command. Shown below are the contents of the file:

💾 encryptdad.bat - Windows

```
SET ORACLE_HOME=C:\oracle\product\10.2.0\ohs
SET ORIGPATH=%PATH%
SET PATH=%ORACLE_HOME%\perl\5.6.1\bin\MSWin32-x86;%PATH%
SET PERL5LIB=%ORACLE_HOME%\perl\5.6.1\lib

perl dadTool.pl -o

SET PATH=%ORIGPATH%
SET ORIGPATH=
SET PERL5LIB=
```

encryptdad.sh – UNIX/Linux

```
#! /bin/ksh

ORACLE_HOME=/u01/app/oracle/product/10.2.0/ohs;export ORACLE_HOME
PATH=$ORACLE_HOME/perl/bin:$PATH;export PATH
PERL5LIB=$ORACLE_HOME/perl/lib/5.6.1 export PERL5LIB

perl dadTool.pl -o
```

The encryptdad.* files should be saved in the same directory as the dads.conf file described above. The dadTool.pl file is also in this directory. The encryptdad.bat file can be run the following ways.

After running the obfuscation utility, the PlsqlDatabasePassword configuration parameter will be modified to something like:

```
PlsqlDatabasePassword          @BUCZxYS3xQEoOxn4UQw981U=
```

> 🔔 The dadTool.pl script makes a copy of the dads.conf file before encrypting the password. For security purposes, it may be desirable to delete this file or move it to a more secure location. The name of the file will be something like: dads.conf.orig.2005-11-17_02-15

At this point, the HTTP Server will have to be stopped and restarted. For UNIX/Linux, the script created in Chapter 1 of this book can be used. For Windows, the Restart HTTP Server shortcut created off the start menu can be used.

Testing Oracle HTML DB

Now that Oracle HTTP Server and the HTML DB engine have been installed, and a Database Access Descriptor configured, it is time to test connectivity to HTML DB.

Open a browser session and type in the appropriate URL. If all the same parameters mentioned in the text of this book have been used during the configuration of the DAD, a URL similar to the following will do the trick. It may be necessary to substitute the text <localhost> below for the name of the server configured with the HTTP Server:

```
http://localhost:7777/pls/htmldb/htmldb
```

If there is a different virtual path configured in the Location directive in the dads.conf, other than <Location /pls/hdb20>, it will have to be changed in the URL.

When a successful connection is made, a screen similar to Figure 2.1 should be displayed.

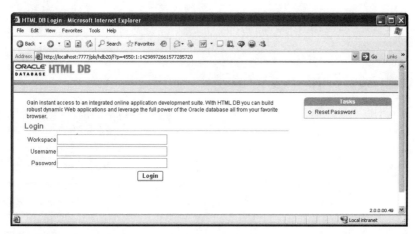

Figure 2.1: *After successful connection to HTML DB*

Troubleshooting Problems with HTML DB Connections

If the screen shown in Figure 2.1 is not displayed, the following information may help with troubleshooting.

Service Temporarily Unavailable

If you receive:

Service Temporarily Unavailable

The server is temporarily unable to service your request due to maintenance downtime or capacity problems. Please try again later.

This error could be due to the PlsqlDatabaseConnectString parameter in the dads.conf file not being configured correctly to connect to the database.

It can also be because the *tnsnames.ora* file is not setup correctly. When both the Oracle HTTP Server and the database are installed on the same machine, there will be two locations where the *tnsnames.ora* file is located. They will each be located in their appropriate home directories: *ORACLE_HOME/network/admin/tnsnames.ora*. Verify these files are configured correctly. The connection can be checked using SQL*Plus. SQL*Plus will also exist in both homes in the *ORACLE_HOME/bin* directory.

The Page Cannot Be Found

The HTTP 404 – File not found error probably means the HTTP Server needs to be restarted. Perhaps the HTTP Server was not restarted after the DAD configuration. This is done by using the Stop HTTP Server followed by the Start HTTP Server shortcuts in Start → Programs → Oracle Application Server - OHS_HOME → Oracle HTTP Server. If the shortcut icons recommended from the previous chapter were created, the Restart HTTP Server icon can be used in lieu of using both Start HTTP Server and Stop HTTP Server.

No Images Show on the Screen

Check to make sure the Alias line is correct. It should have /i/ with a reference to the correct images directory. Also, the end of the line must be a forward slash (/) rather than a backslash. An example is shown below. Note the forward slash at the end of the directory path.

Windows:

```
Alias /i/ "c:\oracle\product\10.2.0\ohs\Apache\Apache\images/"
```

Linux:

```
Alias /i/ "/u01/app/oracle/product/10.2.0/ohs/Apache/Apache/images/"
```

Forbidden

The URL may return a Forbidden message with the following text:

Forbidden

You don't have permission to access /pls/hdb20/htmldb on this server

---

In this case, it may be because an incorrect password was provided or the PlsqlDatabaseConnectString parameter is not set correctly in the dads.conf file. Make sure this is setup correctly and try again.

File Upload Problems

While uploading a file into a workspace or application, the following error may be returned:

HTTP 404 – File not found

Your URL has the wwv_flow.accept at the end of the URL

This may mean one of the configuration parameters has been typed wrong in the dads.conf file. A common problem indicated on the HTML DB Forum is a misspelling where the s is missing just before the $ character for the PlsqlDocumentTablename parameter. Verify the following parameter is correct in the dads.conf file.

```
PlsqlDocumentTablename wwv_flow_file_objects$
```

Conclusion

This chapter covered how to install the HTML DB engine and configured the dads.conf file so the Oracle HTTP Server and mod_plsql module can communicate with the database. The examples also showed how to encrypt the password in the dads.conf file so it is not readily accessible to anyone snooping around.

Finally, troubleshooting was included for some of the more common problems seen when installing and configuring the Oracle HTTP Server and the HTML DB engine.

The next chapter will guide you through the completion of the final steps in preparing for the creation of HTML DB applications. This preparation will include manually creating a workspace and login ID's for an administrator of the workspace and a developer. This developer will be used throughout the book for exercises.

HTML DB
Administration

By now, I hope your excitement for HTML DB is building and if you are like me, you want to get down to business and start learning to write applications using HTML DB. So, this chapter will be brief and show just enough to create a workspace and a user so we can move on with the rest of the book. The basics for HTML DB Administration will be covered here and the more advanced topics in greater detail in a later chapter.

An HTML DB workspace is an area allocated for development of one or more HTML DB applications by one or more developers. For each workspace, there can be one or more Workspace Administrators and one or more Developers. An administrator can also perform development, but it is a good idea to separate the administrative and development tasks because it makes it easier to see who has done what in the activity reports.

The examples in this chapter will accomplish the following:

- Create a Workspace

- Create an Administrator

- Create a Developer

If a workspace on the hosted Oracle site (htmldb.oracle.com) has been requested and granted, this chapter can be skipped for now. Just note that any references to a URL, workspace name, and username will be different when using the hosted oracle site.

Creating a Workspace Using the Manual Method

Use the following URL to gain access to the HTML DB Administration home page. It may be necessary to substitute <localhost> with the correct domain name for your environment:

http://localhost:7777/pls/hdb20/htmldb_admin

---

1. Login to the HTML DB Service Administration screen with the username of ADMIN and the password used during the installation of HTML DB. This was done in the section Create the HTML DB Database Objects in an earlier chapter. Figure 3.1 shows the HTML DB Service Administration page after successful login.

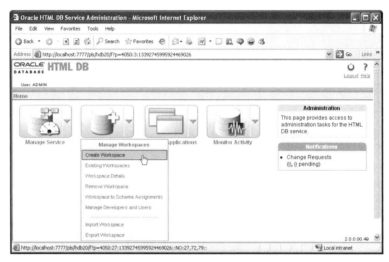

Figure 3.1: *HTML DB Service Administration home page*

2. Click on the down arrow on the Manage Workspaces icon and click on Create Workspace. This will start the Create Workspace wizard.

3. On the Identify Workspace page, enter the following

   - Workspace Name: EASY

   - Click Next

4. The Identify Schema page is where the decision is made to use an existing schema or create a new one. The name of the schema will have to be identified, and if a new schema is to be created, the password to use and the size of the space to set aside for building database objects will have to be specified. For the purposes of following the examples in the book enter the following:

   - Re-use existing schema?: NO

   Schema Name: EASYHDB

- Passwords in HTML DB are case-sensitive. For security purposes, users should choose a different password than the one used in the example.

- Schema Password: easyhdb

- Space Quota: Medium: 5 Megabytes

- Click Next

5. The Identify Administrator page is used to setup an administrator username, password and email contact information on how to get in touch with the Workspace Administrator. Enter the appropriate information:

- Administrator Username: ADMIN

  This is the default. It can be changed, for simplicity, I recommend keeping it set to ADMIN.

- Administrator Password: easyhdb

  For security, a different password should be used for the schema and the ADMIN, but for simplicity the same password has been used in the example.

- First Name and Last Name: Fill in the ADMIN's information

- Email: Fill in the ADMIN's email address

- Click Next

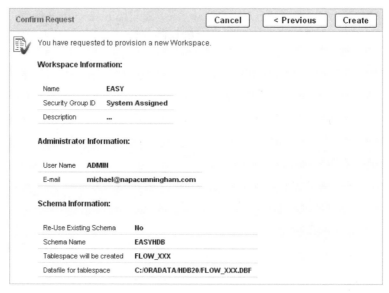

Figure 3.2: *Confirm Provisioning Request*

6. The Confirm Request page, shown in Figure 3.2, allows a review of the information provided before provisioning the workspace. The request can be cancelled at this point, or this is an opportunity to go back and change things. Either way, I find it valuable to print this page out before provisioning the workspace.

7. On the Confirm Provisioning Request screen, the file names for Tablespace will be created and Datafile for tablespace include the letters XXX. The actual names given to the files will be displayed after provisioning.

8. Click the Create button

Figure 3.3: *Provisioning success page.*

9. Figure 3.3 shows the names of the tablespace and data file created to support the new workspace. I usually print the final Provisioning page and keep the two printed pages together as a record.

10. Click the Done button.

Creating a New User

Even though it is possible, it is not always best to do development as the ADMIN user created in the previous section. One reason is if there is more than one developer, each would want their own separate user names. HTML DB tracks changes made by developers and makes it possible to report on who made what changes. The later chapter on Administration covers how to run reports to see which developer has done what.

For the purposes of keeping consistency throughout the book, a developer named EASYDEV will be created.

1. Log out of the HTML DB Administrator application by clicking on the Logout link in the upper right corner of the screen.

2. Navigate to the HTML DB Login page by pointing the browser to the following URL. It may be necessary to replace <localhost> with the correct domain name for your environment:

   http://localhost:7777/pls/htmldb/htmldb_login

3. Login with the ADMIN account created when the EASY workspace was created.

   ▪ Workspace: EASY.

   ▪ Username: ADMIN.

   ▪ Password: easyhdb

      NOTE: Use the password that was entered for the ADMIN user when creating the workspace.

   ▪ Click Login.

   The Workspace home page, shown in Figure 3.4, will be presented upon successful login. It is possible to navigate to the Application Builder, SQL Workshop and Administration here. These will be covered in later chapters of this book.

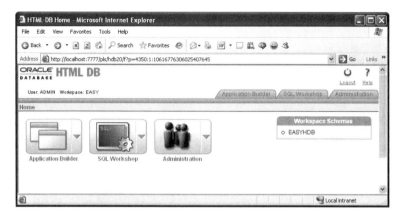

Figure 3.4: *Workspace home page*

Click on the Administration icon.

4. Click on the Manage HTML DB Users icon.

5. Click on the Create Developer icon.

6. On the Create User page complete the following required fields. Any other fields can be filled in, as desired:

   - User Name: easydev

   - Password: easydev

     This password should be changed as necessary for security.

   - First Name and Last Name: Fill in the developer's information

   - Email Address: Fill in the developer's email address

   - Default Schema: EASYHDB

     This schema was created in the section on creating a workspace.

   - User is a developer: YES

     This gives the user permission to develop application pages in the EASY workspace.

   - User is an administrator: NO

   The ADMIN account will be used for workspace administration when necessary.

   - Click the Create User button

This process has created the application developer that will be used throughout the remainder of the book.

Conclusion

Up to this point, a workspace with an administrator account and a separate developer account has been created. Each workspace can contain several applications, and there can be as many workspaces as are necessary for any particular environment. It is also possible to have as many administrators and developers as are needed. This chapter just covered enough of the basics to get you going. HTML DB administration will be covered in greater detail in a later chapter of this book.

The next chapter is where the fun begins; developing an application. The chapter will cover how to use the new EASYDEV account to create an application. It will become clear that it is easy to create a full featured application in a matter of minutes using HTML DB.

Hello World

Introduction

Every book I have ever read that is teaching a programming language or development environment includes a Hello World lesson. This chapter is our equivalent of the traditional Hello World application.

The goal is to provide an exercise leading the reader along the path of building their first application. During the exercise, an application will be built using a Comma Separated Values (CSV) file. This is referred to as Creating an Application from a Spreadsheet.

With little experience, the exercise can be completed in less than ten minutes, but do not let that small amount of time fool you. The wizards in HTML DB can build a feature-packed application in a short time with the steps in which you are about to engage. The application can also be used as a reference when a user wants to go back and see how the wizard did something such as provide navigation for a button.

To complete the lesson in this chapter, the necessary files should have already been downloaded from the Online Code Depot and stored in a directory named C:\htmldb_book\CodeDepot. This process was described earlier in this book. If the files are stored in a different directory, make the necessary changes as the lessons continue.

Building the Application

The creation of a new application starts at the Workspace Home page. Navigate to the Workspace Home by clicking on the breadcrumb menu called Home in the upper left area of the HTML DB development environment and follow these steps:

1. Click on the down arrow of the Application Builder icon. Select the Create Application menu item and click on the Create from Spreadsheet menu item. This is shown in Figure 4.1 below.

2. On the Load Method page click on the Upload file (comma separated or tab delimited) option and click Next.

3. On the Data page:

    - File: Conference_RSVP.csv (from the online Code Depot)

    - Separator: This should be left on the default, which is a comma.

    - Optionally Enclosed By: Since the provided file does not include an enclosed by character, leave this blank.

    - First row contains column names: verify this is checked.

    - File Character Set: leave this on the default

    - Click Next.

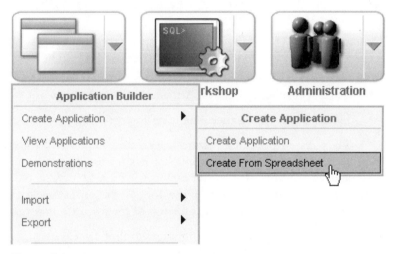

Figure 4.1: *Create Application from Spreadsheet*

4. On the Table Properties page, HTML DB is told how to create the table:

    On this page, one can see that HTML DB has scanned the input file and provided a guess as to the data types for the columns of data. These can be user modified prior to proceeding past this page. The following steps will modify the data types and format to match what the data is in the file being uploaded.

- Schema: EASYHDB

- Table Name: CONFERENCE_RSVP

- For the EMAIL column change the Column Length to a value of 50 from the value of 255.

- For the PHONE column change the Column Length to a value of 20 from the value of 30.

- For the RSVP_DATE column change the Data Type to DATE instead of VARCHAR2 and on the Format field enter MM/DD/YYYY.

- For the COMPANY column change the Column Length to a value of 50 from the value of 255.

- For the DONATION column change the Data Type to NUMBER from VARCHAR2.

- For the PAYMENTcolumn change the Column Length to a value of 20 from the value of 30.

- Click Next.

5. The User Interface Defaults page is shown in Figure 4.2:

- Singular Name: Conference Attendee

- Plural Name: Conference Attendees Report

- The Create Application wizard will create a Report and a Form. The Report is used to display multiple rows from the table being created and the Form is used to edit each row of the table. The plural name will be used as the text at the top of the report region and the singular name will be used at the top of the form region.

- Change the PAYMENT column text to Pmt Type.

- The Column User Interface Defaults region is used to setup defaults for the columns. Whenever a page item is created on a page that refers to the PAYMENT column, HTML DB will create the label next to the page item with the text entered here by the user. This can help make all the labels in a user's applications consistent and their development faster.

- Click Next.

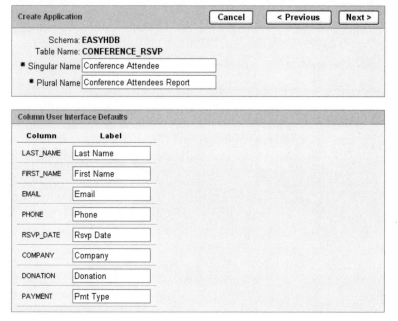

Figure 4.2: *User Interface Defaults while Creating an Application.*

6. On the Summary Page:

    ▪ Summarize By Column: Click the PAYMENT column.

    ▪ Click Next.

7. On the next page:

    ▪ Aggregate by Column: Click on the DONATION column.

    ▪ Aggregate Function to Use: Verify both Sum and Average are selected.

    ▪ Click Next.

8. What was accomplished in steps six and seven is establishing the criteria the wizard will use to build analysis pages. A web page will be built that summarizes the donations and groups them by *payment_type*. This example's data has *payment_type* values of: Cash; Check; VISA; and MasterCard. This part of the wizard will build two pages that sum up the amounts of donations for each payment type as well as the average donation per payment type.

9. On the Application Options page:

- Application Name: Conference RSVP.

- Create Mode: Verify this is set to Read and Write.

- If this were going to be a web application for querying purposes only, the Read Only option would be selected. Setting the Read Only option prevents the creation of several page level buttons such as Apply Changes, Delete, and Create. Leaving the option set to Read and Write will cause the Create Application wizard to add these buttons for proper navigation among the pages.

- Chart Type: This is up to the user, so their personal preference should be selected. The authors like using the Pie Chart for demos like this.

- Click Next.

10. On the User Interface Theme page select Theme 2 and click Next.

   The User Interface page shows a list of the 12 built-in themes from which the user can choose.

11. Finally, the Confirmation page. Click the Create button.

   When the application finishes building, there will be a page that allows the user to either Run the application or to make further edits. Click on the Run Application icon.

If the login page appears, enter the following:

1. User Name: easydev

2. Password: easydev   The password is case-sensitive and must be entered exactly as it was when creating the user.

3. Either press the Submit button or hit the Enter key while focus is still on the password page item.

Congratulations! You have just finished building an application in HTML DB. As I said earlier, as you get comfortable with this type of application building, you will be able to accomplish it in less than 10 minutes. More likely it will be done in less than five minutes.

Exploring the Conference RSVP Application

The previous process created an eight page database web application. Seven of the pages are for the application and page 101 is for the login, which is referred to as authentication in HTML DB. Now it is time to do a little exploring to see what has been accomplished. There is more than most suspect would come from a wizard.

If you are not already running the Conference RSVP application, run it now by clicking on the Run Application icon. This section will provide a look at page one of your application to explain what is there. Refer to Figure 4.3 for this explanation.

If the login page is encountered, follow the steps outlined in the previous section.

In the upper right corner is the Logout link. This is created by a Shared Component called the Navigation Bar. Both of these topics are covered in a later chapter. This might not be very exciting, but the navigation bar can be used to customize Login and Logout to HTML DB applications as well as adding a Printer Friendly link or Help link as is done in the HTML DB development environment.

Figure 4.3: *Conference RSVP Application*

There are also two tabs that were created by the wizard, Conference Attendees Report and Analyze. The text Conference Attendees Report is what was entered by the user as the Plural Name in the user interface defaults.

Now for the fun stuff, the Conference RSVP report. The main body of information presented on the screen is called a Report in HTML DB. An HTML DB Report is a graphical representation of the result of a SQL Select statement.

Page Items

The wizard has created other page items as well such as a Search field, a Reset button, and a Create button. The report also has sorting features built in.

Sorting

The sort feature is indicated by the underline of the column headers such as Last Name, First Name, Email, etc. At first, there should be an arrow next to the ID column heading indicating the column is sorted in ascending order. Clicking again on the ID column heading link will sort the report on the ID column in descending order.

Export to Spreadsheet

It could also be helpful to take note of the Spread Sheet link in the lower left portion of the Report. This link enables the export of the rows in the report to a spread sheet.

Pagination

In the lower right portion of the Report is the Pagination section which is a select list showing which rows of the report are being displayed. This would be rows one through 15 of 50, in this case.

Developer Toolbar

Finally, at the bottom of the page is the Developer Toolbar. The Developer Toolbar will be covered in a later chapter.

Showing Off

Now it is time to show off what has been created. Follow the short exercises below.

1. Type the text *ch* into the Search text field and click the Go button. Notice the built-in functionality of not only finding the text, but highlighting it with Bold, Red text in each of the fields where there is a match.

2. Now click on the column header text Last Name. The report will refresh with the data sorted in ascending order on the Last Name column, and an arrow is displayed next to the column header text indicating the sort order. Click on the Last Name column header again to sort in descending order.

3. Now click on the Reset button to remove the search criteria and refresh the report with all the data. Use of the reset button will not change the sorting properties.

4. On the left-most column of the report there is an edit icon. Click on the ✐ icon on the row for any of the names. This will return you to the Conference Attendee page shown in Figure 4.4. This is where the Singular Name mentioned earlier is used. It represents a single record in the CONFERENCE_RSVP table.

    Figure 4.4 shows what is called a Form Region. Even more specifically, it is an Update Form Region. At this point, you are on the third page of the application, which is a Form allowing modifications to existing rows. The Create button would have navigated to the second page of the application which allows the addition of new rows to the CONFERENCE_RSVP table.

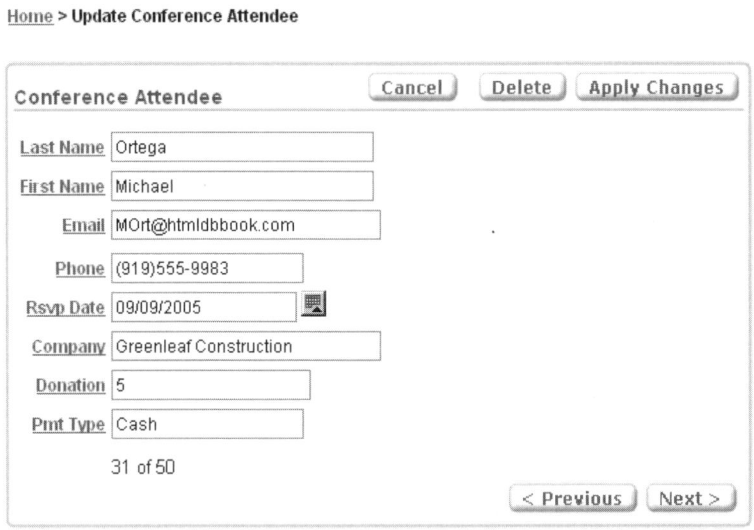

Figure 4.4: *Conference RSVP Editable Form*

On the CONFERENCE_RSVP page, take note of the Breadcrumb Menu in the upper left portion of the page. It is shown in Figure 4.4 above. This is yet another feature provided by the wizard. As one moves through the application, the Breadcrumb Menu provides a hierarchical view of the path taken to get to the current page. It also includes the links to navigate back to previous pages.

Also on the Conference Attendee page, there are buttons to allow the user to navigate to the Next and Previous records in the CONFERENCE_RSVP table.

Try changing the text in one of the fields and click on the Next button. The application will prompt: "Are you sure you want to leave this page without saving?" This is more built-in functionality that helps to prevent the user from moving to another record without saving changes to the current record.

Hey, the showing off is not finished just yet. There is more.

5. It is time to see those summary reports. Click on the Analyze tab in the upper-right portion of the screen.

---

6. Click on the By Pmt Type link in the Charts region. This is one of the charts built from the questions in the wizard from the Building the Application section above. Charts are rendered by either HTML or using the Adobe SVG Viewer add-in for web browsers.

> 🔔 If the user does not have the Adobe SVG Viewer installed, they will receive errors when trying to display the charts on the analysis page. To install the Adobe SVG Viewer, use this link http://www.adobe.com/svg/ and navigate to the downloads page for the SVG Viewer and download and install the SVG Viewer for the user's operating system.

Well that is a look at your first application. During the course of this book, users will be shown how to create and customize all the objects which have been introduced in this simple, but robust, application. Building an HTML DB application can be very EASY!

Conclusion

This chapter showed how to build an application using a spreadsheet. The create application wizard produced an application containing a report with searching capability, a form with the ability to create and edit records, and charts to view data graphically. A good use for the build application wizard is to maintain a contact list of the team with which you work. Using the build application wizard as was illustrated in this chapter is a great way to start new applications and then add on to them. The steps to add application components will be shown in the chapters that follow and yield the tools needed to build larger applications.

HTML DB SQL Workshop

CHAPTER

5

Introduction

This chapter will introduce the SQL Workshop area of the HTML DB Interface. Using the functions available here, users can build and maintain database schemas, query information from the schemas, and load and execute pre-built scripts. It is a powerful interface into the structure and data contained in a database. Users will find themselves using these functions often.

To learn about the SQL Workshop, the first thing to do is access the SQL Workshop area. This can be accomplished in two ways but either way is just a matter of clicking a button or a tab. After logging into the EASY workspace, the three icons for the different HTML DB areas will be presented as shown in Figure 5.1 below.

Application Builder   SQL Workshop   Administration

Figure 5.1: *Main Icon Buttons of HTML DB*

With Version 2.0 of HTML DB, a new type of button has been introduced. This button is a combination of a regular icon button and drop down menu. Clicking on the image section of the button will choose that option. Clicking on the down arrow portion of the button will reveal some drop down menus as shown in Figure 5.2 below. This example shows how to get Data Import/Export utility. Using the drop down menus is typically a much faster means of navigating around HTML DB.

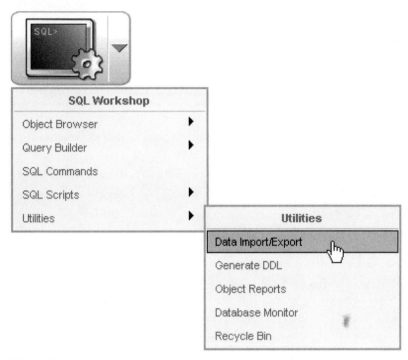

Figure 5.2: *Navigating to the Data Import/Export Utility*

Upon entering the SQL workshop area, three tabs will appear in the upper right hand corner of the page as shown in Figure 5.3 below. These tabs correspond to the three icons shown above in Figure 5.1. The SQL Workshop tab will allow users to jump to this area from anywhere in HTML DB.

Figure 5.3: *The three tabs of HTML DB development*

The SQL Workshop Interface

When accessed, the SQL Workshop is made up of five functional areas: Object Brower; Query Builder; SQL Commands; SQL Scripts; and Utilities. These are represented by the five icon buttons shown in Figure 5.4.

Object Browser   Query Builder   SQL Commands   SQL Scripts   Utilities

Figure 5.4: *The five functional areas of SQL Workshop.*

The five functional areas will be explained in the following sections. Once you become familiar with using these areas, it will be easy to see how the SQL Workshop can help increase productivity.

Object Browser

The Object Browser allows the user to browse any object to which the HTML DB user has access rights. Figure 5.5 shows an example screen of the object browser. The figure shows the list of Tables to which the user has access.

Figure 5.5: *Example screen of the Object Browser*

The drop down list, shown here with the Tables value, allows the selection of the type of object the user wishes to browse. Figure 5.6 show the list of the object types.

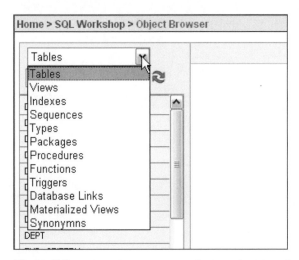

Figure 5.6: *List of Object types available in the Object Browser*

Each time a new type of object to browse is selected, the screen will refresh with the list corresponding to the object type.

When selecting the name of an object in the list, the details for that object will be displayed. For example, when the DEMO_CUSTOMERS table is selected, the screen represented in Figure 5.7 is displayed and the structure of the table is shown. Also, along the top of the window are tabs for different information pertaining to the table. These tabs start with Table, Data, Indexes, and so forth. Each tab will give more and more information about the table.

Below the tabs are actual buttons that can be used to perform operations on the table. The buttons can be used to Add, Modify, Rename, or Drop columns or Rename, Copy, Drop, or Truncate the table. The last option, Create Lookup Table, allows the user to create a lookup type table from the values in a code column in their table. With all this power in HTML DB, it may never be necessary to use SQL Plus or any other tool to interact with the database since it is all built in right here.

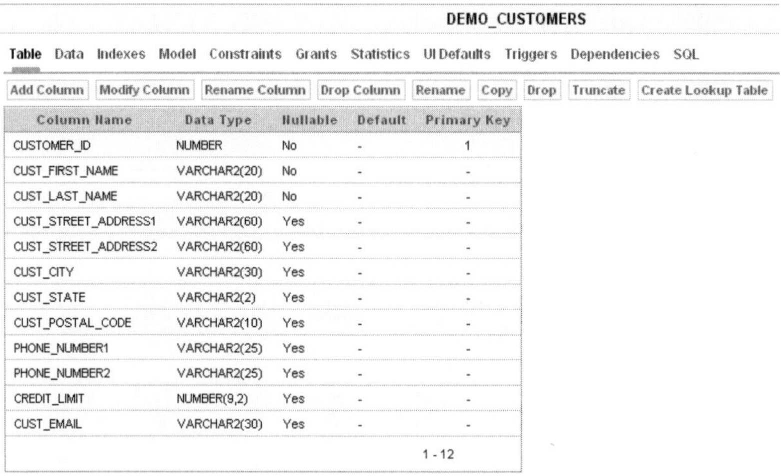

DEMO_CUSTOMERS

Table Data Indexes Model Constraints Grants Statistics UI Defaults Triggers Dependencies SQL

Add Column | Modify Column | Rename Column | Drop Column | Rename | Copy | Drop | Truncate | Create Lookup Table

Column Name	Data Type	Nullable	Default	Primary Key
CUSTOMER_ID	NUMBER	No	-	1
CUST_FIRST_NAME	VARCHAR2(20)	No	-	-
CUST_LAST_NAME	VARCHAR2(20)	No	-	-
CUST_STREET_ADDRESS1	VARCHAR2(60)	Yes	-	-
CUST_STREET_ADDRESS2	VARCHAR2(60)	Yes	-	-
CUST_CITY	VARCHAR2(30)	Yes	-	-
CUST_STATE	VARCHAR2(2)	Yes	-	-
CUST_POSTAL_CODE	VARCHAR2(10)	Yes	-	-
PHONE_NUMBER1	VARCHAR2(25)	Yes	-	-
PHONE_NUMBER2	VARCHAR2(25)	Yes	-	-
CREDIT_LIMIT	NUMBER(9,2)	Yes	-	-
CUST_EMAIL	VARCHAR2(30)	Yes	-	-

1 - 12

Figure 5.7: *List of Object types available in the Object Browser*

Query Builder

The Query Builder is a new feature in HTLM DB version 2.0 and is a very powerful addition. This feature allows queries to be built using a graphical interface. For users who are not familiar with SQL syntax, this is a tool that helps a great deal. Figure 5.8 shows the query builder with two tables selected. The following bullet points explain what is going on in Figure 5.8.

- Select the objects in the left side list of tables and it will build the graphical representation of the table in the top of the query builder canvas.

- Create a join condition, which is represented by the line connecting the two tables, by clicking on a column from one table, holding the mouse button down, and dragging the pointer to the column in the other table. In Figure 5.8, the CUSTOMER_ID column of DEMO_ORDERS was clicked and dragged to the CUSTOMER_ID column of DEMO_CUSTOMERS.

- The columns to query from each of the tables are selected by clicking on the corresponding checkboxes. When selecting the checkboxes, the columns are shown in the Conditions window at the bottom of the canvas. Just three columns have been selected in this example.

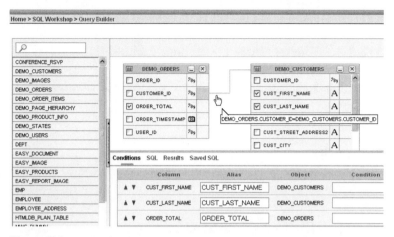

Figure 5.8: *Query Builder.*

- Options for the query can be further selected by choosing Conditions, Sort Order, Group By, and Function. What has been done in this example is the selection of the SUM function so a sum of order totals will be displayed for each customer. The Group By function was then selected for the customer name columns. These actions are shown in Figure 5.9 below.

Condition	Sort Type	Sort Order	Show	Function	Group By	Delete
	Asc		☑		☑	✖
	Asc		☑		☑	✖
	Asc		☑	SUM	☐	✖

Figure 5.9: *Query Builder: The right side of the Conditions canvas.*

Once the query has been built, it can be saved for future use and run at the user's discretion.

The previous figure, Figure 5.8, also shows other selections in the center of the canvas: Conditions; SQL; Results; and Saved SQL. The following is a brief description of how they can be used.

- **Conditions:** The information in this option shows the columns that have been selected to participate in the query and the conditions that have been set for each of the columns.

- **SQL:** Clicking on this option will display the SQL that will be executed. If the user prefers to build queries graphically and get the SQL text from here to use in reports, it can be done. However, while creating reports the query builder can be used to build the SQL statement then return. The SQL statement that is built will be entered as the source SQL for the report.

- **Results:** This option shows the results of the query.

- **Saved SQL:** This option will display a report of all saved queries. Clicking on the saved query will pull the query from the repository and load it into the canvas.

SQL Command Processor

SQL Workshop gives the user access to the SQL Command Processor. It is here that any SQL statement within the rights and permissions of the HTML DB user can be typed in and executed. Any SQL statement or PL/SQL block can be entered and executed. The screen is divided between the statements entered by the user and the results of the statement after execution. The statements can be a SELECT, an UPDATE, a DELETE, INSERT, CREATE TABLE, GRANT, or any other command. It is a great interface that allows users to do exactly what they need to do. Figure 5.10 shows the default display of the SQL Command processor.

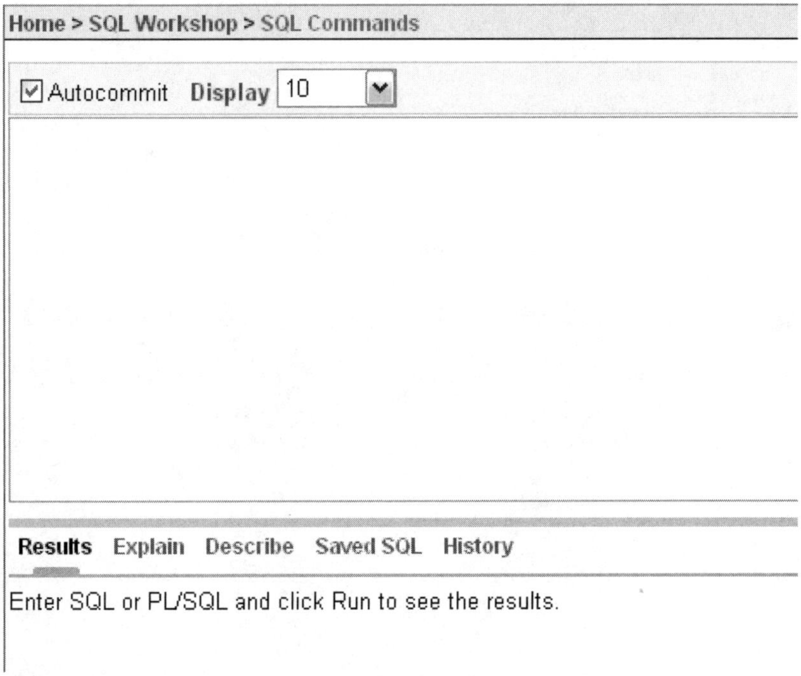

☑ Autocommit   **Display** 10 ▾

Results   Explain   Describe   Saved SQL   History

Enter SQL or PL/SQL and click Run to see the results.

Figure 5.10: *Default screen of the SQL Command processor*

It is a simple matter of entering the statement the user wishes to run and then executing it.   The statements can be executed either by pressing the Run button or by pressing the key combination CTRL+Enter.   I typically use the CTRL+Enter because my hands are already on the keyboard.   In Figure 5.11, a simple SELECT statement has been entered into the SQL Command processor and executed by pressing CTRL+Enter. The results are shown in the results section of the screen.   The Autocommit and Display items at the top of the processor might be unfamiliar.   After each statement is executed, a commit will be issued depending on whether the Autocommit checkbox is checked or not. This will save users from having to commit the data after an INSERT, UPDATE, or DELETE.   The Display drop down offers the option of how many rows to display after a Select statement.   To see more rows than which is shown, simply choose a higher number and re-run the statement.

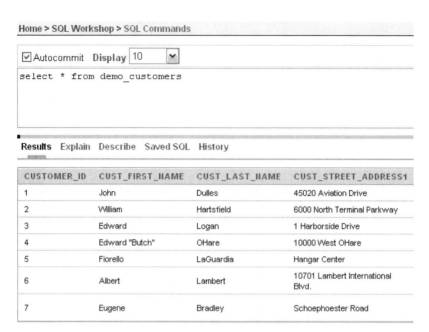

☑ Autocommit Display 10 ▼

```
select * from demo_customers
```

Results Explain Describe Saved SQL History

CUSTOMER_ID	CUST_FIRST_NAME	CUST_LAST_NAME	CUST_STREET_ADDRESS1
1	John	Dulles	45020 Aviation Drive
2	William	Hartsfield	6000 North Terminal Parkway
3	Edward	Logan	1 Harborside Drive
4	Edward "Butch"	OHare	10000 West OHare
5	Fiorello	LaGuardia	Hangar Center
6	Albert	Lambert	10701 Lambert International Blvd.
7	Eugene	Bradley	Schoephoester Road

Figure 5.11: *Sample screen in the SQL Command processor*

🔔 Note: This interface does not support SQL*Plus commands other than the familiar DESCRIBE (DESC) command.

There are also different tabs of the results section. The following table contains an explanation of each:

TAB	DESCRIPTION
Results	Shows the results of the SQL or PL/SQL that have been entered.
Explain	Run the Explain Plan on the SQL statements that are in use. See the detail explanation later in this chapter.
Describe	Describes the structure of a table.
Saved SQL	These are saved SQL statements that all the developers can use. Typically these are saved without values in the statement. These would be supplied when needed.
History	HTML DB will save the last 120 commands that have been run. The history can be used to recall the statement to run again.

Table 5.1: *The functions of the different tabs of the results section*

For practice, create a table using the SQL Command processor. The following *create_easy_products.sql* script shows the CREATE TABLE command for a table called products.

🖫 create_easy_products.sql

```
create table easy_products (
    product_id              number,
    product_name            varchar2(50),
    product_description     varchar2(500),
    product_available       varchar2(1),
    list_price              number(8,2)
)
/
```

This statement can simply be typed into the SQL Command processor and executed. Also, the *create_easy_products.sql* file from the online code depot can be used and executed. Figure 5.12 shows what this step looks like. Assuming all went well, the Table Created message will be displayed. Very simple! If the syntax of the command is incorrect, an error statement will point the user to their mistake. Those familiar with other Oracle products will recognize these errors as the default Oracle errors.

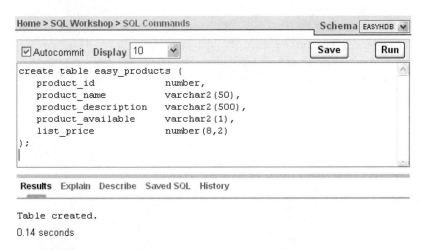

Figure 5.12: *A sample Create Table statement Executed in the Processor*

Figure 5.13 shows the execution of an INSERT statement to add data to the table.

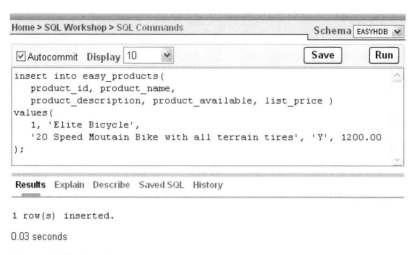

Schema EASYHDB ▼

☑ Autocommit Display 10 ▼   Save   Run

```
insert into easy_products(
    product_id, product_name,
    product_description, product_available, list_price )
values(
    1, 'Elite Bicycle',
    '20 Speed Moutain Bike with all terrain tires', 'Y', 1200.00
);
```

Results Explain Describe Saved SQL History

1 row(s) inserted.

0.03 seconds

Figure 5.13: *Simple insert statement executed in the processor*

Explain Plan

One of the other more useful features incorporated into the HTML DB interface is the Explain Plan, which is shown below in Figure 5.14.   The Explain Plan provides the steps the Oracle Optimizer will use in order to execute any statement against the database schema.   This will provide information which can help diagnose performance problems with applications. The seasoned Oracle developer is well familiar with the Explain Plan.

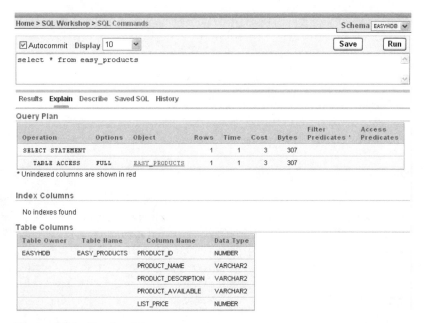

☑ Autocommit Display 10 ⌄   [Save] [Run]

```
select * from easy_products
```

Results **Explain** Describe Saved SQL History

Query Plan

Operation	Options	Object	Rows	Time	Cost	Bytes	Filter Predicates *	Access Predicates
SELECT STATEMENT			1	1	3	307		
TABLE ACCESS	FULL	EASY_PRODUCTS	1	1	3	307		

* Unindexed columns are shown in red

Index Columns

No indexes found

Table Columns

Table Owner	Table Name	Column Name	Data Type
EASYHDB	EASY_PRODUCTS	PRODUCT_ID	NUMBER
		PRODUCT_NAME	VARCHAR2
		PRODUCT_DESCRIPTION	VARCHAR2
		PRODUCT_AVAILABLE	VARCHAR2
		LIST_PRICE	NUMBER

Figure 5.14: *Explain Plan.*

After clicking on the Explain Plan, an interface similar to the SQL Command Processor will be provided. It will be interesting to see what a simple select from the PRODUCTS table will produce. Enter the following in the SQL Command processor and execute it.

```
select * from products
```

After entering in the statement, click on the Explain button. Figure 5.14 shows that the statement will perform a full table scan on the PRODUCTS table, which is normally a very bad thing. If the SELECT statement accesses indexes, it will be indicated here, which is a desired result.

SQL Scripts

Through the SQL Scripts interface, SQL or PL/SQL scripts can be viewed, edited, stored, and edited. It is also possible to upload previously created scripts to execute. This function can save a lot of time.

Figure 5.15 shows the interface to SQL scripts. In this figure, no scripts have been loaded into the system. The next step will be to create a script to load into the application. The script will then be stored and executed. In the SQL Command Processor interface, a single statement can be executed. Loading data one row at a time can be a very long and time consuming process. Scripts will make the process much faster and more efficient!

Figure 5.15: *Interface to the SQL Scripts*

The following code listing has some insert statements we can use to add data to the EASY_PRODUCTS table that was created earlier. The statements are provided in the file named *easy_products_data.sql* in the online code depot for convenience. Notepad in Windows can be used to type these statements and save them to a file. The code listing below shows the file as it would be in the online code depot.

🖫 easy_products_data.sql

```
-- ****************************************************
-- Copyright © 2006 by Rampant TechPress
-- This script is free for non-commercial purposes
-- with no warranties.  Use at your own risk.
--
-- To license this script for a commercial purpose,
-- contact info@rampant.cc
-- ****************************************************
insert into products(
   product_id, product_name,
   product_description, product_available, list_price )
values(
   2, 'The Adventurer',
   '10 speed cruising bike used for street or paved roads', 'Y',
450.00 )
/

insert into products(
   product_id, product_name,
   product_description, product_available, list_price )
values(
   3, 'Toddler Trike',
   '3 wheeled tricycle intended for children under 7 years old',
'Y', 100.00 )
/

insert into products(
   product_id, product_name,
```

```
   product_description, product_available, list_price )
values(
   4, 'Riding on One',
   'Unicycle', 'Y', 300.00 )
/

insert into products(
   product_id, product_name,
   product_description, product_available, list_price )
values(
   5, 'Two for Fun!',
   'Tandem bike intended for 2 people to ride simulateously', 'N',
500.00 )
/
```

Upload this script into the to HTML DB script repository. Click on the
`Upload >` button to begin the process. Figure 5.16 shows the Upload Script
page with the information filled in. Click on the `Upload` button to load the
script into HTML DB's repository.

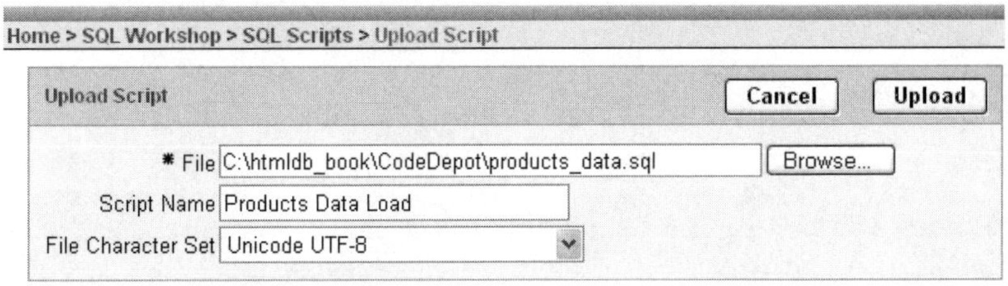

Figure 5.16: *Upload Scripts page*

The script has been loaded into the HTML DB as shown in Figure 5.17.
Notice the view has been changed to Details. This view will yield more
information about the different scripts loaded into the script repository.

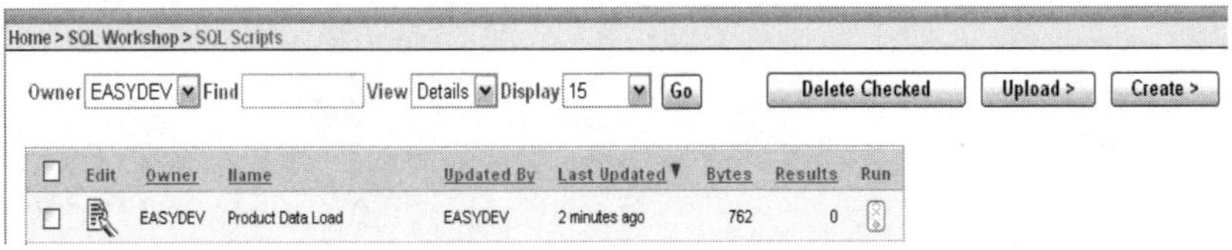

Figure 5.17: *Scripts that exist in the HTML DB Script Repository*

The first icon, which looks like a piece of paper and pencil, allows the script
to be edited and saved back to the database. The checkbox is used to

choose the script to delete. Press the ⊡ for the script to execute and load the records into the products table.

When the script has been run, the results screen will be shown as indicated in Figure 5.18. When first run, the status will be Submitted. By pressing the Go button, it is possible to watch the progress of the script execution. If the script is long, the screen will be updated. When the script has finished running, the status will changed to Complete. When complete, the results of the script can be viewed by pressing the View button. The results will give any statements which failed and the error associated with that failure.

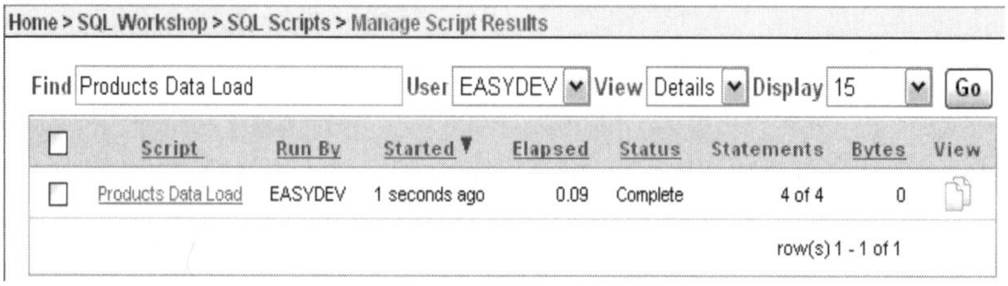

Figure 5.18: *Script completed screen*

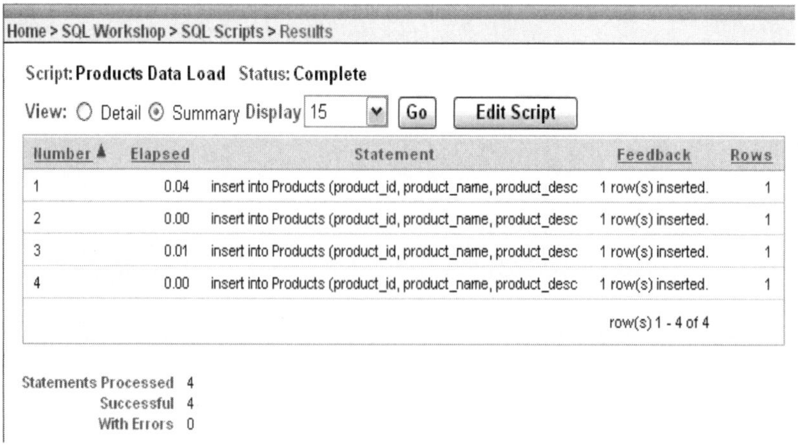

Figure 5.19: *Script results screen*

Utilities

There are several Utilities in the SQL Workshop to help with common tasks performed on the database and reports of the configuration and operation of the database.

Data Import/Export

Data Import/Export is something the user will run across in the HTML DB development environment. It will not be included in this section in great detail because it is covered in a later section in this chapter titled SQL Workshop – Data Import/Export.

Generate DDL

This is used to generate the Data Definition Language (DDL) for a particular schema. It can then be used to deploy the schema to another database or workspace. Figure 5.20 shows the options available to generate the DDL and the objects for which the DDL can be created.

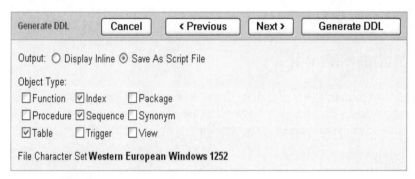

Figure 5.20: *Generating DDL.*

Object Reports

Tables

This option provides reports about the various aspects of a table such as Columns, Comments, Constraints, Statistics, and Storage Sizes.

PL/SQL

This utility provides reports about the PL/SQL in the schema such as Program Unit Arguments, Unit Line Counts, and Search PL/SQL Source Code. The search is a valuable utility enabling the user to search all the PL/SQL for a string such as a table name.

Security

This utility provides reports for User Privileges for grants to objects, Role Privileges, System Privileges, and SQL Injection. The SQL Injection report requires the Oracle 10gR2 database.

All Objects

- **All Objects**: Display all objects in a schema and defaults to the parsing schema.

- **Invalid Objects**: A report of invalid objects such as PL/SQL and Views.

- **Object Calendar**: Displays a calendar of when objects were created.

- **Data Dictionary**: A graphical way to query tables in the data dictionary.

Database Monitor

This is primarily an administrative task, and it requires a privileged connection to the database. The database monitor can be used to view the following information about the database.

Activities

- Sessions

- System Statistics

- Top SQL

- Long Operations

Storage

- Tablespaces

- Data Files

- Free Space

Configuration

- Database: Installed options and feature usage reports.

- Configuration Parameters: *init.ora*

Recycle Bin

This is a convenient feature in HTML DB 2.0. Dropped objects can be viewed and then restored. They can also be purged from the recycle bin.

SQL Workshop: Data Import/Export

The Data Import/Export Utility is used to perform most data export and import functions. Data can be imported into the database either by using simple text or by importing data from a CSV file or a XML file. Data can also be imported manually or through a script using other SQL Workshop facilities. Data Import/Export is an easy method for initially populating a database. This facility is analogous to using the Oracle SQL Loader utility.

In HTML DB 1.6, the Data Import/Export utility was called Data Workshop. In 2.0 it has been incorporated into the SQL Workshop.

Navigating to the Data Import/Export Utility in version 2.0 is performed from either the Workspace Home or by navigating the menus under the SQL Workshop → Utilities → Data Import/Export as shown in Figure 5.2. This is a welcome enhancement in 2.0 as it speeds up navigating through HTML DB. It is also possible to click on the SQL Workshop tab. This method should be employed if version 1.6 is being used.

The Data Import/Export Utility has, quite simply, five wizards to guide the Import or Export of data.

- **Import:** This utility is used for importing text, spreadsheet, and XML data

- **Export:** Used for exporting to Text and XML formatted data

There is no option for exporting to a spreadsheet in the Data Workshop. This task can be accomplished by using other facilities in SQL Workshop. Refer to the chapter on SQL Workshop for complete instructions on Output to Excel.

Importing Text Data

To start the Import Text Data wizard, click on the Import Text data icon in the Data Import/Export home. This wizard allows the user to type text in manually, copy and paste it from another application into HTML DB, or upload it from a file. This is the easiest way to import data from a Microsoft Access or an Excel spreadsheet, a comma delimited file, or other text file with formatted data. The wizard provides guidance through the steps for the import. Later in this chapter, there will be a practice exercise for loading text data from a file.

> Importing text data will commit all successful rows. The rows not successfully imported can be viewed in the Import Repository, which is covered later in this chapter.

If the data being imported is smaller than 30 kilobytes, it is possible to select the Copy and Paste option and paste the data to be loaded into a text area. If it is larger than 30 kilobytes, the Upload file option must be used.

During the import process, the wizard allows the user to either create a new table or add the data to an existing table. One can also choose to copy and paste the data into a text area or upload a file. The exercise at the end of this chapter shows how to import a text file named ch5_1_zip_code.txt, identify records that failed, and to view the file in the Data Workshop repository.

Either a TAB or a single character must delimit the data. The single character is usually a comma, but it can be another character such as a tilde.

XML Import

There is a distinct difference between Importing XML data and the other imports. The user will not be asked if they would like to import into an existing table or a new table as in the other import wizards. The XML Import requires there be an existing table into which to import.

> 🔔 The XML Import is a transactional operation meaning it is all-or-nothing. If one record fails, the entire transaction is rolled back and none of the data will be imported.

It is important to note that HTML DB itself is written with HTML DB. The XML Import wizard is performing the following tasks:

- Uploading an XML file

- Storing the XML file in the database

- Inserting the data from the XML file into the selected table

If HTML DB is doing this, so can you. With the growing popularity of XML formatted files, it may be necessary to write a few web pages to perform this very same function in your own applications. For example, there may be a monthly XML data load from an external source or an XML formatted dump file can be provided to an external source. The same techniques used by HTML DB can be used to write a data import or export screen to deploy with the application.

Import Spreadsheet Data

To start the Import Spreadsheet Data wizard, click on the Import Spreadsheet Data icon in the Import home. The Import Spreadsheet Data wizard uses the same wizard as the Import Text Data wizard so specific details will not be repeated here. They are essentially the same.

Export Text Data

To start the Export Text Data wizard, click on the Export icon in the Data Import/Export home page. The Export Text Data wizard provides a method for exporting all the rows in a table and storing them in a text file. The wizard prompts for the following information:

- Schema from which to export the table

- Which table to export

- Which columns from the table to include in the export

- The column separator character, which is usually a comma

- Whether or not to enclose text data with special characters, which is usually double quotes

- Whether to include the column names as the first row in the export

- Export to DOS or Unix file format

- Which character set to use. This is normally left at the default value.

At the end of the export the user will be prompted to either open the text file or to save it as a file.

XML Export

To start the XML Export wizard, click on the XML Export icon on the Export page. The wizard prompts for the following information:

- Schema from which the table is to be exported. If your workspace is setup with multiple schemas you can select a schema at this point.

- Table from which the data is to be exported.

- Which columns from the table to include in the export.

- Whether or not to Export As File.

   By default, the Export As File check box is not checked. Leaving the Export As File check box unchecked will display the XML data in the web browser. Setting the Export As File checkbox to checked will provide a File Download window where it will be possible to choose to either open the file in the browser or save it as a file to disk.

Import Repository

To view the repository, click on the Import Repository icon on the Data Import/Export page. It is possible to get there by clicking on the SQL Workshop tab, and then use the Utilities → Data Import/Export → Import Repository menus. The two repositories available in the Import Repository are:

- Text Data Import Repository

- Spreadsheet Import Repository

The Text Data Import Repository shows the files that have been uploaded, the table name for where the data was inserted, the status of the imported records including the number of records that succeeded and failed, and more. From here, the file can be viewed by clicking on the link for the file since it is stored in the database. It is also possible to view the failed records and the error text of the failed records as well as the record text that failed. To view the failed records, if there are any, click on the link under the Failed column. This will be covered in detail during the exercise towards the end of this chapter.

The Spreadsheet Import Repository is almost the same. The difference is that since spreadsheet data was copied and pasted into the wizard there is no file. However, the user can see the table where the data was imported and the status of the imported records, which includes the number of records that succeeded and failed.

Import Exercise

The following exercise incorporates:

- Creating a new table by loading data from a text file.

- Using the Import repository to view the status of the import.

- Showing records that failed to load and why they failed.

A new table will be created from a file containing zip code information. The data is stored in a comma-delimited file and has three columns: zip code; city; and state. The file is in the online code depot with the name ch5_1_zip_code.txt.

1. Navigate to the Data Import/Export Utility using one of the following methods

   - From the Workspace home page use the menus by clicking the SQL Workshop → Utilities → Data Import/Export. This was shown in Figure 5.2.

   - From anywhere in HTML DB, click on the SQL Workshop tab, then the Utilities icon, then Data Import/Export icon.

2. Click on the Import icon on the Data Import/Export page.

3. Click on the Import Text Data icon on the Import page.

4. On the Target and Method page make the following selections

   - Import to: New table

   - Import from: Upload file The data must be comma separated or tab delimited

   - Click Next.

The first few lines of the file are shown below:

```
ZIP,CITY,STATE
91773,San Dimas,CA
91798,Ontario,CA
91932,Imperial Beach,CA
```

5. On the File Details page, shown in Figure 5.21, make the following selections

   - Browse for the ch5_1_zip_code.txt file in the c:\htmldb_book\CodeDepot folder

   - Separator: This is a comma.

   - First row contains column names checkbox should be checked

   - The File Character Set should remain set to the default

   - Click Next.

Figure 5.21: *Import Text or Spreadsheet Data*

The separator can be set to whatever character is used in the source file for separating the columns. The most common character used is a comma, but other common choices are ~ (tilde) or the | (vertical bar).

The ch5_1_zip_code.txt file does not require the use of the Optionally Enclosed By option; however, it is common for comma-separated files to include double quotes ("") around text. If a file with this type of formatting is being loaded, the Optionally Enclosed By field is where the proper character, such as the double quote, can be entered.

6. The next screen, Table Properties, is where HTML DB is given the information on what to call the new table and what the data really looks like. The Import wizard does a good job of figuring out what kind of data is in the upload file, but it may not be exact. This is the screen where it will be perfected.

    Since the names of the data columns are included as the first row in the source file, the Import wizard used them to name the columns. However, the data types chosen by the Import wizard are different than is desired. Make the changes to the Data Type and Column Length values as indicated in Figure 5.22.

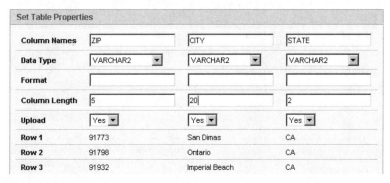

Figure 5.22: *Set table properties for a new table during import.*

  - After making the proposed changes to the Table Properties region as shown in Figure 5.22, click the Next button.

7. The next page of the Import wizard is the Primary Key page. This is where the unique identifier is set for each record. Select or set the following values:

  - Primary Key From: Use an existing column

  - Primary Key: ZIP(VARCHAR2)

  - PK Constraint Name: ZIP_PK

  - Primary Key Population: Not generated

  - Click Import Data

The Import wizard will default the Primary Key From option to Create new column with the name of ID. In some cases, it is possible to load data that does not have a column that uniquely identifies each record being loaded. For HTML DB to work best, a unique identifier must be identified. If the source data does not have a column that can be used as the unique identifier, this method can be used to allow the Import wizard to create one.

Another big option that merits further explanation is the Primary Key Population. This tells HTML DB where to get the value that should be stored in the Primary Key column whenever a new record is added to the table. A sequence is like another table that counts incrementally and will supply a new value for each record inserted. The options and explanations for Primary Key population are shown in Table 5.2 below.

PRIMARY KEY OPTIONS	DESCRIPTION
Generated from a new sequence	The Import wizard will create a new sequence to be used for the population of the Primary Key column.
Generated form and existing sequence	Allows the user to choose a list of existing sequences in which to populate the Primary Key column from.
Not generated	This tells the Import wizard and HTML DB the Primary Key column is not to have any data inserted. In this case, the user will be providing the data.

Table 5.2: *The Primary Key population explanations*

When the import of the source data is complete, the Text Data Import Repository page will appear and the results of the import will be presented. The ch5_1_zip_code.txt file from the online code depot will have two records that failed to import due to bad data. These records have been included on purpose for purposes of explanation.

8. Since there are two records in the data that will produce errors in the Text Data Import Repository, click on the link indicated with the number two in the Failed column, as shown in Figure 5.23.

Type	Schema		Table	Bytes	Succeeded	Failed
Text Import	EASYHDB	ZIP		1,519	72	2

Figure 5.23: *Indication of import status*

9. Clicking the link accesses a Details screen showing detailed information for each of the failed rows. Figure 5.24 shows the two rows with errors and explains the problem with each. The problem for both is the same. The text for the CITY column is too large to fit into the 20-character column defined in step five above. It also shows they are located in row 12 and 49 in the text file that was loaded. This screen provides good information that allows the user to go back, fix the data, and load the two rows again.

Failed Rows

Error	Data
ORA-12899: value too large for column "EASYHDB"."ZIP"."CITY" (actual: 25, maximum: 20)	Row 12: 91766,Phillips Ranch California,CA
ORA-12899: value too large for column "EASYHDB"."ZIP"."CITY" (actual: 24, maximum: 20)	Row 49: 21918,Conowingo is in Maryland,MD
	1-2

Figure 5.24: *Failed Rows from a Text Data Import*

The exercise showed how to load data from a text file, create a new table while defining a primary key, and view the status of the records that were loaded. This case also demonstrated how to view the failed records and the reason for the failure.

Conclusion

This chapter provided a review of:

- The SQL Workshop, which is used to manage the physical objects in the database.

- Scripts to create database objects and to manipulate data.

- The built in utilities.

- The use of the Explain Plan.

- The Query Builder, which is used to graphically build SQL Select statements.

Furthermore, users were shown how to use HTML DB utilities for the import and export of data as well as some of the monitoring utilities available within the HTML DB development environment.

The next chapter will provide an introduction to the application builder.

Learning the HTML DB Application Builder

Introduction

This chapter serves two main purposes. The first is to introduce the HTML DB development environment, and the second is to provide a reference for topics that are not specifically mentioned in other chapters.

The Application Builder is complex, and this book will not cover it all. The book is written for the beginning to intermediate level HTML DB developer, so the most common things any user should know when starting out will be covered.

Instead of taking up space in the individual chapters describing the HTML DB pages used to edit the attributes of various components, they will be included in this chapter. When applicable, more detailed explanations will be included in the other chapters.

Access to the Application Builder is gained from the Workspace home page. While on the workspace home page, click on the Application Builder icon. This will bring up the Application Builder home page as shown in Figure 6.1.

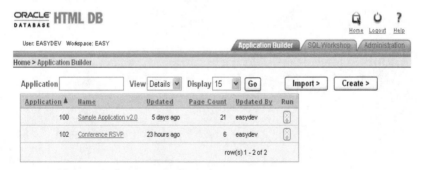

Figure 6.1: *Application Builder home page.*

The screenshot in Figure 6.1 shows the applications in the EASY workspace. The Application display shows properties of the existing applications such as Application ID, Name, last time the application was updated and by whom, and the number of web pages in the application. This page can be used to Import an application from an export file, such as the application included in the on-line code depot. The importing of applications will be covered in another chapter on deployment. Invoking the Create Application wizard is done by clicking the Create button on the Application Builder home page.

Editing an Application

From the Application Builder home page, click on the Conference RSVP application. This will bring up the Application's home page, shown in Figure 6.2.

There are several options available from the Application's home page. The Pages region shows a list of the pages in the application as well as some key attributes of each page, such as page id, the last time and by whom it was updated, and whether the page is locked for development. The application can be run by clicking on the Run Application icon or run a single page by clicking on the run stoplight icon [].

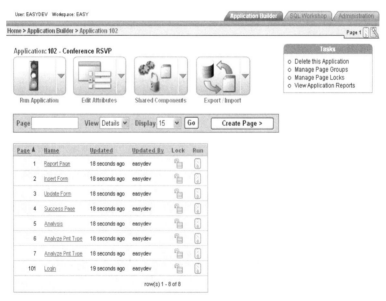

Figure 6.2: *Application Home page for Conference RSVP.*

Run Application

This icon can be used to run the application just as if it were being entered in the browser as a URL. This simulates what a visitor to the web application would encounter upon entering the application.

Edit Attributes

This is used to modify global Application Attributes and is described in greater detail in the Application Attributes section later in this chapter.

Shared Components

Shared Components are parts of an application intended for use on many pages of an application. They are reusable components. Many of the shared components can participate in what is called Publish and Subscribe. For example, a List of Values (LOV) such as Products could be defined in one application and published to other applications. If the LOV were to be modified, the changes can be published to all the subscribing applications. There is also more detail for this option later in the Shared Components section.

Export/Import

This function is used to export the entire application making it easy to deploy to another HTML DB database, or to export various pieces of the application such as Themes, Pages and User Interface Defaults.

Tasks

Many pages in the HTML DB development environment include additional links in the Tasks region in the upper right area of the application home page. These are usually tasks that are not used as often as the tasks available as icons. The tasks available from the Application home page are shown in Table 6.1.

TASK	DESCRIPTION
Delete this Application	This is obvious and will allow the deletion of the application.

TASK	DESCRIPTION
Manage Page Groups	Allows the creation of Page Groups. Page Groups are used as a way to group similar pages together. Some examples are billing, customer maintenance, etc.
Manage Page Locks	This task allows application pages to be locked or unlocked. Locking a page prevents other developers from opening the page for making modifications.
View Application Reports	Navigation to a page that provides links to the many application reports available. There are reports for Shared Components, Page Components, Activity and Cross Application.

Table 6.1: *Application home page tasks*

Standard Attributes

The Application Attributes are where the global properties are set for the application. Navigate to the Edit Application Attributes page by clicking on the down arrow in the Edit Attributes icon and then click on the Edit Definition menu item. The standard attributes are explained in the following sections.

Name

This is where the name of the application is set. It is also the name displayed in the Application Builder home page.

Application Alias

The text entered here can be used in the URL to the application. The application alias can be used in lieu of the application id. For example: if the application id is 102 as in the Conference RSVP application, the application alias can be set to HELLOWORLD. Either of the following can be used on the URL's to get to the application.

```
http://localhost:7777/pls/hdb20/f?p=102
http://localhost:7777/pls/hdb20/f?p=helloworld
```

 Use the Application Alias cautiously. These should be unique in the HTML DB engine. If the same alias name is used more than once, it may confuse the HTML DB engine.

Version

The version field provides a place to set a version that can be used in page templates to indicate the version on every page of the application if the user chooses. To add the version to a page template, use the #APP_VERSION# substitution string in the templates.

Image Prefix

This is set to /i/ by default and represents the same setting as is in the dads.conf file as presented in the section of this book on Database Access Descriptor (DAD). The value here must be the same as in the DAD file.

Logging

This allows the activity to be recorded in activity logs. Each page view will be logged allowing the workspace administrators to monitor the application activity. The activity reports will be covered in the chapter on advanced HTML DB administration.

Parsing Schema

The parsing schema is very important to the application. All SQL statements and PL/SQL are executed as a specific database user known as the parsing schema. This is also the schema that will own the tables, indexes, PL/SQL, etc. that will be created through the SQL Workshop. Although this can be modified for the application, EASYHDB will be used for the parsing schema throughout the book. The EASYHDB parsing schema was created when the easy workspace was created earlier in this book.

Status

This option is used to set the current status and availability of the application. This can be handy when in a development mode for an application or when it is necessary to make an application unavailable during maintenance. The options are shown in Table 6.2 below.

OPTION	DESCRIPTION
Available	The application is available to administrators, developers and other users; however, the developer toolbar will not be displayed on the web pages when they are executed.
Available with Edit Links	The application is available to all and the developer toolbar will be displayed when logged into the Application Builder as an administrator or developer.
Available to Developers Only	Only administrators and developers will be allowed to run the application. Also, a built in authentication scheme must be used. Authentication schemes are covered elsewhere in this book.
Restricted Access	With this option, the Restrict to comma separated user list, where the status must equal Restricted Access, text area is used to build a list of users allowed to use the application.
Unavailable	This option will not allow the application to be executed. The text entered in the Message for unavailable application text area will displayed on the screen to any user attempting to use the application.
Unavailable (Status Shown with PL/SQL)	Use this option to be allowed to write custom PL/SQL that will build html code to display to the user.
Unavailable (Redirect to URL)	This will allow the user to enter a URL to redirect the user to another web site. Make sure to use the full URL including the leading http:// or risk a failure of the redirection action.

Table 6.2: *Status options and their descriptions*

Build Status

There are two settings for build status. The Run Application Only status will allow the application to be executed, but the application will not be displayed on the Application Builder home page. Leaving this setting at the default, Run and Build Application, will allow it to be executed and displayed in the report of applications on the workspace home page.

Global Notification

This is used to display a global, or system wide, notification on pages of an application. A good use of this would be if there was planned maintenance on the weekend. A message to that effect could be displayed during the days prior to the maintenance alerting the users of the application maintenance. The label has #GLOBAL_NOTIFICATION# shown in the text. This is referred to as a substitution string and is very important. A later chapter will cover page templates and how these templates use substitution strings. This particular substitution string would be used in a page template to put the global notification in a strategic location on the page.

Substitutions

HTML DB has several built in substitution strings. This is an area where users can define their own. They can then be used throughout the application. A good use of this may be for a copyright string. One goal might be to create a copyright notification string that reads "Copyright 2005, HTML DB Book. All rights reserved." For this, MSG_COPYRIGHT could be entered for the Substitution String and the copyright notice in the Substitution Value. Then to display the copyright notice in an application it would be referenced with &MSG_COPYRIGHT. including the trailing period. If it is ever necessary to change the copyright notice, this is where it would be changed, and it would instantly be reflected everywhere it is used in the application.

Logo

The built-in page templates are defined with an area in the upper left corner to display a logo, an image file, if the use of one is desirable. This is exactly how the HTML DB development environment displays the image in the upper left corner of the browser. The text used to do this for HTML DB environment is shown below.

The Logo Image Attributes page item is used to set other properties of the <img> tag.

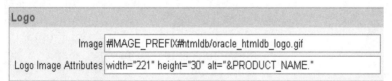

Figure 6.3: *Logo attributes.*

The #IMAGE_PREFIX# text is a substitution string and is substituted with the text /i/ as mentioned earlier in the Image Prefix section. The example above would be translated to:

```
/i/htmldb/oracle_htmldb_logo.gif
```

Security Attributes

Navigate to the Security Attributes page by clicking on the down arrow in the Edit Attributes icon from the Application home page and then click on the Edit Security menu item. Security attributes are explained in the following sections.

Home Link

This indicates the home page of the application. When the Run icon in the application home page is clicked, this is where HTML DB gets the information to know which page is the home page. It is also used in the case where someone types in a URL such as http://localhost:7777/pls/hdb20/f?p=102. The URL tells HTML DB which application ID to run, which is 102 in this example. Then HTML DB uses the value in Home Link to know which application page has been indicated as the home page.

Public User

This is the database user HTML DB uses for logging into the database. It must match the PlsqlDatabaseUsername parameter in the dads.conf file. Looking at the Oracle sessions will reveal a connection to the database with this name as the logged in user.

Authorization Scheme

This option is used to control access to the application. Authorization is different than Authentication. While authentication will confirm who is logged in and that they are permitted to log in, authorization sets the privileges for the user. Custom authorization schemes can be created for an application and can be used at the application level, page level, or down to the component level for each of the page items. If a user does not pass authorization, the page component(s) will not be displayed.

Parsing Schema

This indicates the schema owner for all the database objects the application will use. Each application can use one schema. If there is a need to use multiple schemas, it is usually done by creating a separate application and, if necessary, building navigation to go between the applications. The list of available Parsing Schemas is controlled in HTML DB Administration Services.

Session State Protection

This feature can be used to prevent savvy users from trying different parameters in the URL to gain access to application pages or data to which they should not have access. Session State Protection is explained in the chapter on Advanced Security.

Virtual Private Database (VPD)

This is an advanced feature and can be used to limit the records a user can see. It can be handy for applications where the same SQL select statement would return a different result set depending on who is logged in, such as for different regional salespersons.

Application Pages

Now that the application attributes have been covered, it is time to look at the attributes of an application page. This section will explain many aspects about page attributes, how they are rendered, and attributes of the various components on application pages.

Page Definition

On the Page Definition for an application page, as shown in Figure 6.4, there are three regions.

- Page Rendering: This is the definition of the page components, such as regions, buttons, and items, and the logic controls, such as computations and processes, that will be used in the rendering of the application page.

- Page Processing: This region is where programming logic is defined. These are referred to as logic controls in HTML DB. Logic controls are executed when the application page is submitted to the HTML DB engine.

- Shared Components: This is a list of the shared components used on the current application page. This region can also be used to create new shared components or edit existing ones by clicking on the links for the various shared components.

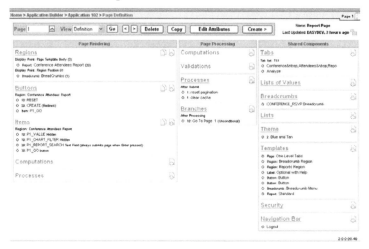

Figure 6.4: *Page Definition for an application page.*

Regions

Regions act as a container for other page components. There are many types of regions such as reports, forms, charts, calendars, web services, TREE's, etc. The components can be a report, text fields, buttons, etc. Regions can then be positioned on the web page, and all the page items in the region will be positioned with it. Regions can also be displayed on the screen or hidden from view based on conditions set by the user.

The following attributes are part of the Region Definition page. The Region Definition page is accessed by clicking on the region link on the applications Page Definition page. The link is shown being selected in Figure 6.5.

Figure 6.5: *Regions section.*

Name

Title

This is the text that will be displayed at the top of the region. This page item supports more that just straight text. A page item can be added to the Title, and it can be made dynamic. A good use for this would be for a policy number. Entering the text Policy - &P1_POLICY_ID.would produce something like Policy - A756123 when the page is rendered.

Another common thing that HTML DB uses in its own development environment is to enter an anchor tag in the Title. For example, it has as the Title a value of <a name="CONDITIONS"></a>Conditions. This serves as a bookmark and allows the development environment to provide bookmark links at the top of pages so it is possible to quickly scroll to that part of the page.

Type

This will dictate how HTML DB will render the region. Types will be covered in greater detail throughout the book, but a brief description is provided here to serve as a point of reference.

The region type is set to instruct HTML DB what type of text is entered in the Region Source text area. That way HTML DB knows how to treat the text when the page is being rendered. Table 6.3 shows the source types used to indicate how a region should be displayed or populated. ...

SOURCE TYPE	DESCRIPTION
HTML Text	Allows the user to enter standard HTML syntax to be rendered in the region. Substitution strings, including page item values, can be inserted into the HTML code by using substitution string syntax such as &APP_USER. The HTML Text type is also used as the region type when a form page is created.
HTML Text (with shortcuts)	Allows the same as HTML Text, but also allows the inclusion of HTML Shortcuts. Shortcuts are pieces of reusable code.
HTML Text (escape special characters)	Allows the same as HTML Text but will render special characters in their original form. As an example: if the user wanted to display the text " in the region. This is the HTML syntax to display a single quote ('). If the region type HTML Text is used, it would be rendered as ('), but setting the region type to HTML Text (escape special characters), the text will display as *"*

SOURCE TYPE	DESCRIPTION
SQL Query	This type of region type is the most common type used when creating a report. The HTML DB engine will execute the SQLselect statement in the region source to populate the report. Even though the Report Wizard will provide a step-by-step guide to build a report, this is more common. Many times an experience programmer will have someone providing them with an SQL select statement they would like to see displayed on a web page and this is the type of report region created when I use the SQL Report wizard.
SQL Query (Structured Query)	This type is assigned to the region when creating a report using the Report Wizard. Regions of this type are not normally created manually.
SQL Query (PL/SQL function body returning SQL Query	This region type can be used to write a PL/SQL function that dynamically builds an SQL select statement and returns the string from the function. HTML DB will then use that string as the select statement to populate the report. This is a powerful feature and can be used by experienced SQL programmers for flexibility.
SQL Query (updateable report)	This type of region is for tabular forms. A tabular form allows the editing of multiple rows for a table at a time. This type of form is best built using the built-in Tabular Form Wizard.
PL/SQL (anonymous block)	This type of region is best used when using the HTML API packages such as the HTF and HTP packages. An example of this would be to put owa_util.print_cgi_env; into the Region source to display the CGI environment in the region.
Chart (HTML) chart	This is a simple chart provided for in the HTML language. This type of chart is rendered using HTML table tags.
Chart (SVG)	This is a more powerful type of chart using the Adobe SVG (Scalable Vector Graphics) standard.
Web Service Result	This type of region permits the use of services provided by other sources. For example: Federal Express provides web services by which one can use to track shipping orders.
Easy Calendar	This is the region type assigned when the calendar was created using the Easy Calendar wizard. This wizard will walk the user through a selection process to pick the table and columns to use for the population of the calendar
Calendar	This is similar to the Easy Calendar except the user will be asked to provide the SQL statement used to populate the calendar.
TREE	A tree provides a page component to represent multi-level information such as a directory tree for a file system, or for District, Store, and Department type of drill down information.
URL	Using this type of region, a URL can be entered and the results of the URL will be rendered inside the region.

Table 6.3: Source types for application page regions.

User Interface

Template

This defines the template that will be used to determine the look of the region.

Display Point

Display points are explained in more detail in a later chapter of this book.

Region HTML table cell attributes

This attribute is only used when there are multiple regions displayed side by side. For example, if there are three regions lined up from left to right instead of top to bottom, regions are across multiple columns. In that case, this attribute can be used to add additional attributes to the region, such as aligning them vertically to the top of the row. This would be accomplished by entering valign="top" for this attribute. To have them display right next to each other, a width would have to be entered on the region to the left that is small enough to allow the region on the right room to move over. To accomplish this, enter width="200" for this attribute.

Source

This is the source code used to populate the region. Depending on whether the user is viewing a report based on a Structured Query, an SQL Query, a Chart, a Calendar, etc. this region will display differently. For example, a Structured Query is not editable except by using the Query Definition tab. If the report is based on an SQL Query, the source region will provide a text area for editing the SQL statement for the report. This is assuming the region type is SQL Query or a similar type as explained above in the Name section. For charts, a Build Query button is provided to guide users through building the SQL statement used to populate the chart.

Conditional Display

The tutorials in this book will provide ample exposure to the user of this attribute, so there will be plenty of opportunities to gain experience with it. There are far too many condition types to explain in detail, but some of the more commonly used conditions are explained in order to provide an understanding of when and where it might be desirable to use them.

The conditional display is used to prevent the rendering of a particular region or page item. Conditions are meant to return a TRUE or FALSE value. TRUE is the default and if returned, the region or page item is rendered. A return value of FALSE will prevent the rendering. Table 6.4 shows the most popular condition types for the conditional display.

CONDITION TYPE	DESCRIPTION
-No Condition -	The Default. This will cause the component to always be rendered.
Exists (SQL query returns at least one row.	This is very common for use when it is desirable to only display a component if a record exists in the database. A common use would be for verifying the user is an administrator.
NOT Exists (SQL query returns no rows)	This is the reverse of the previous item. If a row were to be returned by the query, it would result in a FALSE answer and the component would not be rendered.
SQL Expression	This is similar to the WHERE clause in an SQL statement. A good use for this is when none of the other condition types meets yo For example: you may want to have a condition that the page must be 101 and it is not in print friendly mode. This is similar to having two coi work together to return a true of false value.
Request = Expression1	This condition type is mostly used during page processing on conditions, validations, and processes. For example, a computation does not have a condition where you can specify the button from a select list. So, for computations you would have to use this type of a condition.
Value of Item in expression 1 Is NULL	This type of condition is commonly used on buttons such as a Create or Insert. Let's say you have a page item on a form named P100_CUSTOMER_ID. If that page item is NULL then it would indicate this is a new customer and you would want the Create or Insert buttons to be rendered. This is exactly how the HTML DB wizards setup a form created by a wizard.
Value of Item in expression 1 Is NOT NULL	This type of condition is commonly used on buttons such as a Update or Delete. Let's say you have a page item on a form named P100_CUSTOMER_ID. If the page item has a value then the customer already exists and you would want the Update and Delete buttons to be rendered. This is exactly how the HTML DB wizards setup a form created by a wizard.
Current Page Is Contained Within Expression 1	For this condition you provide a comma delimited list of application page IDs. This type of condition would be used to display Lists or Tabs only for a select list of pages.

CONDITION TYPE	DESCRIPTION
Current page is NOT in Printer Friendly Mode	This condition type is often used on the application page referred to as Page 0 (zero). It is common to display a banner at the top of the page using an after header region. You would use this condition to prevent the region from being rendered when the user put it into the Printer Friendly mode.
User is Authenticated	In the event there is a page that is public and does not require authentication. However, that page is also used by authenticated users. You have one region on the page that you only want to be displayed if the user is authenticated while the rest of the regions can display in either condition. For that one region you could use this type of condition. I've used this type of region on a page so I could see auditing information, but it would not be displayed to the public.
Never	This will prevent the component from being rendered. It's also used to prevent a branch, computation, validation, or process from being executed. I've most often used this computation to prevent certain processes from running while I test an application page.

Table 6.4: *Conditional display types*

Header and Footer

The Header and Footer region is used to modify the look of a region by allowing the user to provide HTML code that will be inserted upon the region being rendered. A common use for this feature within HTML DB is to add descriptive text to the top of a region. For example, the copy region wizard in HTML DB displays helpful text at the top of the regions and this is done by using the Header and Footer.

Authorization

Custom authorization schemes can be created within HTML DB. An authorization scheme may be something like IS_MANAGER or CAN_EDIT_PRODUCTS. These authorization schemes can be created in Shared Components → Authorization Schemes. The authorization scheme either evaluates to TRUE or FALSE. If it evaluates to TRUE, the page component will be rendered. If it evaluates to FALSE, the component will not be rendered.

A common use for this would be for something such as create or edit buttons. If the user has authorization to perform edits, the buttons would be displayed. If not, the buttons would be unavailable.

Customization

Although not a very technical description, this feature is really cool! The developer wants to provide a page with ten regions, which could be reports, forms, or any other type of region, on the page, but some users may only be interested in any combination of three or four regions. Instead of creating several pages to satisfy each application user, all of the regions can be placed on a single page and it can be made customizable. What this feature will do is add a Customize link on the page thereby allowing the user to display a popup with the names of all the regions. The user can then select the regions they want to see and unselect the regions they do not want to see.

In each of the regions, the developer can decide if the region should participate in the customization popup window. There may be one region to be displayed in any situation; whereas, the rest of the regions can participate in user customization.

Customized Option Name

By default, the name to be shown in the popup window will be the Region Title. The Customized Option Name is used to provide an alternate name in the popup Customize Page.

This requires the developer to be using an authentication scheme where each user has a separate login to the HTML DB application. HTML DB must be able to distinguish between users so it knows which regions to display next time the user renders the page.

Configuration

This region allows a Build Option to be selected. A Build Option is used to enable or disable functionality within an application. They are created in Shared Components → Build Options. When a build option is created, it is given a status of INCLUDE or EXCLUDE. If the status is INCLUDE, the components with that build option will be rendered by HTML DB as normal. If the status is EXCLUDE, HTML DB will ignore them during rendering. A build option can be assigned to application pages, regions, page items, page processing, and other page components to include them or exclude them from the rendering process. For example, there may be a build named Version 1.1 that is set to EXCLUDE. This build option may be assigned to page components that are not ready to be rendered. Once testing is completed, the version 1.1 build option could be set to INCLUDE and the page components would be rendered in the application.

Comments

This is a good location to keep notes about the report region. This area could be used to keep track of changes made or perhaps plans to be made in the future.

Page Events View

The Page Events View is accessed by selecting the Events option in the View select list as shown in Figure 6.6 and pressing the Go button.

Page Events are an extremely valuable tool to the HTML DB newcomer. It shows a detailed view of when each page component is being rendered by the HTML DB engine. Figure 6.6 shows page three of application 102, the Conference RSVP application being displayed in the page events view. In order, the After Header processes are executed, the Breadcrumb menu is rendered, and then the Conference Attendee region and page items are rendered. Understanding that one event must occur before another can save hours of frustration. This is one of the tricky things to get the hang of when learning HTML DB.

Page rendering events and page processing events are explained in greater detail in a later chapter of this book.

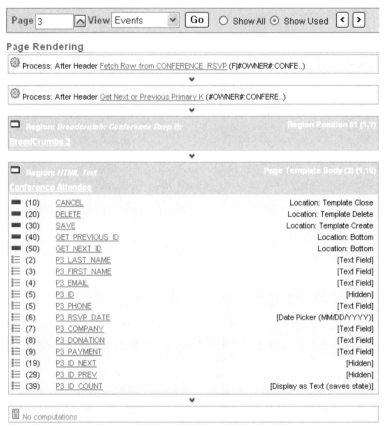

Figure 6.6: *Page rendering events view.*

Page Objects View

This view is used to see the database objects on the application page.

The Page Objects View is accessed by selecting the Objects option in the View select list as shown in Figure 6.6 and pressing the Go button.

Page History View

This view is used to see the history of changes made to page components on the application page. It will show the changes made and by which developer. It is also possible to see the history of when the page was locked and unlocked.

Page Export View

This view provides another way of exporting an application page. This option has generated a lot of questions on the HTML DB forum. The export implies that it would be possible to import the page into any other application, but that is not the case. An exported page can only be imported back into the same application id that exported the page. The value of exporting an application is so modifications can be made to the application, and if something goes wrong, the page can be re-imported to get back to where you started.

Page Groups View

This view will show the other pages that belong to the same group as the current page.

Page References View

This view displays the other application components that reference this application page. Figure 6.7 shows that a breadcrumb menu, two branches on pages one and three, and a tab have links to this page.

Application	From Component	Relation	To Page
102	CONFERENCE_RSVP Breadcrumb	Breadcrumb	1
	Page 1	Branch	1
	Page 3	Branch	1
	Conference Attendees Report	Tab	1
		row(s) 1 - 4 of 4	

Figure 6.7: *Other pages that reference the current application page.*

Page Rendering

Page rendering is the action taken by the HTML DB engine to render the application page in a browser. The Events view of an application page shows the Page Rendering execution order, shown previously in Figure 6.6. The events view shows the order in which page components such as regions, buttons, items, computations, and processes are executed. Page rendering is also covered later in this book in the section on Page Processing.

Page Level Computations

Computations can either be processed while the page is being rendered or while the page is being submitted. A page level computation can be used to set the current date and time of a page item.

Page Level Processes

Processes can either be executed while the page is being rendered or while the page is being submitted. There is a significant difference with each. Page level processes are considered for execution as the page is being rendered. This is handy for executing a page process that is used to populate the page items on the page.

Session State

To the seasoned developer, session state can best be defined in terms of global variables. Session state is the storing of page item values in the database. Their values can be referenced from any page in an application. Since they are stored in a database table and are specific to each HTML DB session, their values can be referenced in stored procedures.

A big benefit any experienced web developer will notice immediately is that session state is managed by HTML DB. Nothing special like saving them in hidden page values has to be done. Just being able to reference session state from a stored procedure will show how valuable it is to have HTML DB provide this ability.

Session state for page items are tied to a page so all the page items can be set to NULL values by clearing the cache for a page. It is also possible to set all the page items in the entire application to NULL by clearing the cache for the application.

Viewing the values in session state can be done by using the Session link on the developer toolbar. It is also possible to view session state for the whole workspace by logging in as an administrator and navigating to HTML DB Workspace Administration → Manage Services → Session State

Navigating to the HTML DB Workspace Administration is accomplished by clicking on the Administration tab.

Reference Types for Page Items

While using HTML DB, it will be necessary to reference the session state for page items. There are several ways, or reference types, for referring to the page item depending on the type of code the HTML DB engine is executing. For the most part, page items in SQL are referenced using the Bind Variable syntax and when editing page items, their values are set using the Substitution String syntax.

Bind Variable: Syntax :P100_CUSTOMER_ID

This syntax is used within the SQL statements for page processes, page computations, and page validations.

Substitution String: Syntax &P100_CUSTOMERID.

When a page is rendered, the HTML DB engine will substitute the text of the substitution string &P100_CUSTOMER_ID. with the value of the session state, such as the value 231. The syntax of the substitution string includes a leading ampersand (&) and a trailing period (.). The substitution strings can be used in region titles, page items, URL's, and other locations.

PL/SQL: Syntax V('P100_CUSTOMER')

This is used to reference the session state of page items from a PL/SQL stored procedure. When the page is submitted, the session state is stored in HTML DB tables for each of the page items. The session state can then be referenced by using the V and NV functions. The V function is for alphanumeric values and the NV function will return the value as a number.

Template Substitution: Syntax #P100_CUSTOMER_ID#

This syntax is primarily used in templates to reference attributes set on attributes pages such as application attributes, page definition, etc. This syntax is also used on reports to reference the values returned for columns in an SQL select statement. One example is to use this syntax in a report column link to refer to the column in the SQL statement.

Preferences

Preferences comprise a persistent session state that is maintained between user sessions. That is, when a user logs out and logs back in, the Preferences can be re-read and used. They are like variables that last forever between uses of the application.

In HTML DB, the developer may have chosen to modify the default view from Icons to Details, so HTML DB saved that selection as a user preference. HTML DB then uses the stored user preference to know how to display the screen the next time the developer logs in to do development.

Preferences are user specific. If public authentication, Page Is Public, is being used for web pages, all users are authenticated with the same user preferences. Since public pages do not require a valid user login id, HTML DB uses the username of NOBODY; therefore, since everyone using public pages is known to HTML DB as nobody, the preferences are shared among all web users. If the previous visitor to the web page sorted the report by the Payment Type column, the next user to visit would see the same sorting due to the preference being reused. In this case, the developer may want to create a page process that will reset the preferences as the page is being rendered. That can be done by creating a Session State page process with the type set to Reset Preferences (remove all preferences for current user). This can be handy on report pages where data can be sorted. In the description above, the preferences are being reset before loading a report page to restore the default sorting of how the report was designed. The section in this book on HTML DB APIs provides more information on the htmldb_util.remove_sort_preferences procedure.

HTML DB URL Format

Understanding the URL used in HTML DB will help improve a developer's efficiency. The URL has several distinct parts. For reference look at the sample URL that follows.

```
http://localhost:7777/pls/hdb20/f?p=102:3:7646151020298818363::NO::P
3_ID:28
```

http://localhost:7777/pls/hdb20 is the address used to navigate to HTML DB.

The rest of the URL is actually a call to a stored procedure within the database named F. The parameter being passed is a colon delimited string to the P parameter in the procedure. The values in the colon delimited string have a specific position they must be presented to the procedure. These positions are referred to as arguments. The arguments are shown here.

```
f?p=App:Page:Session:Request:Debug:ClearCache:itemNames:itemValues:P
rinterFriendly
```

- App: This is the application ID or the alias of the application.

- Page: The page ID to render or the alias name of the page.

- Session: A numeric value indicating the session ID. The session ID is needed so HTML DB knows which session state to reference.

- Request: When buttons are pressed, they set the REQUEST, normally to the name of the button. The next page can then reference the REQUEST to know the name of the button the user pressed.

- Debug: Set this value to YES to display debug information in the page being rendered.

- ClearCache: This will clear the cache for an application page. To clear the cache for multiple pages, a comma delimited string of page ID's can be provided. This is a URL argument to remember. It will be used quite often during development and testing. It is argument six in the colon delimited string. To clear cache for the entire application, enter the value APP for this argument.

- itemNames: This argument is used to set the session state of page items. Multiple page items can be set here by using a comma delimited list. Page items are global so even though the goal is to navigate to page 100, the session state can be set for items on other pages or application level items.

- itemValues: This is partner to the itemNames argument. These are the values used to set the session state for the items listed in the itemNames argument.

- PrinterFriendly: To render the page in a mode that is better for printing, set this argument to YES. It is then possible to set the conditional display to Current page is NOT in Printer Fiendly Mode. The page component would then not be rendered if the PrintFriendly argument is set to YES.

Shared Components

There is an icon on the Application Home page to access shared components. Shared Components are used by many pages in an application. In some cases, using the publish and subscribe feature of HTML DB, these shared components can actually be used by other applications.

Logic: Application Level Components

Most documentation of Shared Components will not mention Application Level Components. That is because, technically, they are not defined in HTML DB as a shared component. However, an application level component can be used anywhere within the application. Application Level Components consist of those described in Table 6.5.

COMPONENT	DESCRIPTION
Application Items	Application Level Items are similar to hidden page level items. They have session state and are not visible page components. One difference is they are not named with the page prefix (P100_). Instead, they will be named with the application prefix F102 for app id 102, or another prefix such as G_ can be chosen. This has been used to indicate Global.
Application Processes	These are globally defined processes that can execute for every page in the application. It could be handy for inserting a record into a table to indicate a page is being viewed. Another great use for an Application Process is the ability to define a process here and call it on the appropriate pages by creating an On Demand process on an application page.
Application Computations	An Application Computation would be setup if there is a computation the developer wants to execute for every page in the application or if they simply wanted it to execute when the user creates a new session, which is when the user first accesses an application page. The On New Instance computation point is the one that executes when the user first accesses the application and is commonly used to read browser cookies.

Table 6.5: *Application level components*

Web Services

The building of web services is covered later in this book in the section on Creating Other Components with HTML DB.

Build Option

Using build options can disable certain functionality. This is done by creating a build option and setting the page component attribute called build option. Figure 6.8 depicts that a build option named Version 1.1 has been created. It will be turned on, and at a later time, set to INCLUDE when the new features are ready for the public. Another use for this is if there are problems discovered with the new features after the application is in production, the developer can simply change the build option back to EXCLUDE and HTML DB will not render the new features. If used cautiously, this feature could be used to back-out changes in the middle of the day.

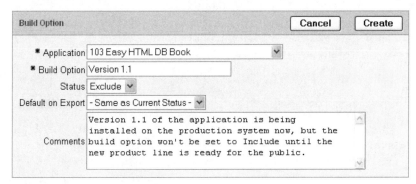

Figure 6.8: *Creating a build option.*

Security

Security will be covered in detail later in this book in the chapter on HTML DB Administration II.

Navigation

The components responsible for HTML DB navigation are covered in detail in a later chapter in this book.

User Interface

The user interface section includes Themes, Templates, User Interface Defaults, Lists of Values (LOV's), and Shortcuts.

Themes and Templates are covered in a later chapter of this book.

User Interface Defaults

User Interface Defaults provide the ability to set default properties for tables and views and columns. These defaults are used by the wizards when creating reports and forms. Not only does this feature provide a consistent name for the components placed on an application page, but it also saves time because they are defined ahead of time.

To create a user interface default, navigate to the Shared Components page and click on the User Interface Defaults link. This will bring up a list of the tables in the parsing schema. An experienced developer would encourage new developers to switch the view to Details by selecting the Details item in the View select list and clicking the Go button.

1. Click on the DEMO_ORDERS table link.

2. On the next page, click on the Create User Interface Defaults button.

    The next page is the Table Defaults page shown in Figure 6.9. It shows several attributes for each column. When a report or a form is created and columns are added to that report or form, they will obtain the defaults set here. The order in which the column will be displayed can be established by setting the sequence and whether or not the column should be included.

Column Name	Label	Include In Reports	Report Sequence ▲	Searchable
ORDER ITEM ID	Order Item Id	✓	1	-
ORDER ID	Order Id	✓	2	-
PRODUCT ID	Product Id	✓	3	-
UNIT PRICE	Unit Price	✓	4	-
QUANTITY	Quantity	✓	5	-

Group By	Aggregate By	Include In Forms	Form Sequence	Required
-	-	✓	1	✓
-	-	✓	2	✓
-	-	✓	3	✓
-	-	✓	4	✓
-	-	✓	5	✓

Figure 6.9: *Table Defaults.*

3. Click on the UNIT_PRICE column link to edit the default properties.

4. There are several properties that can be set for the UNIT_PRICE column. Some of them are:

- Label: This is the default label, or column heading, for the page item when it is added to a page.

- Mask: For dates and numbers, this is valuable because the formatting can be set here once and it will not have to be done every time a report or form is created.

- Display As: For dates, the developer may want the default to be a Date Picker. This is also really helpful for large text fields where it is desirable to default this to Text Area.

- Default Value: This is another valuable property to set for a date. An example of this is setting the default to today's date by entering the following text in this property.

  ```
  ( select to_char( sysdate, :PICK_DATE_FORMAT_MASK ) from dual )
  ```

- Help Text: If the Help Text feature is used in an application, this can be an incredible time saver.

- List of Values: If the column is a select list and uses a List of Values, it can be defined by using the List of Values tab.

5. For the UNIT_PRICE column, make the following selections:

- Report Defaults → Mask: &PICK_DATE_FORMAT_MASK.

- Tabular Form Default → Display As: Date Picker (use application format mask).

- Form Defaults → Mask: &PICK_DATE_FORMAT_MASK.

- Default Value: Use the query shown above in the Default Value bullet point.

6. Click the Apply Changes button.

The authors of this book believe that user interface defaults are an underutilized feature in HTML DB. To not use this feature should be considered cruel and unusual punishment to the developer, because they will find themselves making the same attribute changes to page item after page item to keep things consistent.

Lists of Values (LOV)

A LOV is a reusable list that can be built dynamically with a SQL select statement or with a static set of values typed in by the developer. Examples of static LOVs are:

- Gender: Male, Female

- Days of Week: Monday, Tuesday, Wednesday, etc…

The values in dynamic LOV's are populated using a SQL select statement such as:

```
select description d, manufacturer_id r
from   manufacturer
order by 1;
```

LOV's can be used in forms, in tabular form columns, in reports using Display as Text based on LOV, and select lists. More explanation on creating and using LOV's is included later in this book.

Shortcuts

Shortcuts enable the creation of reusable HTML or PL/SQL code. For an idea of how this is used, the select list in the Conditional Display region for a button is shown in Figure 6.10. There is a button displayed after the select list followed by a list of items shown directly below the select list. In the HTML DB development environment, this was done using a shortcut. The name of the shortcut is then placed in the Post Element Text of the select list item. This example shows that HTML DB is actually written in HTML DB.

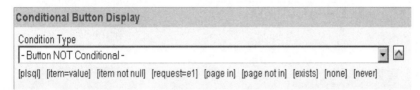

Figure 6.10: *Shortcut use in HTML DB Development Environment*

As an exercise to demonstrate how to create and use the developer's own shortcut, a page item that displays a date page item will be created. A link will be provided on the side of the page item that will allow the user to click on it and set the item to today's date.

This is defined in the following four step process:

1. Create a blank application page named Shortcuts. In the Page Attributes, add the following text to the HTML Header section. This is using the functions.js script provided as part of HTML DB. It provides the source code for the setValue() function used later in the shortcut. What is being accomplished here is borrowing some code provided with the installation of HTML DB.

    ```
    <script src="#IMAGE_PREFIX#javascript/functions.js"
    type="text/javascript"></script>
    ```

2. Create a shortcut from scratch by going to Shared Components →Shortcuts.

    ▪ On the Creation Method page, select From Scratch and click Next.

    ▪ On the Shortcut Attributes page:

        o Name: SET_TODAYS_DATE.

        o Type: PL/SQL Function Body.

        o Shortcut: Enter the text from below. The file is in the Code Depot.

    ▪ Click Create.

plsql_shortcut.sql

```
declare
    r   varchar2(32767) := null;
    d   varchar2(11) := null;
begin
    d := to_char( sysdate, :PICK_DATE_FORMAT_MASK );
    r := '<a href="javascript:setValue(''#CURRENT_ITEM_NAME#'',''' 
         || d || ''');">';
    r := r || '<img src="#IMAGE_PREFIX#r_blue_arrow.gif"
         width="16" height="16"></a>';
    return r;
end;
```

> In the Listing above, make sure there are not any extra lines or characters after the final semi-colon (end;). This will cause a PL/SQL error.

Not only is the setValue JavaScript function provided by HTML DB going to be used in this example, the above script references a gif image named r_blue_arrow.gif, which is provided with HTML DB. Take note of the date format. It is possible to change the date format to the developer's preferred format. Another thing that can be done is the use of a substitution string for the date format to keep the date format consistent throughout the application. One such substitution string would be PICK_DATE_FORMAT_MASK. If so, the statement would look something like this:

```
d := to_char( sysdate, :PICK_DATE_FORMAT_MASK );.
```

> When using the PICK_DATE_FORMAT_MASK as mentioned above, the page item would be created as a Date Picker (with application format mask).

3. Create an HTML region on the page and then a Date Picker on the page. This way the formats will always stay consistent whether the Date Picker icon or the Shortcut icon is used.

4. After the page item is created, edit the new page item and add the text SET_TODAYS_DATE to Post Element Text (include the double quotes), as shown in Figure 6.11.

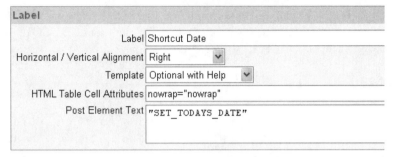

Figure 6.11: *Using a Shortcut in the Post Element Text.*

 Be careful: Shortcuts are case-sensitive. It is recommended that developers use the same case as the HTML DB development team, which is UPPERCASE.

Apply Changes to the page item and run the page. It should look similar to Figure 6.12. What has happened with the SET_TODAYS_DATE shortcut is HTML DB has executed the PL/SQL block and returned the following HTML code.

```
<a href="javascript:setValue('P2910_SHORTCUT_DATE','01/24/2006');">
<img src="/i/r_blue_arrow.gif" width="16" height="16"></a>
```

It is this HTML code that was rendered as the Post Element Text for the page item. It creates an anchor tag and an image tag displaying a blue arrow. Clicking on the blue arrow executes the JavaScript in the anchor tag.

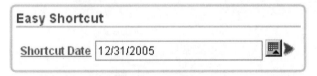

Figure 6.12: *Using a Shortcut to Set the Date.*

The example above used the PICK_DATE_FORMAT_MASK substitution string. This is a best practice method of keeping all dates consistent throughout an application.

This is not the extent of the usefulness of shortcuts. The sample in Figure 6.10 is created with a shortcut that is an elaborate PL/SQL program returning a string of HTML source code.

Files

The files in this shared component are stored in the HTML DB repository. From the repository, they can be referenced in HTML code as described below.

Cascading Style Sheets and Static Files from the information on JavaScript are covered in a later chapter of this book.

Images

Images can be stored in the HTML DB repository and rendered in an application page. The process and explanation of adding an image to the repository follows:

1. Navigate to the Shared Components page.

2. Click on the Images link.

3. Click on the Create button.

4. On the Create Image page:

    - Application: Select the application this image will be used in.

    There are two ways to add the image to the repository. It can either be associated with an application or with the workspace. Adding it to the workspace is done by selecting the No Application Associated option. If the image is added to the workspace, it can be referenced by all applications in the workspace. If it is added to a particular application, it can only be referenced by that application.

    - Upload New Image: Browse for the file name to upload.

    - Notes: Enter notes if desired.

    - Click Upload.

5. Upon completion, the program will return to the Images page showing a list of images in the repository.

Referencing Images

When images are referenced from the repository, it is done by using substitution strings. The two options are:

- #WORKSPACE_IMAGES#: Use this substitution string if the image is either associated with an application other than the developer's own or associated with the workspace using the No Application Associated option.

- #APP_IMAGES#: Use this substitution string if the image is loaded into the repository and associated with the current application.

Examples

The image can be rendered into a region of type PL/SQL by adding the following code for the region source:

```
htp.img( '#WORKSPACE_IMAGES#EasyHTMLDB.gif' );

htp.img( '#APP_IMAGES#EasyHTMLDB.gif' );
```

To use a loaded image as the logo for the application, it can be set in the Application Attributes page as shown in Figure 6.13.

Figure 6.13: *Using substitution strings.*

There is additional information about working with images in a later section of this book.

Export/Import

Export/Import is a utility to export various pieces of an application. Using this utility, the following application pieces can be exported: an application; an application page; CSS files; Image Files; other Files (i.e. JavaScript); Themes; and, User Interface Defaults. The export/import utilities are used for backing up data or for deploying an application to another location.

Application Deployment is covered in more detail later in this book and more information about export/import is included there.

Developer Toolbar

The developer toolbar is displayed at the bottom of web pages when a developer or administrator is logged into the HTML DB development environment. It provides quick links to several common tasks.

- Edit Application: Goes straight to the Application's home page described earlier in the chapter.

- Edit Page 1: The page id (1) will depend on which page you are on. This will take you to the Page Definition screen.

- Create: Runs the Create wizard allowing the developer to select whether they want to create a New Page, new Region on the current page, new Control on the current page, or a new Shared Component.

- Session: It is difficult to express enough how important this link is to an HTML DB developer. Clicking this link will display a popup window showing the current status session state. Session state will become very important as new developers dive into the world of developing HTML DB applications.

- Debug: This is another very important link. It causes the current web page to be re-posted with debug information shown inline. Some of the valuable information displayed is the amount of time each step took to process while rendering the page. There is a section on debugging later in the book.

- Show Edit Links: This link will display a little icon ⁛ next to each of the components on the page. Clicking on the icon will display a popup window allowing the developer to change the properties of the component without leaving the current page. This is a very handy productivity feature in HTML DB.

Page Zero

Page Zero is a special application page that must be deliberately created by the developer. It is not created by default when using the Create Application wizards.

The intended purpose of Page Zero is that any items created on Page Zero will be rendered on every other page of the application. The only restriction is Page Zero will only render the following types of components:

- Regions

- Buttons

- Items

An example use for Page Zero would be for a banner, footer, or a sidebar table of contents the developer wants displayed on every page of their application.

In the HTML DB development environment Page Zero is used to display the main tab list you see at the top of every page in the Application Builder, SQL Workshop, and Administration applications.

Creating a Page Zero

1. From the application builder page click the Create Page button.

2. Choose Blank Page, click Next.

3. On the Page Attributes page enter 0 in the Page field, click Next.

4. On the Page Name page, enter Page Zero for Name, click Next.

5. On the Tabs page, select the No option, click Next.

6. Click Finish.

There, now the application will have a Page Zero. Any item placed on this page will be rendered on every other page in the application. Viewing the page definition of Page Zero will display a page as shown below.

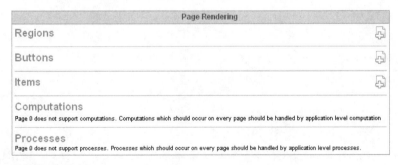

Figure 6.14: *Page Definition for a Page Zero application page.*

> 💣 Even though figure 6.14 shows regions for defining Computations and Processes, they are not processed by the HTML DB engine. Also, any JavaScript placed in Page Zero attributes such as in the HTML Header area, are not processed by the HTML DB engine.

Easy HTML DB Book application

During the course of this book, there are several exercises that can be built and used for later reference. So far, the Conference RSVP application has been created and the following exercises will create an application named Easy HTML DB Book. This application will be used to build the pages in the exercises in the following chapters.

The code depot also includes an application named Easy Samples that is similar to the Easy HTML DB Book application. It has all the pages the author built while working on the book and documenting the exercises. This application can be installed and is a great source for looking at how to do perform a certain task in HTML DB.

1. Navigate to the Application Builder home page and click on the Create application link as shown in Figure 6.9.

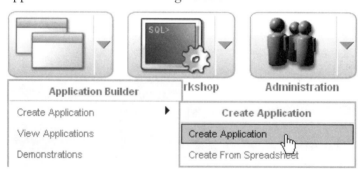

Figure 6.9: *Create a new Application.*

2. On the Name page:

   ▪ Name: Easy HTML DB Book.

   ▪ Application: 103 If ID 103 is not available, another ID should be used.

- Create Application: Choose the From scratch option.

- Schema: User the EASYHDB schema already created. When using a workspace on the hosted Oracle site, use the schema available.

- Click Next.

3. On the Pages page:

   - Page Name: Enter Home as the page name.

   - Click the Add Page button. The application must have at least one application, and this is the starting point.

   - Click Next.

4. On the Tabs page, choose the No Tabs option and click Next.

5. On the Shared Components page, choose No and click Next.

6. On the Attributes page, leave the defaults and click Next.

7. On the User Interface page, choose Theme 2 and click Next. In truth, any theme can be chosen, but the figures used throughout the book are using Theme 2.

8. On the Confirm page click the Create button.

That completes the building of the Easy HTML DB Book application.

Conclusion

This chapter described many of the attributes that can be set for an application, application pages, and page level components. It should serve as a place of reference when it becomes necessary to understand what each attribute is providing.

The topic of Session State was also covered. The session state can be thought of as HTML DB's way of managing variables. The examples showed how to create the Easy HTML DB Book application that will be used in the exercises throughout the book.

The next chapter will begin with the most common type of application page used in HTML DB; the Report. An HTLM DB report is a graphical representation of an SQL Select statement and has many built in features.

Creating Reports

Introduction

An HTML DB report is, simply put, a graphical representation of a query. The query is executed during the page rendering event.

Reports can be built by either using the Report Wizard or by entering SQL statements for the SQL Report. If the SQL Report option is used, there will also be an opportunity to use the graphical query builder. This is a welcome feature of HTML DB version 2.0 and is easy for users transitioning from Microsoft Access to HTML DB.

Building a Report Using the Report Wizard

The report wizard will help build a report very quickly. In most cases, the initial report can be built in two to three minutes. No joke! The more comfortable one gets with HTML DB, the easier it will be to do the same.

Do not let the fact that a report can be built in a matter of minutes fool you into thinking it is not valuable. After the initial report is created, there are several customizations that can be made to the report to provide additional features.

This section of the chapter is focused on rebuilding the report part of the Conference RSVP report in the application that was created earlier. This is page one of the Conference RSVP application. Some of the columns will be formatted, and in the following sections, a couple of features will be added.

This is a lengthy tutorial, but these exercises will provide exposure to a few of the more esoteric features of HTML DB. The skills learned here can be applied to other areas of HTML DB development. It should be well worth the time.

Navigate to the Conference RSVP application by clicking on the Application Builder icon and then by clicking on the Conference RSVP link in the report of applications.

1. Click on the Create Page button.

2. Choose the Report option and click Next.

3. Choose the SQL Report option and click Next.

   This is the most common way to create reports for beginners. As new users get more comfortable with HTML DB, they may choose either method, but I still prefer using the Wizard Report wizard.

4. On the Page Attributes page:

   ▪ Page: Enter 11

   ▪ Page Title: Conference RSVP Report

   This is the text that will be displayed on the caption bar of the browser. It is also displayed as the name when viewing all pages in an application.

5. On the Tab (optional) page:

   ▪ Choose the Do not use tabs option.

   ▪ Click Next.

6. On the SQL Query page, enter the following in the text area and click Next. Use file ch7_1.sql from code depot.

   💾 **ch7_1.sql**

```
select
    id, last_name, first_name,
    email, phone, rsvp_date,
    company, donation, payment
from
    conference_rsvp
```

> 🔔 Notice there is no semi-colon on the end of the SQL statement. This is because HTML DB appends more SQL on the end of this statement if sorting in reports is allowed. Having the semi-colon will produce a common error (ORA-00911: invalid character) and can lead to more debugging.

7. On the Report Attributes page:

- Region Template: Reports Region.

- Report Template: template: 2. Standard

- Region Name: Conference – Confirmed Attendees

- Maximum Rows per Page: 15

At this point, the number of rows that will appear on each page can be changed. This is referred to as pagination and is used to restrict the number of rows displayed at a time. Later, a Select List will be added to the application page to make this a user selectable option.

- Click Next.

8. On the Confirm page click Finish.

9. When the success page displays, click on the Run Page icon.

Conference – Confirmed Attendees

ID	LAST_NAME	FIRST_NAME	EMAIL	PHONE	RSVP_DATE	COMPANY	DONATION	PAYMENT
1	Vorse	Robert	RVorse@htmldbbook.com	(919)555-8393	02-SEP-05	Smyth Industries	5	Check
2	Hill	Alan	Alan.Hill@htmldbbook.com	(919)555-2832	02-SEP-05	TechDyne Consulting	10	Cash
3	Azordegan	George	GAzo@htmldbbook.com	(919)555-8290	02-SEP-05	Applied Cryogenics	5	Check
4	Jones	Albert	Albert@htmldbbook.com	(919)555-1243	02-SEP-05	CompuTech	5	Check
5	Davis	Philip	PDavis@htmldbbook.com	(919)555-7362	09-SEP-05	Strickland Propane		
6	Eads	Robert	Robert.Eads@htmldbbook.com	(919)555-2638	23-SEP-05	Cyberbiotics	5	Cash
7	Lilly	Joseph	JLil@htmldbbook.com	(850)555-5378	02-SEP-05	Bank of Springfield		
8	Bloomstrom	Luke	Luke@htmldbbook.com	(704)555-3722	09-SEP-05	Transworld Consortium	10	Visa
9	Gardner	Vasanti	VGardner@htmldbbook.com	(423)555-2623	02-SEP-05	Railinc Corporation		
10	Yoell	Patrick	Patrick.Yoell@htmldbbook.com	(919)555-2737	02-SEP-05	Landacorp	7	Check
11	Crotty	Kent	KCro@htmldbbook.com	(919)555-6282	27-AUG-05	Scolex Industries	3	Cash
12	Sommer	Eugenia	Eugenia@htmldbbook.com	(860)555-2233	22-SEP-05	GlaxoSmithKline	15	Mastercard
13	Pierce	Robert	RPierce@htmldbbook.com	(919)555-2723	02-SEP-05	Scolex Industries	5	Check
14	Fouladi	Afroze	Afroze.Fouladi@htmldbbook.com	(423)555-9483	22-SEP-05	Management Dynamics	10	Cash
15	Little	Milton	MLit@htmldbbook.com	(919)555-4744	02-SEP-05	Scolex Industries	20	Visa

row(s) 1 - 15 of 50 ☑ Next ▣

Figure 7.1: *Running the first report.*

At this point, the report shown in Figure 7.1 will have been created. There is still some customizing to do to add the Spread Sheet link, some buttons, the search field, and number of rows to display.

Adding the Spread Sheet link

This is made simple by the Report Attributes page in HTML DB. Navigate to this page by clicking on the Edit Page 11 link in the developer toolbar at the bottom of the Conference RSVP Report web page. Then, click on the Report Attributes (RPT) link as shown in Figure 7.2. This link goes directly to the Report Attributes page for the report. Clicking on the Conference - Confirmed Attendees link goes directly to the Region Definition page.

Figure 7.2: *Report Region links.*

Once on the Report Attributes page, navigate to the Report Export region. Use the hot link provided near the top of the page, which is shown in Figure 7.3, for faster navigation to save the need to scroll the page manually.

Figure 7.3: *Using the hot links for faster navigating.*

In the Report Export region set the following:

- Enable CSV Output: YES

- Separator: Leave this column blank, which is the default

This is the character that will be used to separate each of the columns of data in the export file. The default value of the separator is dependent on the NLS setting. Most likely this is either a comma (,) or a semi-colon (;). Some common alternative choices are the tilde (~) or vertical bar (|).

- Enclosed By: Leave this column blank (default)

This is the character that will be used to enclose the data in the export file. The default value is a double-quote ("). The resulting text in the output file would look like this: "Bloomstrom".

- Link Label: Enter the text Spread Sheet.

This is the text that will be displayed as the link in the report.

- Filename: Enter the text Conference_RSVP.csv

This is the name to be given to the file when the report is exported. The default name of the report is the name of the region, with spaces replaced by an underscore (_), and a file extension of CSV. The default name of the example file would have been conference_-_confirmed_attendees.csv.

- At the top of the page, click the Apply Changes button.

- Run the page by clicking on the ⊡ icon in the upper right corner of the Page Definition page.

A link with the name Spread Sheet will now be visible in the lower left corner of the report region. Clicking on this link will offer the user the option of saving the report to a file named Conference_RSVP.csv.

Adding the Search Field to the Report

Adding a search field to the report is a two step process:

- Create a page item for the search value.

- Modify the query for the report to use the value in the page item.

This same process would be used to provide several search fields. That will be covered in the Add Query By Example to a Report section later in this chapter.

To create the search page item in the report region, click on the Edit Page 11 link in the developer toolbar. This goes to the Page Definition page.

1. On the Page Definition page, click on the ⊡ icon in the Items section.

2. On the Item Type page choose the Text option and click Next.

3. On the next page choose the Text Field (always submits page when Enter pressed) option and click Next.

   This option will do just what it says. When the user presses the Enter key while in the search page item, the page will be submitted.

4. On the Display Position and Name page:

   - Item Name: P11_REPORT_SEARCH

   - Sequence: 10

   - Region: Conference - Confirmed Attendees.

   - Click Next.

5. On the Item Attributes page:

- Label: Search.

- Label Alignment: Right.

- Field Width: 50

The field width is used to indicate how wide to make the page item when rendering it in an HTML web page. The field width in this example will be set at 50 since that is the text length of the largest column that will be searched.

- Field Alignment: Left.

- Label Template: Optional with Help.

- Click Next.

6. On the Source page:

- Leave all the items on this page on the default values and click Next. These are explained in detail in another chapter in the book.

- Click the Create Item button.

Adding the Go Button to the Report

The next step is to create a Go button to serve as the submit button for the user when they enter new search criteria. This will also happen when the user presses the Enter key while in the Search field (P11_REPORT_SEARCH) created above.

Buttons are covered in great detail in the chapter on Creating Other Page Components, so extensive detail will not be provided here.

1. On the Page Definition page, click on the ⬓ icon in the Buttons section.

2. On the Button Region page, click Next.

3. On the Button Position page, choose the Create a button displayed among this region's items option and click Next.

4. On the Button Attributes page:

- Button Name: P11_GO

- Sequence: 20

- Beginning on New Line: NO, which is indicated by the lack of a check mark

- Beginning on New Field: YES

- Label: Go

- Request: Go

- Button Style: Template Based Button

- Template: Button

- Click the Create Button button.

At this point, the program returns to the Page Definition page. Click on the Run button to run the page.

Modifying the Query on the Report

In order for the report to use the new P11_REPORT_SEARCH field for filtering, the query must be modified. For this, a WHERE clause will be added to the SQL statement used to populate the report.

1. Click on the Conference - Confirmed Attendees link in the Region section of the Page Definition page as shown in Figure 7.2.

2. Modify the text in the Region Source, shown above, to what is shown in the listing below. The ch7_2.sql file in the code depot should be used.

🖫 ch7_2.sql

```
select
    id, last_name, first_name,
    email, phone, rsvp_date,
    company, donation, payment
from
    conference_rsvp
where

instr(upper(LAST_NAME),upper(nvl(:P11_REPORT_SEARCH,LAST_NAME)))
> 0  or

instr(upper(FIRST_NAME),upper(nvl(:P11_REPORT_SEARCH,FIRST_NAME))
) > 0  or
    instr(upper(EMAIL),upper(nvl(:P11_REPORT_SEARCH,EMAIL))) > 0
or
    instr(upper(PHONE),upper(nvl(:P11_REPORT_SEARCH,PHONE))) > 0
or
    instr(upper(COMPANY),upper(nvl(:P11_REPORT_SEARCH,COMPANY))) >
0  or
```

```
instr(upper(PAYMENT),upper(nvl(:P11_REPORT_SEARCH,PAYMENT))) >
0
```

3. When the modification is complete, click Apply Changes.

4. Run the report by clicking on the ⬚ icon.

Enter the value AM in the Search field and either press the Enter key or click the Go button. The filter is applied to the results of the report.

Highlighting Words in a Report

As we saw in chapter 4 when we did a search the search word was highlighted in each of the fields wherever it was found in the report. The next step will be to show you how to do that in this report.

1. Once again click on the Edit Page 11 link in the developer toolbar.

2. Click on the Report link as shown in Figure 7.2 to navigate directly to the Report Attributes page.

3. Click on the ⬚ link next to the LAST_NAME column.

4. Go to the Highlight Words page item in the Column Formatting region and enter the text: &P11_REPORT_SEARCH.

5. Take note the trailing period that must be there as shown in Figure 7.4. This is referred to as Exact Substitution.

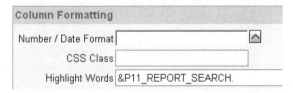

Figure 7.4: *Shows proper syntax for exact substitution.*

6. Click Apply Changes.

> 🔔 Save time by using the ⊡ button in the upper right area of the Column Attributes page. This will save the changes and navigate to each of the next columns in the report. On the last page click Apply Changes.

7. Repeat the setting of the Highlight Words page item for the following report columns: FIRST_NAME, EMAIL, COMPANY, PAYMENT TYPE.

Test the work by running the report.

8. Type in the text AM in the Search page item and press the Enter key.

A full screen of results should be visible with the text am in red, bold letters everywhere there is a match. Isn't this exciting! These are the kinds of things that are built into HTML DB that eliminate developers from having to develop their own programming logic to do it.

Report Pagination

Report Pagination is the control of which series of rows are being displayed to the user based on the entire set of data in the report.

The goal of this section is to give an understanding of what is pagination, how to setup pagination in reports, and how it is reset. The reason it would need to be reset is so any subsequent searches would not leave the user in an undesirable place in regards to the pagination. For example, select the pagination to view rows 31 – 45. Then change the search page item and return a different result set. If the pagination were not reset, we would automatically be taken to rows 31 – 45 of the new result set. This is not the desired result. So, the pagination should be reset any time a new search is submitted.

The easiest way to explain resetting pagination is with the use of Figure 7.5. The figure shows a user looking at the pagination of rows 31 – 45. A reset of the pagination would return the user back to the beginning to rows 1 – 15.

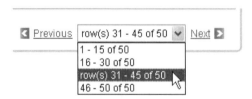

Figure 7.5: *Report Pagination*

Resetting the pagination is done by creating a Page Process. There is a wizard that makes this step very easy.

1. Navigate to the page definition page and click on the  icon in the Processes section under the Page Processing region.

2. On the Process Type page: choose the Reset Pagination option and click Next.

3. On the Create Page Process page, leave everything at the default value except the following

   ▪ Condition Type: Request Is Contained within Expression 1.

   ▪ Expression 1: Go,P11_REPORT_SEARCH.

     This setting is case sensitive and must be typed as shown. This step is setting up the process to only process when the Go button is pressed or when the user is in the P11_REPORT_SEARCH page item and presses the Enter key. Under these two conditions, the Reset Pagination process will be processed. Any other time the page is submitted and rendered again, this process will be ignored. This performs an If … Then logic statement.

   ▪ Click Create Process.

Whenever the page is resubmitted with new search criteria, the report will automatically be returned to the first set of rows in the result set.

Adding the Number of Rows Item to a Report

This feature allows the user to control pagination of the report by selecting how many rows will be displayed on each page. This feature is used often on various pages in HTML DB. Figure 7.6 shows this feature being used on the Application home page.

Figure 7.6: *Display Select List used for Report Pagination.*

Providing user selectable pagination is a two step process.

▪ Create the Select List for the user to select from.

▪ Modify the Report Attributes to use the value from the Select List.

Since select list components are covered in greater detail in the chapter on Creating Other HTML DB Components, only brief step-by-step instructions will be given here.

Create the Number of Rows Select List

This is an item that is not present on the original Report page of the Conference RSVP application. However, it is a common feature to provide on reports. It is created as follows:

1. While running the page, click on the Edit Page 11 link in the developer toolbar.

2. Click on the ⎘ icon in the Items section.

3. Choose the Select List option and click Next.

4. For Select List Control Type, leave the default: Select List – and click Next.

5. On the Display Position and Name page:

    - Item Name: P11_ROWS

    - Sequence: 15

      The sequence will be set to 15 because this Select List is to be displayed between the Search page item and the Go button. The Search page item has a sequence of 10, and the Go button has a sequence of 20. Setting the p11_rows select list to a sequence of 15 will cause the HTML DB engine to put it between the other page components.

    - Region: Conference - Confirmed Attendees

    - Click Next.

6. On the List of Values page

    - Display Null Option: NO

    - List of Values Query:
      ```
      STATIC2:5;5,10;10,15;15,25;25,50;50,100;100
      ```

      What this does is create a static list of values to display in the select list. After entering the static text, click on the link Create or edit static List of Values to view a popup that will guide you through the creation. If the developer is the kind of person who finds it difficult to remember the proper syntax to use when creating the static list, using the link will help.

- Leave all the other values with the default values and click Next.

7. On the Item Attributes page:

- Label: Enter the text Display.

8. Leave all the other values with the default values and click Next.

9. On the next page click the Create Item button.

   Once back on the Page Definition page, it will be necessary to make a couple change to the P11_ROWS select list.

10. Click on the P11_ROWS Select List link.

11. On the Edit Page Item page:

- In the Displayed region, change the Begin On New Line value to NO.

   The reason behind this setting is covered later in this book in the section called Controlling Form Layout.

- In the Default region set the Default Value to 15.

- Click on the Apply Changes button.

Modify the Report to use the Number of Rows Select List

1. From the Page Definition page, click on the Report link as shown in Figure 7.2.

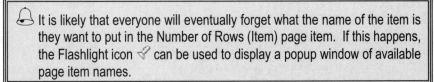

It is likely that everyone will eventually forget what the name of the item is they want to put in the Number of Rows (Item) page item. If this happens, the Flashlight icon can be used to display a popup window of available page item names.

2. In the Layout and Pagination region, enter the text P11_ROWS, which is the Select List item created earlier, in Number of Rows (Item). Then click Apply Changes.

3. Run the page with the new modifications.

4. Clear the text in the Search page item and click the Go button.

5. Change the value in the Display select list to 25 and click the Go button.

What was accomplished in this section was learning how to add a page component that enables a user to customize the way they see the data in a report. However, it was still necessary to manually delete the data from the Search page item. The next logical step is to provide a button for the user that enables them to Reset the page.

Creating a Reset button for the Report

This section will not just be used to create a button. A process will also be created to reset the various page items. The detailed explanation on processes is contained in the chapter on Page Processing.

The tasks in this section require two steps

- Create the Reset button

- Create a Reset Report Search process

To create the reset button, follow the abbreviated steps below:

1. On the Page Definition page click on the icon in the Buttons section.

2. On the Button Region page click Next.

3. Button Position: Create a button in a region position and click Next.

4. On the Button Attributes page:

   - Button Name: RESET

   - Label: Reset

   - Default for the rest and click Next.

5. Image Attributes page: Click Next.

6. On the Create Button page:

   - Position: Region Template Position #CLOSE#

     The [Close] link below the Position select list can be used to help make this faster.

   - Default the rest and click Next.

7. On the Branching page:

- Branch to Page: &APP_PAGE_ID. Be sure to remember the ending period.

- Click Create Button.

At this point, the program returns to the Page Definition page, and it is time to create the processes.

Creating the Reset Report Search Process

It is common to provide users of a web site with a button to reset the page, especially when it includes filtering page items. The process created here will be set to process only in the condition where the Reset button was pressed. The reset button will submit the page and set the REQUEST = 'RESET'. This will be explained better in the following pages.

1. On the Page Definition screen, click on the icon in the Processes section under the Page Processes region.

2. On the Process Type page: Choose the Session State option and click Next.

   Session State was explained in a previous chapter and will not be covered again here. However, this type of process does warrant further explanation. In order to change session state while processing a page, a Session State process is created. The type of Session State process picked should be one that will deal with the level of session state that is needed, such as application level, page level, page item level, etc. If one session state process will not handle everything that is needed, it may be necessary to use several session state processes on the same page to handle it all.

3. On the next Process Type page choose the Clear Cache for items (ITEM,ITEM,ITEM) option and click Next.

   This is the option to select to clear the session state for multiple page items on the current application page.

4. On the Process Attributes page:

   - Name: Reset Report Search

   - Leave the others defaulted and click Next.

5. On the Process page:

   - Enter items delimited by ",": P11_REPORT_SEARCH,P11_ROWS

This will cause the session state for the two items listed to be cleared when the page is submitted. In the case of the P11_ROWS page item, it will be cleared and then set to its default value.

- Click Next.

6. On the Messages page:

- Success message: It is not necessary to be notified when this process is successful, so leave this blank.

- Failure Message: Unable to clear cache.

- Click Next.

7. On the Process Conditions page:

- When Button Pressed: RESET

    This is telling the HTML DB engine to only allow processing of this process when the RESET button is pressed.

- Click Create Process.

Creating a Report Link

Until now, every time the report was submitted it returned to the same report. In other words, there was no navigation to another web page. Now it is time to see how to navigate from the report page to another application page. The report shows a list of the rows, but the rows cannot be edited in a report, so the goal is to navigate to a form page to edit a single record at a time. Until our own form page is created in the next chapter, the navigation will be to the existing form page that was created when the Conference RSVP application was built in a previous chapter. The form page to which the navigation will go is application page three.

The idea here is to modify the ID column in the report to be a linked column that will navigate the user to page three when the link is clicked. Navigating to the page is not all that is needed. It will also be necessary to let page three know which record the user wants to edit. This is done by sending the value of the ID column in the URL when navigating to page three. Believe it or not, all this work is handled in one section while modifying the properties of the ID report column.

Before this lesson commences, take note of the ID column in the report. It is a column with a column heading of ID and it can be sorted. When finished, the column heading will be blank, not sortable, and will have an icon the user can click on to be navigated to the form page so the row can be edited.

Navigate to the page definition page and click on the Report link as was shown in Figure 7.2.

1. Before changing the heading of the ID column, first set the Headings Type to Custom. Click on the Custom option in the Column Attributes region, as shown in Figure 7.7.

Headings Type: ○ Column Names ○ Column Names (InitCap) ◉ Custom ○ PL/SQL ○ None

Figure 7.7: *Set Headings Type to Custom.*

2. In the Column Attributes region, click on the ⃠ icon next to the ID column.

    This navigates to the page where all the changes necessary to alter the look, feel, and behavior of the column will be made.

3. On the Column Attributes page:

    ▪ In the Column Definition region, clear the text in the Column Heading page item.

    ▪ In the Column Link region: Link Text: Click on the [Icon 2] link below the Link Text page item.

    The proper syntax for the <img> tag will be filled in automatically. As the mouse pointer is placed over each of the links, an image is displayed in the area to the right.

    ▪ Modify the text in the Link Text page item. Change the alt tag text from alt="Icon 2" to the following:

    ```
    alt="Click to edit #FIRST_NAME# #LAST_NAME#"
    ```

The columns returned in the query are usable as substitution strings. This provides a good deal of flexibility in the way they can be used to display information to the user. What is happening here is modification of the text that will be displayed when the mouse pointer is scrolled over the icon in the report row, as shown in Figure 7.8. By using the query columns as substitution strings, it is possible to display bubble text with data from the report row.

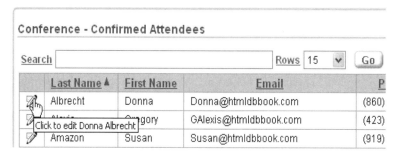

Figure 7.8: *Using Substitution Strings in Bubble Text.*

4. Target: Page in this Application.

   Choosing this option just means the plan is to navigate to another page in this application. To navigate to a page in a different HTML DB application, the URL option would be chosen.

5. Page: Enter the value 3 to indicate to the page to which to navigate when the Link icon is clicked.

6. Item 1 Name: Use the ✓ icon next to the Item 1 Name page item. This will display a popup window. Click on the P3_ID link.

   This is indicating a page item on another page that will have its session state set when navigation is transferred to the next page. If the name of the page item you are going to set is known, it can be typed in manually. This method is useful when you cannot remember the name of the item on the next page.

7. Item 1 Value: Again, use the flashlight icon next to the Item 1 Value page item to display the popup window. Then click on the #ID# link in the popup. If known, the value needed in this page item can be typed in manually, but this way can be more useful when first starting out with HTML DB because it is not always possible to remember the correct syntax to use here.

8. Click Apply Changes.

Run the report to see the link that will now show up where the ID column is. Place the mouse over one of the links to see the bubble text display with the First and Last name as shown in Figure 7.8. Finally, click on one of the ✎ icons to be navigated to the Form page that allows the row to be edited.

> 🔔 Click the back button on the browser to go back to the Report page. Do not click on the Cancel button as this will navigate to page one in the application since that is how it was built by the create application wizard.

Creating the Create Button

At this point, there is one button missing. The missing button is the Create button that is used to navigate to the application page where a form will allow the creation of new rows. Since our own form has not been created yet, the Create button will be added and it will navigate to application page two for now.

Navigate to the Page Definition page for the Report, which is application page 11. If an application page is running, click on the Edit Application link in the developer toolbar, and then click on the Conference RSVP Report link in the Application home page.

1. From the Page Definition page, click on the 🔲 icon in the Buttons region.

2. On the Button Region, page click Next.

3. On the Button Position page, choose the Create a button in a region position option and click Next.

4. On the Button Attributes page:

   ▪ Button Name: CREATE

     The [Create] link can be used to do this.

   ▪ Label: Create

   ▪ Button Type: Template Driven

   ▪ Action: choose the Redirect to URL without submitting page option.

     What this does is prevent the creation of a separate Branch. Since the goal is to get the Report page to redirect (navigate) to page two, and a branch is not required, this option can be chosen. Even though a branch can do the same thing, there is no need to have one. The maintenance of the page components can be kept lower by not creating the branch.

   ▪ Click Next.

5. On the Image Attributes page leave the default and click Next.

6. On the Display Properties page:

   - Position: Region Template Position #CREATE#

     The [Create] link can be used to do this.

   - Leave the rest default and click Next.

7. On the Branching page:

   - Target: Page in this Application.

   - Page: 2

   - Request: leave blank

     Leaving this option blank will cause HTML DB to set the request to the Button Name (CREATE). If the developer wanted to have a different request name, it could be entered here. The request can be used in Conditional Display properties to detect what the request was set to when the page was submitted.

   - Clear Cache: 2

     This clears the session state for all page items on page two. All the page items will be set to null. The cache for multiple pages can be cleared by separating them by a comma.

   - There are no Conditional Display attributes that need to be set for this button, so it is not necessary to go to the next page. Click the Create Button button.

Run the report by clicking the ⬚ icon in the upper right corner of the Page Definition page.

The finished report is shown in Figure 7.9. You may ask yourself "Why would I want to build a report manually instead of use the wizard?" Well, with more experience, developers usually find that a wizard will not always do what is needed. The steps in the previous lessons will give the experience needed to build your own reports or modify those that have already been built using the wizard.

Later in this chapter there are other tips on how to do even more with reports, but due to space constraints it is not possible provide step-by-step instructions for all of them. The experience gained so far will be valuable in knowing how to accomplish those later lessons.

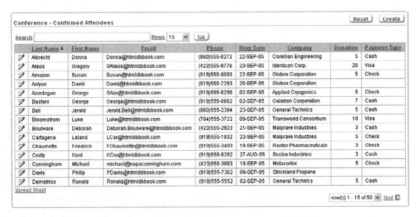

Figure 7.9: *Results of Creating a Report.*

Add Query By Example to a Report

In the previous sections of this chapter, a report was created and several modifications made. The search page item allowed the report to be resubmitted to filter the data containing a match to what was typed in. However, this is not always what is wanted. What if the user wanted to search for all records where Payment Type = Visa, and the Donation was greater than ten? This would not be possible with the current search method. What needs to be done is the creation of another region on the application page and the addition of page items to be used to filter the query used to populate the report.

The next exercise is indicative of what I've seen performed quite a lot. The developer creates a report using the wizard and gives it to user community. Then, they ask for a change to the report so they can filter the report with different data for each field in the report. This exercise will guide you in that process.

Navigate to the page definition page for application page 11.

Create the Filter Region

1. On the Page Definition page click on 🔲 icon in the Regions section.
2. On the Region page choose the HTML option and click Next.

The HTML region type creates a blank region with no page items allowing the developer to create them themselves.

3. On the Display Attributes page:

- Title: Filter Criteria.

- Region Template: Reports Region.

- Display Point: Page Template Body (2. items below region content).

  Another way to do this is to make this selection by clicking on the ✏ icon to the right of the Display Point select list. This is a valuable popup allowing the developer to see graphically the location of each of the region display points on the page as shown in Figure 7.10. The developer would then click on the <u>Page Template Body (2)</u> link as shown in Figure 7.10.

- Sequence: This can be left at the current value.

  The sequence is often a matter of personal preference. Since the new region is being placed in at a different display point and since it is the only region in that display point, the sequence becomes irrelevant. A later chapter in this book will cover form layout using region position and sequence in detail.

- Click Next.

4. On the Source page click Create Region.

Now that the Filter Criteria region is created, it is time to add page items to the region. These page items will later be used in the WHERE clause of the SQL statement in the report region to filter the results. Currently the report is filtered by the P11_REPORT_SEARCH page item, but when this exercise is complete it will be filtered by the page items in the Filter Criteria region.

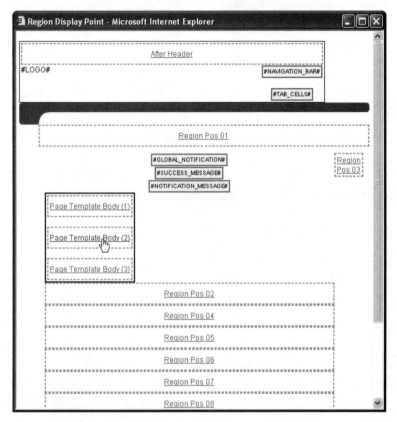

Figure 7.10: *Graphical display of region placement for a page.*

The following example walks through creating one page item and modifying the SQL statement for the report. After creating that page item, the example will move on to create the rest of the page items using a feature named Create multiple items.

First off, move the Go button to the Filter Criteria region and hide the P11_REPORT_SEARCH page item.

Navigate to the page definition page for page 11.

5. Click on the link for the P11_GO button.

6. Change the Sequence to 100 so it displays after all other page items in the region.

7. Change the Region to Filter Criteria.

8. Apply Changes.

   Now, hide the P11_REPORT_SEARCH page item

9. Click on the P11_REPORT_SEARCH link in the page definition page.

10. In the Conditions region, change the Condition Type to Never. The [never] link can be used to speed up the process.

11. Apply Changes.

Create an Item to use in the Filter Criteria

The next step will create a page item to use in the WHERE clause of the report SQL statement to filter the Last Name column. This process should be familiar by now. It is the same process used when creating the P11_REPORT_SEARCH page item earlier in the chapter.

Create a new Text item, named P11_LAST_NAME, sequence set to 20, in the Filter Criteria region, the rest is default.

Add a Page Item to the Filter the SQL Report

The previous example created a page item to use in the WHERE clause. Now it needs to be added to the SQL statement for the report.

Navigate to the Region Definition page for the Conference – Confirmed Attendees report. Replace the current statement in the Region Source to the statement in the file ch7_3.sql in the code depot.

🖫 ch7_3.sql

```
select
   id, last_name, first_name,
   email, phone, rsvp_date,
   company, donation, payment
from
   conference_rsvp
where
   instr(upper(LAST_NAME),upper(nvl(:P11_LAST_NAME,LAST_NAME))) > 0
```

Save the changes and can run the report to see how it works.

Creating Multiple Items

This feature allows the creation of multiple items on an application page in a very short time. These items can be built in multiple regions. I once used this feature to build ten pages in one evening so a colleague could show them to the client the next morning. I can't begin to tell you how excited they were to come in the next morning to see their vision of an application before their eyes.

To create the remaining page items, navigate to the page definitions page and click on the 🔲 icon in the Items area.

On the Item Type page, click on the Create multiple items link below the Create Item region. This will navigate to a page similar to the one shown in Figure 7.11. In Figure 7.11, all the items have been filled in. Do the same making sure to select the Region as shown and number the sequences indicated.

Once all the information has been filled in, click the Create Multiple Items button.

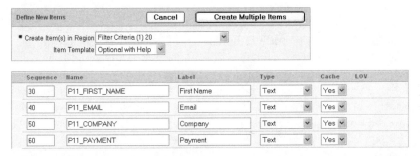

Figure 7.11: *Creating Multiple Items*

Once the page items are created, it will be necessary to modify the SQL statement for the report one final time. Change it to the SQL contained in file ch7_4.sql:

💾 **ch7_4.sql**

```
select
   id, last_name, first_name,
   email, phone, rsvp_date,
```

```
    company, donation, payment
from
    conference_rsvp
where
    instr(upper(LAST_NAME),upper(nvl(:P11_LAST_NAME,LAST_NAME))) > 0
and
    instr(upper(FIRST_NAME),upper(nvl(:P11_FIRST_NAME,FIRST_NAME))) >
0 and
    instr(upper(EMAIL),upper(nvl(:P11_EMAIL,EMAIL))) > 0 and
    instr(upper(COMPANY),upper(nvl(:P11_COMPANY,COMPANY))) > 0 and
    instr(upper(PAYMENT),upper(nvl(:P11_PAYMENT,PAYMENT))) > 0
```

Run the report again and try entering some values for the filter criteria and press the Go button. The Filter Criteria region may not be laid out as you would like. A later chapter will cover how to format page layout

Another desirable thing to do is modify the Reset Report Search process for the page so it clears the page cache for all items in the Filter Criteria region.

Using HTML Expressions

Understanding HTML Expressions can be bit tricky. However, once you get the hang of them there is almost nothing that cannot be done with a report column.

An HTML Expression modifies how the column will be displayed to the user and gives a great deal of flexibility. An earlier section covered how to add a column link to a report column to provide navigation to another page. The HTML Expression allows the same thing but takes it a step further. Knowing how to write HTML code will enable the use of the HTML Expression to its full potential.

This tutorial will show how to modify a report column in order to display images that reside on the file system in the directory referenced by the #IMAGE_PREFIX# substitution string. The names of the image files are stored in a table in the database. The HTML Expression will use the values from the report and display the image using HTML tags. It will also show how to deal with thumbnails and full size images. This is a common task for developers of web sites to provide, which is a small image that loads quickly and a link for the user to see the full size image.

To follow this tutorial, load and run the script named easy_report_image.sql from the code depot into the SQL Script Repository of the SQL Workshop.

This script creates a table and loads the names of several image files included with the installation of HTML DB. The data in the table is shown in Figure 7.12.

ID	IMAGE_THUMBNAIL	IMAGE_FULL_SIZE
1	b-rename.gif	b-rename.gif
2	b-unlock-1.gif	b-unlock-1.gif
3	b-upload.gif	b-upload.gif
4	b-version.gif	b-version.gif
5	b-lock-1.gif	b-lock-1.gif
6	b-login.gif	b-login.gif
7	b-move.gif	b-move.gif
8	b-new_fold.gif	b-new_fold.gif
9	cancel.gif	cancel.gif

Figure 7.12: *Contents of the easy_report_image table.*

To keep this example simple, the same filename is loaded into both the IMAGE_THUMBNAIL and IMAGE_FULL_SIZE columns. In a real situation, there would be two separate file names, but this will give an idea of how this can be put to use in your own applications.

Navigate to the Easy HTML DB Book application and create a new report page. To do this:

1. Click on the Application Builder tab at the top of the window.

2. Click on the Easy HTML DB Book application link.

3. On the Application Home page, click the Create Page button.

4. On the Create Page screen, choose the Report option and click Next.

5. On the next page, choose the Wizard Report option and click Next.

6. Previously in this chapter, a report was created using the SQL Report type. For that wizard, a SQL statement was provided. For the Wizard Report, it will be possible to select Tables and Columns and build the query

7. On the Page Attributes page:

   ▪ Page: 1070

- Page Title: Reports - HTML Expression
- Region Title: Images
- Region Template: Reports Region, Alternative 1
- Click Next.

8. On the Tab page click Next.

9. On the Tables and Columns page:

   - Table/View: EASY_REPORT_IMAGE
   - Select all available columns and move them to the Displayed Columns list by clicking on the ⊙ icon.
   - Click Next.

   Figure 7.13 shows the columns being selected for the EASY_REPORT_IMAGE table. The ID column has already been moved over and the remaining columns are selected to be moved also. Building a query for the report using the Wizard Report will create what is referred to as a structured query.

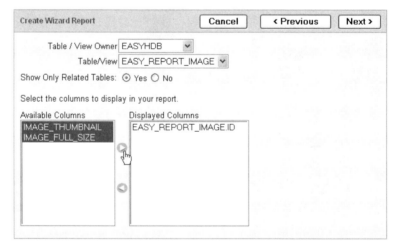

Figure 7.13: *Table and Column selection for a structured query.*

10. On the Report Options page click Next.

11. Finally, click the Create Report Page button.

12. Click on the Run Page icon.

    Take a look at the report because the HTML Expression is going to be used to change the way it looks.

13. Click on the Edit Page 1070 link in the developer toolbar.

14. Click on the RPT link for the Images regions.

15. On the Report Attributes page:

    - Click off the Show checkbox for the IMAGE_FULL_SIZE column.

      The IMAGE_FULL_SIZE column will not be displayed, but it still has to be selected so the value can be used in the HTML Expression. In this example, both images are the same, but as mentioned, in a real life application there would be another image file for the full size.

    - Click on the Edit icon to the left of the IMAGE_THUBMNAIL column.

16. On the Column Attributes page, enter the following text in the HTML Expression text area and click Apply Changes.

💾 ch7_5.txt

```
<a href="#IMAGE_PREFIX##IMAGE_FULL_SIZE#" target="_blank">
<img src="#IMAGE_PREFIX##IMAGE_THUMBNAIL#"></a>
```

This is creating an anchor tag to provide a link to the full size image. It is also displaying the thumbnail image in the report column. The #IMAGE_PREFIX# substitution string is used because the image files are stored in that location in the file system. If the developer is using a windows machine that location is:

```
C:\oracle\product\10.2.0\ohs\Apache\Apache\images
```

To create a sub-directory under the \images directory such as \images\easy_image, and store the images there, it would be referenced as follows:

```
<a href="#IMAGE_PREFIX#easy_image/#IMAGE_FULL_SIZE#"
target="_blank">
<img src="#IMAGE_PREFIX#easy_image/#IMAGE_THUMBNAIL#"></a>
```

> 🔔 It is not necessary to put a forward-slash after the #IMAGE_PREFIX# substitution string because it is included in the dads.conf alias parameter.

Run the report. The images will be displayed in the report. Clicking on the images in the report will display another browser window with the full size image.

Report Attributes

Throughout the exercises in this chapter, the Region Definition and Report Attributes pages have been used several times. The Region Definition page was described in an earlier chapter. This section will describe, in detail, the regions and attributes on the Report Attributes page.

Column Attributes

This region represents the most common attributes a developer would want to make changes to. To make addition changes to a column click on ✎.

Headings Type

This will dictate the way the column headings are displayed. The options are self-explanatory except for the PL/SQL type. The PL/SQL option could be selected to dynamically have the column headings generated at run time. A PL/SQL function could then be provided that returns a colon delimited list of values to be rendered as the column headings. A simple example for page 11 from above would be:

```
return 'id:last:first:email:phone:rsvp:company:donation:pmt';
```

This is not used very often, but it could be used in a multi-language implementation. One use for something like this would be in a banking application. At one bank, the teller can hit a button and the text on the screen switches to Spanish so the customer can read the information on the screen. Using PL/SQL, the data could be queried from a language translation table in the database and return the colon delimited string. The return values would then be used in the report headings.

Layout and Pagination

Report Template

Report templates control how the rows are displayed in reports. Several templates are built-in and available regardless of the theme used, and several templates are provided in the themes.

Built in Report Templates

Figure 7.14 shows the list of report templates. Notice the prefixes in the list are default:, export:, and template: 2.

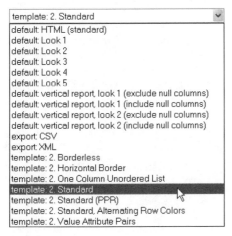

Figure 7.14: *Report Templates*

Table 7.1 below includes descriptions for the types of report templates.

DEFAULT	BUILT-IN TEMPLATES.
Export	The user is provided with a File Download dialog box when this type of report is rendered. This type of report makes it very easy to provide download capabilities. The report can be developed using another template, then once it is perfected, change it to export before deployment. If this type of template is used, it is best not to have other page components; just the report.
Template: 2.	This indicates the report template is provided as a template in Theme 2.

Table 7.1: *Report template prefixes*

Pagination Scheme

The Pagination Scheme will select the look of the pagination area on the report. Table 7.2 shows examples of the selection:

PAGINATION SCHEME	EXAMPLE
Row Ranges 1-15 16-30 (with set pagination)	**1-15** 16-30 31-45 46-50
Row Ranges 1-15 16-30 in select list (with pagination)	row(s) 1 - 15 of 50 ▼ Next ▶
Row Ranges X to Y (no pagination)	row(s) 1 - 15 of 16
Row Ranges X to Y of Z (no pagination)	row(s) 16 - 30 of 50
Row Ranges X to Y of Z (with pagination)	◀ Previous row(s) 16 - 30 of 50 Next ▶
Search Engine 1,2,3,4 (set based pagination)	1 2 3 4
Row Ranges X to Y (with next and previous links)	◀ Previous 16 - 30 Next ▶

Table 7.2: *Pagination scheme examples*

Display Position

The display position indicates where the pagination will be displayed in relation to the report region.

Number of Rows

Defines the maximum number of rows displayed in the report at one time. If the Number of Rows attribute is used, this attribute will be ignored.

Max Row Count

This is the maximum number of rows the HTML DB engine will count if one of the pagination schemes that display X to Y of Z is used. This helps prevent huge performance problems if the query returns thousands of rows.

Strip HTML

This will allow HTML DB to strip out any HTML tags and will prevent conflicts. This option should almost always be set to YES. The reason for this is that if data is selected from the database and it contains HTML tags, it can cause conflicts with the page being rendered.

Sorting

These are the sorting icons displayed in the column headings of the sorted row. They are different depending on whether the row is sorted ascending or descending. Use the links provided [▼ ▼] to change the sorting icon. It is also possible to provide the developers own images to display here.

Messages

These are messages displayed to the user in the report region. The When more data found message item works together with the Max Row Count. If more rows exist than were allowed by the setting in Max Row Count, this message will be displayed at the end of the report.

Report Export

This was detailed in the Adding the Spread Sheet link section earlier in the chapter.

Break Formatting

 To keep the figures in the book small, the list of columns has been narrowed and a WHERE clause added that reads: (WHERE first_name like '%an%'). So, do not be alarmed if your results look different.

The best way to explain this is to create a report and put Break Formatting to work. You already know how to create a new SQL Report using the wizard. Navigate to the Easy HTML DB Book application and create a SQL report with page id 1071 using the SQL statement from file ch7_1.sql. Name the page Break Formatting for easy reference later.

After the report has been created, navigate to the Report Attributes page. Figure 7.16 shows what the Break Formatting region should look like before the Apply Changes, but here is an explanation of what is done.

- The first thing was to move the PAYMENT column into the first column position. This is done by clicking on arrows shown in Figure 7.15.

Figure 7.15: *Moving column positions.*

- Display this text when printing report sums: This is the text that will be printed at the end of the report for the grand total of the report. This is printed at the bottom of Figure 7.17.

- Breaks: This has a couple of options such as First Column, First and Second Columns, and First, Second and Third Columns. Since the break group was to be on the payment, that column was moved to the first position and selected the First Column option.

- Display this text on report breaks using #SUM_COLUMN_HEADER# substitutions: The column heading of the payment column is Pmt Type. This is the heading that will be substituted for the #SUM_COLUMN_HEADER# substitution string in each of the break groups. The text Total for: has been added. To see how this is displayed in the report, refer to Figure 7.17.

- Identify how you would like your breaks to be displayed: The truth is there are some things that are just too difficult to explain. They are much easier done than said! So, I encourage you to change this setting to other options and see how it looks.

- For repeating heading breaks use this format: The #COLUMN_VALUE# substitution string is taken directly from the value of the break column. In Figure 7.17 it is being displayed with the values Cash, Check, and -null- from records with no payment data. Some font tags have also been added for formatting as well as the text "Payment Type:". This text is only displayed if the Repeat Headings on Break option was used from above. That phenomenon will be observable if the value is changed and the page rendered to see the difference.

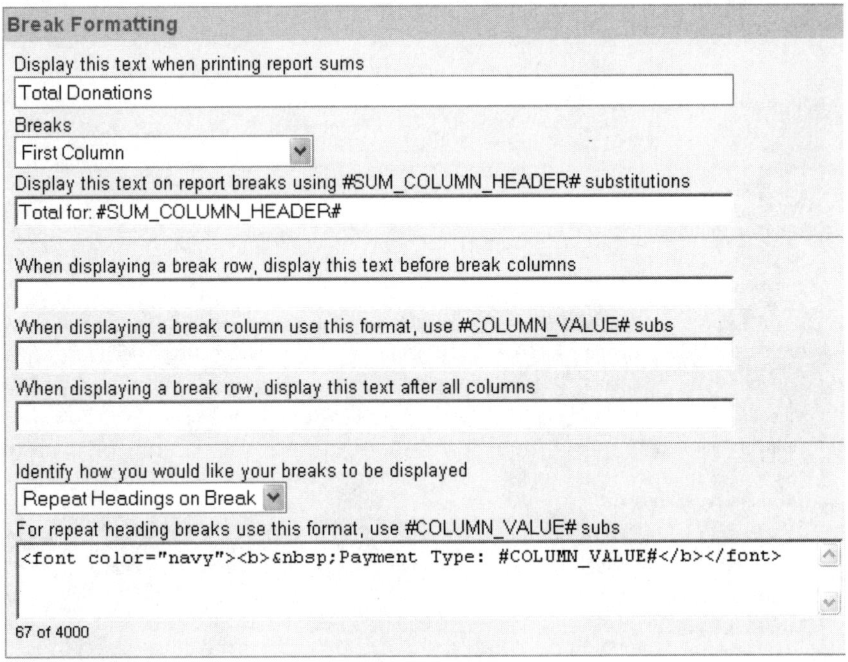

Figure 7.16: *Setting up Break Groups.*

Break Formatting

Payment Type: Cash

Last Name	First Name	Email	Company	Donation
Hill	Alan	Alan.Hill@htmldbbook.com	TechDyne Consulting	10.00
Najafi	Alan	ANaj@htmldbbook.com	Smyth Industries	5.00
Total for: Pmt Type				**15.00**

Payment Type: Check

Last Name	First Name	Email	Company	Donation
Amazon	Susan	Susan@htmldbbook.com	Globex Corporation	5.00
Cartagena	Leland	LCar@htmldbbook.com	Malprave Industries	5.00
Villanueva	Alanson	AVillanueva@htmldbbook.com	Cyberbiotics	7.00
Total for: Pmt Type				**17.00**

Payment Type: - null -

Last Name	First Name	Email	Company	Donation
Gardner	Vasanti	VGardner@htmldbbook.com	Railinc Corporation	- null -
Total for: Pmt Type				**0.00**
Total Donations				**32.00**

1 - 6

Figure 7.17: *Results of a Break Report.*

Column Attributes

To view the Column Attributes page, navigate to the Report Attributes page for a report region. Click on the edit icon 📝 to the left of the column names.

Column Definition

- **Show Column**: Select whether or not the column should be visible to the user. For columns such as primary key columns, it may be necessary to select the data but you may not necessarily want to display it to the user. This data is generally used for link columns.

- **Sum**: Calculates the sum of the column and displays it at the end of the report.

- **Sort**: Select YES if the user should be able to sort the column.

- **Heading Alignment**: Indicates where the text should be placed in the column heading.

- **Column Alignment**: Indicates the alignment of the data in the report column.

Column Formatting

Number / Date Format

When selecting data from a table, HTML DB can convert it to the format of the developer's choice by entering the format here. Since text on web pages is displayed in alphanumeric format, this attribute will most often be used for numeric and date type data columns.

Cascading Style Sheets (CSS) Class

If the developer has created custom cascading style sheets or would like to use one provided by HTLM DB, it can be entered here. The text entered here is simply the name of the class, such as navybold. It will be expanded and rendered by HTML DB as:

```
<span class="navybold">Last Name</span>
```

CSS Style

This attribute is provided to permit the developer to provide their own inline cascading style sheet code. Only the style element, such as color:blue;, is entered by the developer. It will be expanded and rendered by HTML DB as:

```
<span style="color:blue;">Email</span>
```

Highlighting Words and HTML Expression were both covered in detail earlier in the chapter.

Tabular Form Element

Display As

This attribute will dictate how the report column is to be rendered. There are several options from which to choose. Some of them are used most commonly in Reports and others are used in Tabular Forms. Table 7.3 shows the options available as the Display As attribute.

DISPLAY AS ATTRIBUTE	DESCRIPTION
Standard Report Column	The default style to display a report column. Just displays un-editable text in the report column.
Display as Text	The value displayed in the report column will be derived from an LOV. For example, if you select an 'M' from the table for this column, and it is based on the Gender LOV the value displayed would be 'Male' instead of 'M'.
Date Picker	Used in Tabular Forms to provide an editable date picker column.
Text Field	Displays an editable text field
Text Area	Displays an editable text area
Select List	Displays a select list in the report column. It can be populated by any of the methods shown in parenthesis. LOV's are explained in chapter 10.
Hidden	Does not display the column in the report.
Popup LOV	The column will be displayed with an icon that will display a popup window with the values from an LOV.

Table 7.3: *Display As attribute options.*

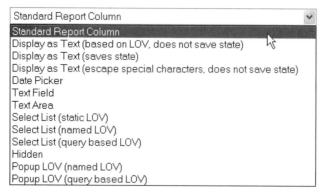

Figure 7.18: *Display As options for Tabular Form Element.*

- Element Width: Used to set the width of form elements such as a text field.

- Number of Rows: Used to set the height of a text area.

- Element Attributes: Used to set attributes of form elements.

  For example, there is no way to set the maxlength for a text field in a tabular form column using the HTML DB development environment. However, the maxlength can be set using JavaScript. The Element Attributes field can be used for this by entering the following text into the attribute.

  ```
  onFocus="javascript:this.maxLength=20;"
  ```

- Element Option Attributes: Used to set attributes for radio buttons and checkboxes.

- Default Type: This select list is used to set the type of code to be used to set the default value of the report column. The options are:

  - No Default: There is no default value specified for the element.

  - Item (application or page item name): Set the default value to the value of another page item, such as a text field. This can also use any value in session state.

  - PL/SQL Expression of Function: With this, a PL/SQL function returning the value is provided to set as the default or a SQL expression to calculate the default.

- Default: The default text or PL/SQL function used as the default. If the PL/SQL Expression or Function is used, this text will be embedded in the SQL as a column. Therefore the proper syntax must be included. The syntax to use is:

  ```
  ( select sysdate from dual )
  with the parenthesis and no semi-colon

  The text shown above will be embedded in a SQL statement as:

  select customer_id, customer_name,
        ( select sysdate from dual )
  from    . . .
  ```

- Reference Table Owner: When using the column in a tabular form and using automatic row processing, this attribute is used to select the schema owner of the table being updated.

- Reference Table Name: Used with the previous attribute, this is the name of the table.

- Reference Column Name: Used with the previous attribute, this is the name of the column.

The reference attributes above will be explained further in a later chapter about tabular forms.

List of Values

This is used in both reports and tabular forms. In reports this is used when the Display As attribute is set to Display as Text, based on LOV. When that Display As type is used, the LOV information is defined in this region. Using LOV's is explained in more detail in the section on Select Lists.

Column Link

This was described in detail, but there was no explanation on how to create a column link for a text column. Assuming about the focus is still on page 11 in the Conference RSVP application, the only thing that would be changed from the link discussion earlier is to change the Link Text. In this case, the Link Text will be set to #LAST_NAME#. Figure 7.19 shows what the link would look like for a link on the Last Name column. For further information, refer to the discussion earlier in the chapter.

Many documents pertaining to HTML DB reports talk about drill down reports. This is how drill down reports are created. If the developer has a series of reports, they would create links to navigate to each of the reports as shown here.

	Last Name	First Name	Email	Phone	Rsvp Date
✎	Vorse	Robert	RVorse@htmldbbook.com	(919)555-8393	02-SEP-05
✎	Hill	Alan	Alan.Hill@htmldbbook.com	(919)555-2832	02-SEP-05
✎	Azordegan	George	GAzo@htmldbbook.com	(919)555-8290	02-SEP-05

Figure 7.19: *Using links on report column text.*

Authorization and Conditional Display are covered in several other places in the book. These apply here as well, except here it refers to the report column.

Formatting Numeric and Date Columns

Text displayed in a web page has no data type; it is all just text. HTML DB provides a mechanism for developers to convert data types, such as numbers and dates, into a format consistent with the data being displayed. Displaying dates in the default Oracle format is not generally how users expect to see their dates. Also, a dollar amount is much prettier if it is formatted accordingly. The next two exercises are meant to show how easy it is to render this type of data in a more natural format.

The following exercises continue to work with page 11 in the Conference RSVP application.

Formatting a Numeric column

1. Navigate to page 11 in the Conference RSVP application.
2. Click on the Report link next to the Conference – Confirmed Attendees report region.
3. Click on the edit link for the DONATION column.
4. For the Number / Date Format attribute click on the ▨ icon.
5. When the popup is displayed, click on one of the currency style formats.
6. Click the Apply Changes button to return to the Report Attributes page.
7. On the Report Attributes page, change the Column Alignment for the DONATION column to right.
8. Click the Apply Changes button to finish.
9. Run the report to see the changes.

Formatting a Date column

1. Navigate to page 11 in the Conference RSVP application.
2. Click on the Report link next to the Conference – Confirmed Attendees report region.
3. Click on the edit link for the RSVP_DATE column.
4. For the Number/Date Format attribute click on the ▨ icon.

---

5. When the popup is displayed, click on one of the date formats.

    If none of the formats are acceptable and the developer knows how to type in a preferable date format, that can be done instead.

6. Click the Apply Changes button to finish.

7. Run the report to see the changes.

Conclusion

This chapter covered information on HTML DB reports. Reports are a graphical representation of the results of a SQL Select statement. Although reports are simple to create, there are several customizations, such as navigation links, images, sorting, and exporting to a file, all of which enhance the presentation of the information. The examples also showed how to add several other page components manually to a report. The proper way to use Break Formatting in reports was also covered. These skills will be valuable as you continue building application pages.

The next chapter will cover Forms. An HTML DB form is commonly used to edit a single record in a table. The chapter also includes details on Tabular Forms which can be used to edit multiple records in a table.

Creating Forms

An HTML DB form is a web page that is built to edit a single record from a table or view. Although this chapter covers building only one form region, the same techniques can be used to build multiple regions on a page in order to edit records from multiple tables.

Building a Form Using the Form Wizards

To follow along with the exercises in this section, navigate the Conference RSVP application built in Chapter 4. The Create Application from the Spreadsheet wizard in Chapter 4 actually built two forms in the application: one for INSERTs, and one for UPDATEs and DELETEs. This exercise will cover building a single page that will perform INSERTs, UPDATEs, and DELETEs.

The exercise will build an application page with the following page components.

- An HTML region to contain the Conference Attendee buttons and page items.

- Buttons

- Page Items

- Page Rendering process: For populating the form

- Page Processing process: For updating the database

- Branch

1. Navigate to the Application home page the Conference RSVP application and click the Create Page button.

2. On the next page choose the Form option and click Next.

---

3. On the next page, there will be several wizards that offer guidance through the building of various types of forms. Select the Form on a Table or View option and click Next.

4. On the Table / View Owner page the EASYHDB schema will be selected. Click Next.

5. On the Table / View Name page type in CONFERENCE_RSVP or select it using the popup from the ⌂ icon. Then click Next.

6. On the Page and Region Attributes page:

   - Page: 12.

   - Page Name: Edit Conference RSVP.

   - Region Title: Conference Attendee.

   - Region Template: Leave the default of Form Region.

   - Click Next.

7. No tabs and click Next.

8. On the Primary Key page:

   - Primary Key: ID

     Observe that there are only two selections. The form wizards used Automatic Row processes that only support the use of two column primary keys, only two columns can be chosen here. For tables with multiple columns in the primary key, this is not the choice to use. For that, developers may find themselves creating forms with the Form on a SQL Query wizard and then creating their own buttons, processes, and branches.

   - Click Next.

9. On the Primary Key page:

   - Choose the Existing trigger option.

     When the create application wizard imported the conference_rsvp.csv file, it created a trigger on the table to populate the value of the primary key column. This step reuses it.

   - Click Next.

10. On the Columns page:

- Select every column except for the COMPANY column, as shown in Figure 8.1. The COMPANY column will be added later in another exercise.

  The COMPANY column can be deselected by holding down the Control key and clicking on it.

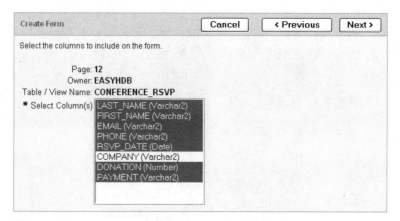

Figure 8.1: *Selecting all column except the company column.*

11. On the Process Options page, leave all the defaults as shown in Figure 8.2 and click Next

    This is where the text displayed on buttons can be changed. It is also to time to decide whether or not to include a button. For example, some of today's databases are FINO (First In, Never Out) systems, meaning data is never deleted. The developer may therefore wish to select NO for the Show Delete Button option.

12. On the Branching page:

    - After Page Submit and Processing Branch to Page: 11.

    - When Cancel Button Pressed Branch to this Page: 11.

      For this page, the plan is to branch back to the report page created in Chapter 7. That was page 11. If your report page has a different page ID, enter that number here instead of 11.

    - Click Next.

13. Finally, click the Finish button.

---

1. Before continuing, for the purposes of this example, it may be helpful to go back to the reports page created in Chapter 7 and modify the following:

2. Report Column Links: Change these so they navigate to page 12 instead of page three. It will also be necessary to change the Item for the link from P3_ID to P12_ID. There are two links: one for the ID column, and one for the LAST_NAME column.

3. Create Button: Modify the button in the Optional URL Redirect section and set the Page and Clear Cache both to 12.

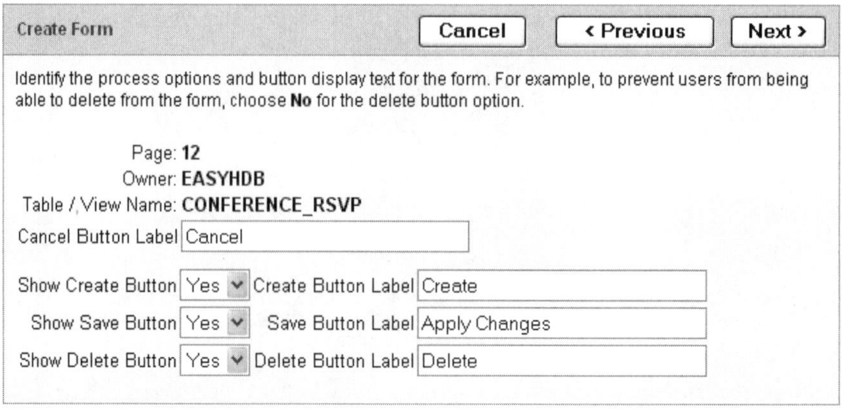

Figure 8.2: *Process Options*

Examining the Results of the Form Wizard

The Form Wizard creates several page components which warrant some explanation. Figure 8.3 shows the Page Rendering region for the new application page.

Figure 8.3: *Page Rendering region for Form created with a wizard.*

- **Regions**: In the regions section, it is apparent that an HTML region has been created to contain the buttons and page items.

- **Buttons**: Four buttons were created by the wizard. The cancel button is a simple redirect, which means it will not execute page processes. The other three buttons, Delete, Save, and Create are used to issue specific database manipulation requests. Buttons will be explained in more detail later in the Examining Buttons section.

- **Page Items**: These, of course, are the page items to display the data. The one exception is the P12_ID hidden page item. This is not displayed but is used as a variable on the page. The page item attributes are set up to participate in dynamic SQL with the Automatic Row processing processes. This will be covered in the section Adding a Page Item to a Form.

- **Processes**: An Automatic Row Fetch process was also created. This process dynamically builds SQL Select statements and populates page items. The Automatic Row Fetch is explained in detail in the section on Examining Automatic Row Fetch.

Examining Buttons

These buttons are special because they have the Database Action attribute set to a particular setting corresponding to their participation in the Automatic Row Processing process. It would be advantageous to navigate to the button attributes page as a reference while viewing the following description of the button attributes.

The conditional display on the buttons is based on the P12_ID page item. The idea is if there is a value in the P12_ID item, then the record exists and can therefore be UPDATEd or DELETEd. If the P12_ID item is NULL, no record exists and therefore the record needs an INSERT action.

DELETE button

Table 8.1 shows the important attributes of the Delete button.

Database Action	SQL DELETE action
Conditional display	When P12_ID is NOT NULL.
Optional URL Redirect	The Delete button also has the special function of asking the user if they are sure they want to delete the record before actually performing the delete. This is done by using the Optional URL Redirect attributes of the delete button.

Table 8.1: *Delete button attributes.*

SAVE button

Table 8.2 shows the important attributes of the Save button.

Database Action	SQL UPDATE action
Conditional display	When P12_ID is NOT NULL.

Table 8.2: *Save button attributes.*

CREATE button

Table 8.3 shows the important attributes for the Create button.

Database Action	SQL INSERT action
Conditional display	When P12_ID is NULL.

Table 8.3: *Create button attributes.*

Examining Automatic Row Fetch

It is important to understand what the Automatic Row Fetch is doing. This, and the next topic, can be difficult concepts to understand so I will attempt to break them down into manageable pieces. There are several regions on the edit process page for an Automatic Row Fetch (ARF) process, but the most important region is the Source region as seen in Figure 8.4.

The ARF dynamically performs SQL SELECT statements to populate the session state for page items. The ARF is set to a process point of On Load – After Header.

Figure 8.4 can be used to illustrate several attributes:

- Table Owner: Select the schema name for the owner of the table.

- Table Name: Enter the table name or view. An ARF can only dynamically build SQL Select statements for a single table or view.

- Item Containing Primary Key Column Value: This is the page item for the first primary key column. This item is used to build the WHERE clause of the dynamic SQL statement. It is common to set this page item in the URL while navigating to the page. The ARF then uses the value in session state for the WHERE clause and populates the rest of the page items.

- Primary Key Column: This is also used in the building of the WHERE clause. Looking at Figure 8.4, the ARF would build a WHERE clause something like:

```
WHERE ID = :P12_ID.
```

- Item Containing Second Key Column Value: This is the page item for the second primary key column. It is also used in the building of the dynamic WHERE clause and mention above.

- Second Key Column: The column name for the second database column making up the primary key for the table. The ARF can only be used for tables that have two or fewer columns making up the primary key. If the tables have more than two columns for the primary key, it will be necessary to write custom PL/SQL processes. The realization that ARF only allows for two column primary keys may influence database design.

- DML Fetch Mode: There are two modes from which to choose, and how the session state behaves during page rendering depends on this setting. The recommended setting for this is Set Memory Cache on Fetch.

  - Set Memory Cache on Fetch: With this setting, the session state for the page items will be set immediately after the dynamic SQL Select is executed. If there are other page rendering processes that use the values for page items being populated by this ARF, this is the mode that must be used.

  - Set Memory Cache On Display: Using this setting will not set session state until the page is rendered. If the developer needs to hide the session state of page items being populated with this process until the page is completely rendered, this is the setting to use.

The explanation of the Valid Request information is in the Examining Automatic Row Processing (DML) section below.

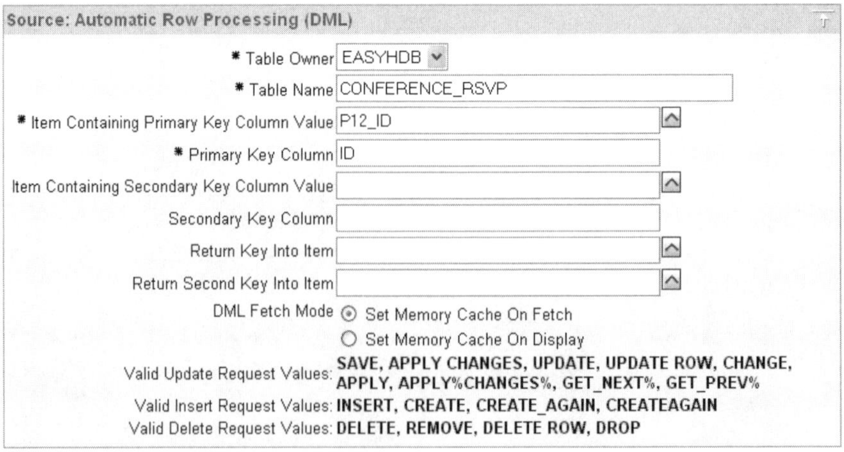

Figure 8.4: *Source Region for an Automatic Row Fetch Process.*

Examining Automatic Row Processing (DML)

It is also important to understand what the Automatic Row Processing is doing for us. Navigate to the Process Row of CONFERENCE_RSVP page process by clicking on the link in the Processes section under Page Processing. Not to diminish the importance of the other regions, the most important region in the Automatic Row Processing (DML) process in the Source region as shown in Figure 8.5. For the rest of the discussion, Automatic Row Processing will be referred to as ARP.

The ARP dynamically performs SQL INSERTs, UPDATEs, and DELETEs. Page items can either be set to participate in the dynamic SQL statements or not. Adding a page item to participate in the dynamic SQL statements is explained later in the section, Adding a Page Item to a Form. The ARP is set to a process point of On Submit – After Computations and Validations. That way validation for all page items can be performed before attempting to update the data in the database.

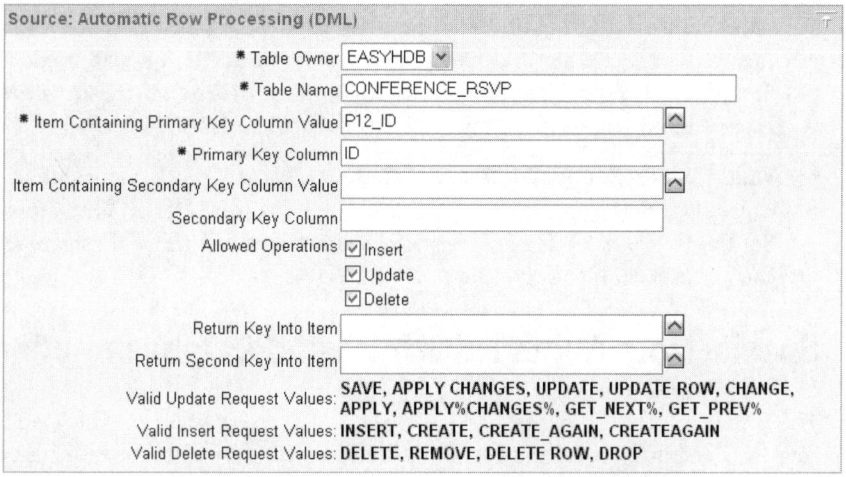

Figure 8.5: *Source Region for Automatic Row Processing (DML) Process.*

Figure 8.5 shows several attributes. The attributes not explained above in the Examining Automatic Row Fetch section will be explained here.

- **Allowed Operations:** The values here indicate the types of dynamic SQL that can be utilized by this ARP. For example, if the developer does not want to allow any DELETE operations, the Delete option would be unchecked. Many database systems today do not do DELETEs; they simply mark the row as an inactive row. In that case, a custom page process would be created to update the database record.

- **Return Key Into Item:** During an INSERT process, there may be triggers that populate the primary key columns during INSERT. The value returned will be based on the column identified in the Primary Key Column above and will be returned into a page item entered here. In the example in Figure 8.5, the value inserted in the *id* column would be returned and the session state would be set for the item entered in the Return Key Into Item field. The value returned could then be used by subsequent page processes.

- **Valid Update Request Values:** These are REQUEST values that will cause the ARP to generate and execute the dynamic UPDATE statement. Developers need to know this if they create their own buttons on a page. The REQUEST for the button must be set to one of these values if the developer wants the button to cause the ARP to perform an UPDATE.

- **Valid Insert Request Values:** These are REQUEST values that will cause the ARP to generate and execute the dynamic INSERT statement. Set the REQUEST for any user created buttons to one of these values to cause the button to drive the ARP to perform an INSERT.

- **Valid Delete Request Values:** These are REQUEST values that will cause the ARP to generate and execute the dynamic DELETE statement. Set the REQUEST for any user created buttons to one of these values to cause the button to drive the ARP to perform an DELETE.

Special Note About REQUEST and Database Action

The previous section mentioned the Valid … Request Values. The Database Action was also mentioned earlier. Either one of these can cause the Automatic Row Processing (DML) to produce dynamic SQL.

- **Example 1:** If we were to change the name of the SAVE button to SAVESOMETHING, the ARP would still perform an UPDATE because the Database Action is set to SQL UPDATE action. At that point, the Database Action takes precedence over the name of the button. In fact, the SQL UPDATE action sets the REQUEST to SAVE.

- **Example 2:** If we kept the button name as SAVE and removed the Database Action, the ARP would again work because the REQUEST is set to a value matching the name of the button. In this case, the REQUEST would be SAVE. Since SAVE is one of the Valid Update Request Values, the ARP will still produce a dynamic UPDATE statement.

It is apparent that there is more than one way to cause the ARP to produce dynamic SQL.

Adding a Page Item to a Form

If the form wizard is used to build forms, it will eventually be necessary to add another page item to the form. In the section above, the COMPANY field was left off the form on purpose. The following instructions will show how to add the COMPANY column as a page item and have it participate in the automatic row processing for the page.

To create the COMPANY page item, navigate to the Page Definition screen for the application page that was just created.

1. Click on the Create Item icon 🔲.

2. On the Item Type page, select the Text option and click Next.

3. On the next page, choose Text Field and click Next.

4. On the Display position and Name page:

   ▪ Item Name: P12_COMPANY.

   ▪ Sequence: Leave this at the default value. This will be changed this later in the section named Controlling Form Layout.

   ▪ Click Next.

5. On the Item Attributes page accept the defaults and click Next.

6. On the Source page, shown in Figure 8.6:

   ▪ Item Source: Database Column.

   Selecting Database Column permits the new page item to participate in Automatic Row processing, both Fetch and DML.

   ▪ Database Column Name: COMPANY.

   This is telling the Automatic Row processor which database column this page item is tied to.

- Click Next.

7. On the Caching page, make sure the From source each time item is displayed option is selected and click the Create Item button.

The caching is set differently for page items participating in Automatic Row Processing because when the data is selected, the session state will be replaced with the new value. If this is not desired, set the option to Only when the value is null.

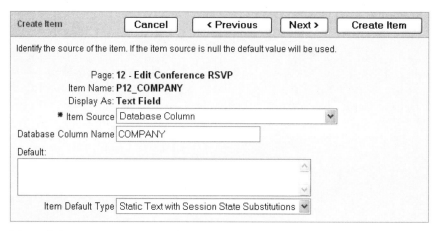

Figure 8.6: *Setting the source for a new page item.*

Controlling Form Layout

Form layout for the newcomer to HTML DB can be confusing at first. This section will show how to position page items in a region. The same techniques learned here can be used for laying out regions on a page.

First of all, Figure 8.7 shows what has been done so far. This is most likely not a layout for deployment as the final product. For reference, Figure 8.12 shows the final product. The explanations between here and there will give details on the steps taken.

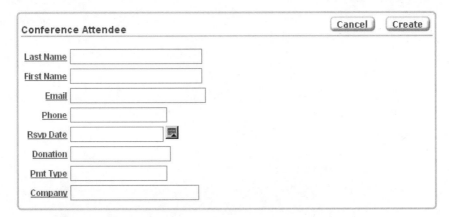

Figure 8.7: *The Form before modifications to layout.*

Re-Sequencing the Page Items

For the first step, the Company field needs to be moved up. Since the form wizard numbered the page items with sequences of 1, 2, 3, 4....9, all page items will have to be re-sequenced before the Company field can be moved up.

1. Navigate to the Page Definition page and click on the Items link as shown in Figure 8.8. This navigates to a page allowing multiple edits at a time.

Figure 8.8: *Items link to edit multiple items at a time.*

2. On the Page Items page do the following:

- Re-Sequence the page items as show in Figure 8.9. Notice all sequences are being changed to increment by 10. Some page items have also been moved by changing their sequence order.

- While on the Page Items screen, modify the width of some of the items as shown. This is so the page item sizes more match their data sizes in the CONFERENCE_RSVP table.

- Finish the modifications and click the Apply Changes button. The Page Items screen will then be displayed with the new sequences and widths for the page items.

	Sequence ▲	Name	Prompt	New Line	New Field	Width
📝	10	P12_ID	Id	Yes	Yes	30
📝	30	P12_LAST_NAME	Last Name	Yes	Yes	31
📝	20	P12_FIRST_NAME	First Name	Yes	Yes	31
📝	50	P12_EMAIL	Email	Yes	Yes	50
📝	60	P12_PHONE	Phone	Yes	Yes	15
📝	70	P12_RSVP_DATE	Rsvp Date	Yes	Yes	10
📝	80	P12_DONATION	Donation	Yes	Yes	5
📝	90	P12_PAYMENT	Pmt Type	Yes	Yes	21
📝	40	P12_COMPANY	Company	Yes	Yes	50

Figure 8.9: *Re-Sequencing page items.*

3. Navigate back to the Page Definition screen by clicking on the Page Definition link in the Breadcrumb menu.

Moving a Page Item

Before showing another image of the layout, the Last Name field will be changed to display next to the First Name field.

1. Click on the P12_LAST_NAME link in the Items section.

2. On the Edit Page Item screen, which is shown in Figure 8.10, modify the Begin On New Line selection to NO. Then click Apply Changes.

Figure 8.10: *Modifying the Begin on New Line attribute.*

Running the application page as it is now configured will look like Figure 8.11.

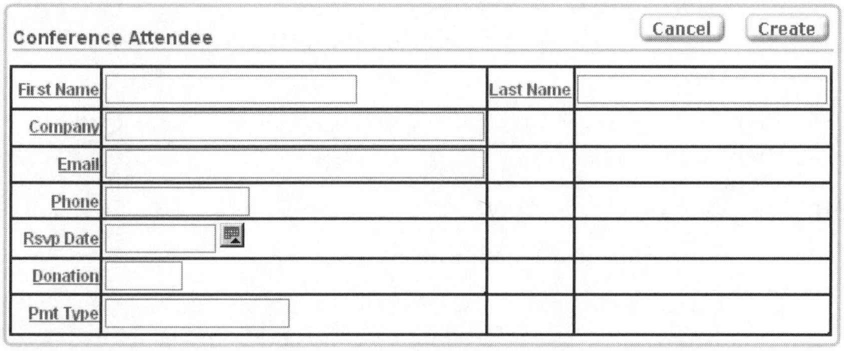

Figure 8.11: *Page items and labels laid out in HTML table cells.*

In Figure 8.11, the HTML table cells have been drawn in. The labels are placed into a cell of their own as are the fields. Also, notice how the Last Name page item is pushed to the right. This is due to the width of the Company and Email fields. In HTML, there is a table cell property called COLSPAN. If the COLSPAN property on the Company and Email columns is set to two, it will then allow those fields to stretch into the column with the Last Name label. This would, in affect, allow the Last Name page to display more to the left. Or, if the COLSPAN were set to three, they would be rendered into the column with the Last Name field. This is how the movement of page items, both label and field, can be controlled among the columns.

Finishing the Page Item Placement

With the detailed explanation behind us let's continue.

1. Navigate to the Page Definition Page and click on the P12_COMPANY item.

2. On the Edit Page Item screen for P12_COMPANY modify:

   - ColSpan: 2

   - Click the Next Item button. This is next to the Apply Changes button and looks like ⊡.

3. For the P12_EMAIL item:

   - ColSpan: 2

   - Click the Next Item button.

4. For the P12_PHONE item, no changes are needed. Click the Next Item button.

5. For the P12_RSVP_DATE item, no changes are needed. Click the Next Item button.

6. For the P12_DONATION item:

   - Post Element Text:

     This is being done because on the next page item, P12_PAYMENT, the Begin On New Line and Field should both bet set to NO. This would cause the Payment label to position itself right next to the P12_DONATION page item. Since that will not look good, some space will be provided using the Post Element Text attribute.

   - Click the Next Item button.

7. For the P12_PAYMENT page item:

   - Display As: Select List.

   - Begin On New Line: NO.

   - … Field: NO.

   - List of values definition (scroll down the page):
     ```
     select distinct payment d, payment r
     from   conference_rsvp
     order by 1
     ```

   - Click the Apply Changes button.

Running the application page will display the new form shown in Figure 8.12.

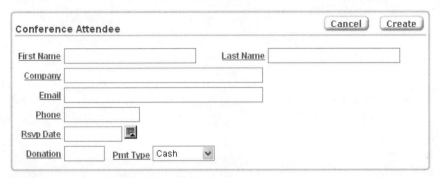

Figure 8.12: *The new layout for the form.*

This section illustrated how to manipulate the position of page items using the item Sequence, the Begin On New Line, Begin On New Field, and ColSpan attributes. Although a region does not have all of these attributes, these same techniques can be applied to regions to manipulate their positions in an application page.

Building Tabular Forms

A tabular form enables the editing of multiple records of a table or view all at once. Submitting the form will then perform updates or deletes on all the modified rows in the tabular form. Editing lookup tables is an excellent use for Tabular Forms.

This exercise will create a tabular form on the CONFERENCE_RSVP table. The COMPANY column will purposely be left out again so it can be added in a different section.

1. To create the tabular form, navigate to the Easy HTML DB Book application's home page and click the Create Page button.

2. Choose the Form option and click Next.

3. Choose the Tabular Form option and click Next.

4. On the Table / View Owner page:

    - Table / View Owner: EASYHDB.

    - Allowed Operations: Allow all, UPDATE, INSERT and DELETE.

    - Click Next.

5. On the Table/View Name page type in CONFERENCE_RSVP or select it using the popup from the ▣ icon. Then click Next.

6. On the Displayed Columns page:

   ▪ Select all columns except for the ID and COMPANY columns. The COMPANY column will be added later in another exercise. In this case, displaying the ID column is not desirable since it is the primary key column.

     The ID and COMPANY columns can be deselected by holding down the Control key and clicking on them.

   ▪ Click Next.

7. On the Primary Key page:

   ▪ Primary Key: ID

     There are only two selections. The form wizards used Automatic Row processes that only support the use of two column primary keys, so two columns can be chosen here. Tables that have more that two column primary keys would require custom programming and advanced use of the HTML DB API. That explanation is beyond the scope of the book.

   ▪ Click Next.

8. On the Primary Key Source page:

   ▪ Choose the Existing trigger option.

   ▪ Click Next.

9. On the Updateable Columns page select all columns and click Next.

   To keep a column from being editable in the Tabular Form, it would be de-selected here.

10. On the Page and Region Attributes page:

    ▪ Page: 1081.

    ▪ Page Name: Tabular Form - CONFERENCE_RSVP.

    ▪ Region Title: Conference Attendees.

    ▪ Region Template: Leave the default of Report Region.

    ▪ Report Template: Leave the default of template: Standard.

- Click Next.

11. No tabs and click Next.

12. On the Button Labels page leave the defaults and click Next.

13. On the Branching page leave the defaults and click Next.

14. Finally, click Finish then Run the page.

Figure 8.13 shows the completed page as it is now. Later, the COMPANY column will be added.

	Last Name	First Name	Email	Phone	Rsvp Date	Donation	Pmt Type
☐	Vorse	Robert	RVorse@htmldbbor	(919)555-8393	09/02/2005	5	Check
☐	Hill	Alan	Alan.Hill@htmldbbo	(919)555-2832	09/02/2005	10	Cash
☐	Azordegan	Georgey	GAzo@htmldbbook.	(919)555-8290	09/02/2005	5	Check
☐	Jones	Albert	Albert@htmldbbook	(919)555-1243	09/02/2005	5	Check
☐	Davis	Philip	PDavis@htmldbboc	(919)555-7362	09/09/2005		
☐	Eads	Robert	Robert.Eads@htmlc	(919)555-2638	09/23/2005	5	Cash
☐	Lilly	Joseph	JLil@htmldbbook.cc	(850)555-5378	09/02/2005		
☐	Bloomstrom	Luke	Luke@htmldbbook.	(704)555-3722	09/09/2005	10	Visa
☐	Gardner	Vasanti	VGardner@htmldbb	(423)555-2623	09/02/2005		
☐	Yoell	Patrick	Patrick.Yoell@htmlc	(919)555-2737	09/02/2005	7	Check

Conference Attendees — Cancel Delete Submit

row(s) 1 - 10 of 49 ▾ Next ▶

Add Row

Figure 8.13: *A Tabular Form.*

Examining the Results of the Tabular Form Wizard

The Form Wizard creates a report region, some buttons, some processes, and a branch.

- **Report Region:** In the regions section, a Report region has been created. Tabular Forms are really reports with editable fields.

- **Buttons:** Four buttons were created by the wizard. The cancel button is a simple redirect, which means it will not execute page processes. The other three buttons, Multi-Row Delete, Submit, and Add, are used in the conditional processing of the automatic row processes. More about the buttons will be included later in the Examining Tabular Form Buttons section.

- **Processes**: The Automatic Row processes were explained in the section on Forms. Tabular forms have something similar called Multi Row processes. There are three processes that work on Tabular Forms: Multi Row Update, Multi Row Delete, and the Add Rows to Tabular Form process. These processes dynamically build the SQL statements for updating the data in the database table.

Examining Tabular Form Buttons

There is something special about the Tabular Form MULTI_ROW_DELETE button. The others simply submit the page and the processes use the REQUEST in the conditional processing. However, the MULTI_ROW_DELETE button has the Optional URL Redirect set to confirm with the user they really want to perform the delete action. The URL Target attribute is set to the following.

```
javascript:confirmDelete(htmldb_delete_message,'MULTI_ROW_DELETE');
```

The confirmDelete function asks the user if they really want to delete data. If they answer yes, the page is submitted and the REQUEST is set to MULTI_ROW_DELETE. The ApplyMRD process on the page has the conditional processing set to respond to this REQUEST.

Examining the Multi Row Processes

There are two Multi Row processes: Multi Row Update (MRU) and Multi Row Delete (MRD). Their names explain the function they perform. These processes write dynamic SQL statements to update the database from the Tabular Form. When these processes are used, they are set to execute On Submit – After Computations and Validations.

The MRU and MRD processes have the same attributes. The most important section is the Source section shown in Figure 8.14. The attributes are explained here:

- **Table Owner:** The schema name for the owner of the table.

- **Table Name:** Enter the table name or view. MRD's and MRU's can only dynamically build SQL statements for a single table or view.

- **Primary Key Column:** This is the first column of the primary key for the table. It is used for building the WHERE clause for the dynamic statement.

- **Second Key Column:** This is the column name for the second database column making up the primary key for the table. The MRU and MRD processes can only be used for tables that have two or fewer columns making up the primary key.

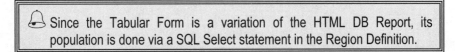

Figure 8.14: *Source for Multi Row processes.*

> There are two Multi Row Update processes. This is because one of them executes when the Add Rows button is pressed and the other executes when the Submit button is pressed.

Add Rows to a Tabular Form Process

The Add Rows to a Tabular Form process is used to go to the end of the records set for the Tabular Form and open a new row for editing. There is no Multi Row Insert process because the MRU also takes care of the Inserts.

Adding a Column to a Tabular Form

This section will show how to add another column to the tabular form so it can also participate in the Multi Row processes for updating to the database.

> Since the Tabular Form is a variation of the HTML DB Report, its population is done via a SQL Select statement in the Region Definition.

1. To start, modify the Select statement that populates the Tabular Form. Navigate to the Page Definition screen and click on the Conference Attendees link to edit the Region Definition.

---

2. On the Region Definition page, modify the region source and add the COMPANY column. The Select statement should then look something like this:

```
select
"ID",
"LAST_NAME",
"FIRST_NAME",
"EMAIL",
"PHONE",
"COMPANY",
"RSVP_DATE",
"DONATION",
"PAYMENT"
from "#OWNER#"."CONFERENCE_RSVP"
```

3. After modifying the region source, click the Apply Changes button.

   At this point, it would be useful to run the page. The Company column is now there, but it is not editable. The next step is to make the column editable and to configure it to participate in the Multi Row processes.

4. Click on the Edit Page 1081 link in the developer toolbar to get back to the Page Definition screen.

5. Click on the Report link for the Conference Attendees region. This will navigate to the Report Attributes page.

6. On the Report Attributes page, click on the edit icon next to the COMPANY column.

7. On the Column Attributes page, scroll down to the Tabular Form Element section and make the following changes. The completed changes are shown in Figure 8.15.

   - Display As: Text Field.

   - Reference Table Owner: EASYHDB.

   - Reference Table Name: CONFERENCE_RSVP.

     This must be the same as the table name in the MRD and MRU processes.

   - Reference Column Name: COMPANY.

   - Click Apply Changes.

Run the page to see the changes to the Tabular Form. New developers are encouraged to make some data changes and try out the various functions on the page.

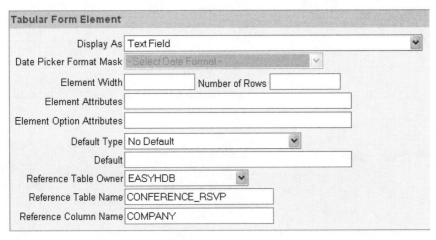

Figure 8.15: *Configuring a Tabular Form column.*

The preceding sections have shown how to create a tabular form, how to add a column to a tabular form, how to make it editable, and have it participate in the Multi Row processes. It also showed what the role of a Multi Row processes is in a Tabular Form.

Creating a Form on a Table with Report

A popular wizard to use when building applications is the Form on a Table with Report. This wizard will build two application pages complete with navigation to go back and forth between the two pages. The first page is a report and the second page is a form for editing a row in the report.

At this point, readers might be thinking the author is a masochist. They might be asking themselves, "Why did he take us the long route of making the report and the form when we could have just done it this way?" It is because the wizards will not do everything, and it is vital to know how to add page components to reports and forms with HTML DB.

The following exercise walks through the creation of the Form on a Table with Report for the CONFERENCE_RSVP table.

1. To create a Form on a Table with Report, navigate to the application home page for the Easy HTML DB Book application and click on Create Page.

2. Choose the Form option and click Next.

3. Choose the Form on a Table with Report option and click Next.

4. On the Table / View Owner page the EASYHDB schema will be selected. Click Next.

5. On the next page enter CONFERENCE_RSVP for the table name and click Next.

6. On the Define Report page:

   - Page: 1082.

   - Page Name: Report - Conference Attendees.

   - Region Title: Conference Attendees.

   - Leave the rest defaulted and click Next.

7. No tabs and click Next.

8. On the next page leave all columns selected and click Next.

9. On the next page click the edit icon of your choice and click Next.

10. On the Define Form Page screen:

    - Page 1083.

    - Page Name: Edit – Conference Attendee.

    - Region Title – Conference Attendee.

    - Click Next.

11. No tabs and click Next.

12. On the next page leave the default primary key (ID) and click Next.

13. On the next page choose the Existing trigger option and click Next.

14. On the next page leave all column selected and click Next.

15. On the Identify Process Options page leave the defaults and click Next.

16. Finally, click Finish and Run the page.

The use of this wizard results in the creation of pages very quickly in HTML DB. In fact, while writing this part of the chapter, I ran through this exercise several times. Although I did not enter the page names and titles each time, I was able to create the two pages in less than 40 seconds. Setting up User Interface Default for the CONFERENCE_RSVP would produce two pages that needed very little customization. The only customization I can think of would be modifying the form layout.

Creating a Master Detail Form

A Master Detail form includes several of the features that have been covered so far. The Master Detail wizard will create two application pages. One page is a report and the other has a form and a tabular form on the page. There is the option of separating the second page into two separate pages. At the developer's request, the wizard will put the form on one page with a standard report, and another page will have a form to edit a single detail record for a total of three application pages.

For this example, the DEPT and *EMP* tables will be included with HTML DB. The *DEPT* table is the Master and the *EMP* table is the Detail.

The two following sequences can be used for the population of the primary key columns of the *DEPT* and *EMP* tables. In the SQL Workshop → SQL Commands window, run the following SQL statements.

```
create sequence dept_seq start with 10000
/
create sequence emp_seq start with 10000
/
```

Next, create the Master Detail form.

1. Navigate to the application home page for the Easy HTML DB Book application and click on the Create Page button.

2. On the next page, choose the Form option and click Next.

3. On the next page, choose the Master Detail Form page and click Next.

4. On the Master Table page:

   - Table / View Owner: *EASYHDB.*

   - Table / View Name: *DEPT.*

   - For the Available Columns, select the ⟲ icon to move all columns to the Displayed Columns list, and then click Next.

5. On the Detail Table page:

- Table / View Owner: *EASYHDB*.

- Table / View Name: *EMP*.

  EMP is the only table in the select list. This is because the Show Only Related Tables item is set to YES. Therefore, only tables having a foreign key relationship to the Master (*DEPT*) table will be in the select list. If there is no foreign key relationship or to see all tables, the Show Only Related Tables can be set to NO.

- For the Available Columns, select the ⊘ icon to move all columns to the Displayed Columns list, and then click Next.

6. On the Primary Key source page, which will be the primary key for the Master table:

- Primary Key Source: Select the Existing sequence option.

- Sequence: DEPT_SEQ. This is the sequence created earlier.

- Click Next.

7. On the next Primary Key source page, which will be the primary key for the Detail table:

- Primary Key Source: Select the Existing sequence option.

- Sequence: EMP_SEQ. This is the sequence created earlier.

- Click Next.

8. On the Master Options page:

- Include master row navigation?: YES.

  The master row navigation option will add two buttons, Previous and Next, to the Master part of the Master Detail page. These buttons are shown in Figure 8.18. These buttons will scroll through the records in the Master (*DEPT*) table one at a time.

- Master Row Navigation Order: DNAME.

  The Master Row Navigation Order will provide the sorting for the data in the Master part of the Master Detail page. If no selection is made here, the sorting will be determined by the primary key. Choosing a different sorting order may impact the performance.

- Include master report: YES.

This option is what indicates to the wizard you also want the report page. The report page that will be built by the wizard is shown in Figure 8.17. If a Report page has already been created, NO can be selected here to prevent the wizard from creating another one.

- Click Next.

9. On the Layout page, select the Edit detail as tabular form on same page option and click Next.

To get the wizard to create two separate pages, choose the Edit detail on separate page option. What this will do is put a standard report in place of the tabular form in Figure 8.18. A separate form page will be built to allow edits on the Detail (*EMP*) records.

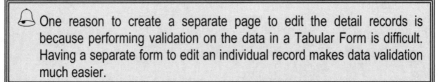

> One reason to create a separate page to edit the detail records is because performing validation on the data in a Tabular Form is difficult. Having a separate form to edit an individual record makes data validation much easier.

10. On the Page Attributes page, enter the data as shown in Figure 8.16. This is where the names of the pages and regions the wizard is going to create are setup. When the entries are completed, click Next.

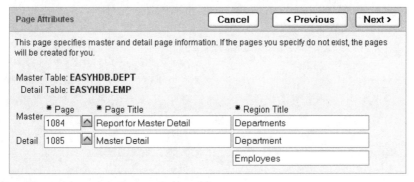

Figure 8.16: *Master Detail page attributes.*

11. No tabs and click Next.

12. Finally, click Create and then, Run Page.

The pages produced from the wizard are shown in Figures 8.17 and 8.18. From here the developer can go into the pages and regions and do any customizations as they choose. Also, as mentioned during the exercise, some developers may also have chosen to provide their own report to replace the report created by the Master Detail wizard. In this case, they will go to their custom report and add the navigation links to navigate to the Master Detail page.

Figure 8.17: *Report page from Master/Detail wizard.*

Figure 8.18: *Master/Detail page from the wizard.*

Creating a Form for Email

Not only will this section show a simple form for emailing, but it will also introduce the HTMLDB_MAIL package. The HTMLDB_MAIL package is used by the developer to send email from within HTML DB.

For information on setting up Email, refer to Chapter 15 – HTML DB Administration II.

In the following example, it will be necessary to build a new page with page ID 1080. The page created by the author is shown in Figure 8.19 and is included in the EASY Sample application in the code depot. Building pages, buttons, and page items have already been introduced, so those steps will not be repeated here. Since many text messages are limited to maximum length, the text area was limited to 160 characters.

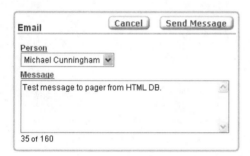

Figure 8.19: *Simple emailing form.*

The data in the select list is populated from a table named EASY_PERSON. The table contains a column with an email address that can be used to send text messages to a person's cell phone.

To send the text message, an After Submit page process will be created that executes on the condition when the Send Message button is pressed. The code used for the email process is shown in file ch8_1.sql contained in the code depot.

The HTMLDB_MAIL.SEND procedure can send text of data type VARCHAR2 or CLOB; however, the limit for the length of any single line is 1000 characters. After the 1000 character limit, a new line must be included before continuing the email message.

The person's pager address is being selected and used in the p_to parameter of the send procedure. The message body is taken from the P1080_MSGTEXT page item.

Also, take notice of the use of htmldb_mail.push_queue procedure. Email in HTML DB is placed into a message queue and processed every ten minutes. However, since text messages can sometimes be urgent, such as a production database issue, the htmldb_mail_push_queue procedure has been used to force the email queue to send all messages immediately.

ch8_1.sql

```
declare
   s_pager easy_person.pager%type;
begin
   select
      pager
   into
      s_pager
   from
      easy_person
   where  id = :P1080_ID;

   htmldb_mail.send(
      p_to => s_pager,
      p_from => 'easyhtmldb@rampant.cc',
      p_body => :P1080_TEXTMSG,
      p_subj => 'HTML DB Email' );
   htmldb_mail.push_queue( 'localhost', 25 );
end;
```

Conclusion

This chapter covered a lot of information in regards to building forms. The simple task of creating a form was covered, followed by the manual process of adding page components to the form. The details of how to add page components and have them use the automatic row fetch and automatic row processing for DML were included. The examples then showed how to create tabular forms and how to manually add tabular form columns. Another topic covered was how to control form layout using the item sequence and begin on new line and begin on new field attributes.

Finally, the method for creating a Form on a Table with Report, which creates two pages, one report and one form page, was covered as was how to create a Master/Detail Form followed by details on the importance of the REQUEST. The REQUEST can be used during page processing and is set back to NULL after HTML DB branches to a different page.

Now that the basics of forms have been covered, it is time to move on to other development items such as images and documents.

Working with Images and Documents

Any kind of file can be stored in the HTML DB repository, but most commonly the files stored there are images and documents. Learning how to store images and documents and the various ways to either render them in a web page or provide the ability to download them will give developers the basic tools for working with other types of files.

Storing Files in HTML DB

Uploading files is very easy in HTML DB if the plan is to store them in the provided table WWV_FLOW_FILES. It may not seem so at first, but after just a few samples you will know exactly how to do it. The goal of this section is to provide a couple examples of the more common uses for uploading files. Those uses are to store images for later display in a web page and storing documents either for downloading or for display into a browser such as a PDF file. These two examples will yield the tools necessary to provide the same functionality in a very short time.

Explaining WWV_FLOW_FILES

Loading scripts and other files into the repository have been mentioned throughout this book. The files uploaded are put into a table in the FLOWS_FILES schema named wwv_flow_file_objects$. This table name is indicated in the dads.conf file with the parameter PlsqlDocumentTablename. How it looks in the dads.conf file is shown here:

```
PlsqlDocumentTablename   wwv_flow_file_objects$
```

HTML DB then provides a view to this table named WWV_FLOW_FILES. Running the following script in a SQL Command window will reveal the files currently loaded into the repository.

```
select
   id, flow_id, name,
```

```
   filename, title, mime_type,
   doc_size, dad_charset, created_by,
   created_on, updated_by, updated_on,
   last_updated, content_type, language,
   description, file_type, file_charset
from
   wwv_flow_files;
```

The only column missing from the WWV_FLOW_FILES view in the query above is the BLOB_CONTENT column. This is because the SQL Command window will give an inconsistent data type error when querying a column of BLOB data type.

Loading and Displaying Images

Loading images is very easy in HTML DB. What you do with them after they are loaded is another thing. When an application page is built to upload an image, it will be stored in the WWV_FLOW_FILES view. It is really stored in the wwv_flow_file_objects$ table, but for explanation purposes it will be called wwv_flow_files since this is how it would be referred in queries.

Even though the uploaded image is initially stored in WWV_FLOW_FILES, it is not desirable to keep it there. This is because sometimes it is better to store it in a table in the parsing schema. That way it is easier to write PL/SQL to access it and makes it easier to export and import the entire schema, including the images, when deploying the application.

Once the image is stored in the developer's own table, which will be called EASY_IMAGE, then a stored procedure can be created to display the image in an HTML DB Report.

The following tutorial will:

- Create the EASY_IMAGE table.

- Create an application page to load the image.

- Create a process to move the image to the EASY_IMAGE table.

- Create a stored procedure to pull the image from the EASY_IMAGE table and using some API procedures, display it in an HTML DB Report.

- Create an application page with a report region to display the image.

Create the EASY_IMAGE Table

In a SQL Command window, run the statements below. The file named create_easy_image_table.sql in the online code depot can be used. Another option is to load the file into the SQL Script repository and run it that way.

🖫 **create_easy_image_table.sql**

```
create table easy_image (
    image_id            number not null,
    name                varchar2(90) not null,
    filename            varchar2(400),
    mime_type           varchar2(48),
    doc_size            number,
    created_by          varchar2(255),
    created_on          date,
    content_type        varchar2(128),
    blob_content        blob null
)
/

create unique index ak1_easy_image on easy_image( image_id )
/

create unique index ak2_easy_image on easy_image( name )
/
```

Creating the Image Upload Application Page

Navigate to the EASY HTML DB Book application and click the Create Page button.

1. On the Create page, choose the Blank Page option and click Next.

2. On the Page Attributes page, enter 1090 for the Page number and click Next.

3. On the Page Name page, enter Easy Image Upload and click Next.

4. No tabs and click Next.

5. Click Finish.

6. On the Success page, click the Edit Page link.

7. Click on the ⬚ icon in the Regions area.

8. Choose the HTML option and click Next.

9. On the Display Attributes page, enter Image Upload for the Title and click Next.

10. On the next page, click Create Region.

Create the File Browse... Item

1. Click the ⬚ icon in the Items area.

2. On the Item Type page, choose the File Browse option and click Next.

3. On the Display Position page:
   - Item Name: P1090_NAME
   - Sequence: 10
   - Region: Image Upload
   - Click Next.

4. On the Item Attributes page:
   - Label: Image File Name.
   - Field Width: 80
   - Click Next.

5. On the next page click on the Create Item button.

Create the Upload Button

Now it is time to provide a button to submit the page. The file will be uploaded when the page is submitted.

1. Click the ⬚ icon in the Buttons area.

2. On the Button Region page, click Next.

3. On the Button Position page, choose the Create a button in a region position option and click Next.

4. On the Button Attributes page, enter UPLOAD for the Button Name and click Next.

5. On the Image Attributes page, click Next.

6. On the Display Properties page, click Next.

7. On the Branching page enter &APP_PAGE_ID. for the Branch to Page field and click Create Button. Remember the ending period!

Create the Copy Image Process

This process is going to move the record inserted into the wwv_flow_files view over to the new easy_image table.

1. Click on the ⊡ icon in the Processes area of the Page Processing region.

2. On the Process Type page, choose the PL/SQL option and click Next.

3. On the Process Attributes page:

   - Name: Copy Image

   - Sequence: 10

   - Point: On Submit – After Computation and Validations

   - Click Next.

4. On the Process page, enter the following for the PL/SQL Page Process and click Next. The full text can be found in file copy_image_process.sql in the online code depot.

🖫 **copy_image_process.sql**

```
begin
    --
    -- When an image is uploaded it is stored in the
    -- FLOW_FILES.WWV_FLOW_FILE_OBJECTS$ table.
    -- The wwv_flow_file_objects$ table is identified in the
dads.conf
    -- file in the PlsqlDocumentTablename parameter.
    -- WWV_FLOW_FILES is a view to this table.
    --
    -- We want to keep the image in our own table.
    -- Copy the image from WWV_FLOW_FILES to our own EASY_IMAGE
table.
    --
    insert into easy_image(
            image_id, name, filename,
            mime_type, doc_size, created_by,
            created_on, content_type, blob_content )
    select id, name, filename,
            mime_type, doc_size, created_by,
            created_on, content_type, blob_content
    from   wwv_flow_files
    where  name = :P1090_NAME;

    --
```

```
   -- Now that we have copied the image to our own EASY_IMAGE
table
   -- delete it from the WWV_FLOW_FILES table.  That way we can
keep
   -- the files from growing too much in the WWV_FLOW_FILES and
make
   -- it easier for use to make backups of our data.
   -- Deleting the record is done by referencing the NAME column.
   -- When the file is uploaded the P14_NAME page item will be
set to
   -- the value of NAME that was put into the WWV_FLOW_FILES
table
   -- and we can use it for reference.
   --
   delete from wwv_flow_files where name = :P1090_NAME;
end;
```

5. On the Message page:

    - Success Message: Image successfully loaded.

    - Failure Message: Image could not be loaded.

    - Click Next.

6. On the Process Conditions page:

    - When Button Pressed: Select the UPLOAD item.

    - Click Create Process.

The page to upload an image is now complete. Run the new application page and take a look. The finished page is shown in Figure 9.1 with the Image File Name filled in.

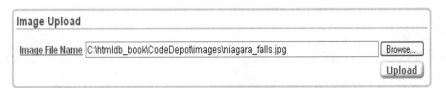

Figure 9.1: *Completed Image Upload Application Page.*

Uploading an Image

On the newly created application page, click on the Browse... button and navigate to the C:\htmldb_book\CodeDepot\images\niagara_falls.jpg file. After selecting the file, click the Upload button.

The following is going to happen when the button is clicked:

- The application page is submitted and the fact that is being submitted by pressing the Upload button is stored in the HTML request as UPLOAD.

- The image is automatically inserted into the wwv_flow_files view.

- When the image is inserted the P1090_NAME page item will be set to a value of F22557/niagara_falls.jpg. NOTE: the F22557 will be different on each system. Since the wwv_flow_files has a unique index in the NAME column, the value in the P1090_NAME page item can be used to select information about the image that was just inserted.

- The page process Copy Image will be executed to move the image record to the EASY_IMAGE table. The process is executed on the condition of the UPLOAD button being pressed. Also, the process uses the P1090_NAME page item in the SQL statements to copy the image.

- The page will be rendered and the results will be displayed.

Creating the PL/SQL Procedure to Display the Image

At this point, the PL/SQL procedure that will be used to download the image into the browser has to be created. Navigate to the SQL Workshop and click on the SQL Script icon.

1. On the SQL Scripts page click the Upload button.

2. On the Upload Script page:

   - File: C:\htmldb_book\CodeDepot\plsql_display_easy_image.sql

   - Script Name: Display Easy Image PLSQL.

   - Click Upload.

3. Once the script is uploaded, click on the run button to the right of the Display Easy Image PLSQL script. Tip: If it is sorted by Last Updated in descending order it will be the first row in the report.

4. Click the Run button on the next page also.

5. Now that the PL/SQL Procedure has been created and the execute privilege has been granted to public, click on the Application Builder tab to go back to the Application Builder Home page. Then click on the Easy HTML DB Book link. You are now at the Application Home page and ready to continue on to Create the next application page.

The text of the plsql_display_easy_images.sql file is shown here to make referencing it convenient.

 Take note of the fact that this procedure must be granted execute to public. Forgetting this little detail can be the source of great frustration.

plsql_display_easy_image.sql

```
create or replace procedure display_easy_image( p_id number ) as
   s_mime_type   varchar2(48);
   n_length      number;
   s_filename    varchar2(400);
   lob_image     blob;
begin
   select mime_type, dbms_lob.getlength( blob_content ), filename,
blob_content
   into   s_mime_type, n_length, s_filename, lob_image
   from   easy_image
   where  image_id = p_id;

   owa_util.mime_header( nvl( s_mime_type, 'application/octet' ),
FALSE );

   -- Set the size so the browser knows how much it will be
downloading.
   htp.p( 'Content-length: ' || n_length );

   -- The filename will be used by the browser if the users does a
"Save as"
   htp.p( 'Content-Disposition: filename="' || s_filename || '"' );

   owa_util.http_header_close;

   -- Download the BLOB
   wpg_docload.download_file( lob_image );

end display_easy_image;
/

--
-- This is very important.  I can't tell you how many times I've
-- forgotten to do this and cost myself time in troubleshooting.
--
grant execute on display_easy_image to public
/
```

Creating the Display Image Application Page

1. Click on the Create Page button from the Application home page.

2. Choose the Report option and click Next.

3. Choose the SQL Report option and click Next.

4. On the Page Attributes page:

   ▪ Page: 1091

   ▪ Page Name: Easy Image Display.

   ▪ Click Next.

5. On the next page, leave Do not use tabs and click Next.

6. On the SQL Query page, enter the following as the SQL SELECT statement and click Next. It will select every record from the EASY_IMAGE table. Only select the IMAGE_ID column because this is what needs to be sent to the DISPLAY_EASY_IMAGE procedure.

   ```
   select image_id from easy_image;
   ```

7. On the Report Attributes page:

   ▪ Region Template: Report Region, Alternative 1.

   ▪ Report Template: default: Look 1.

   ▪ The two options above are chosen to give an idea of other templates and how they look.

   ▪ Region Name: Easy Images.

   ▪ Click Next.

8. Click Finish.

9. On the Success page, click the Run Page icon.

At this point, the only data in the report is that of the IMAGE_ID column. Next, the HTML Expression property of the IMAGE_ID report column will be used to pull the image from the table using the DISPLAY_EASY_IMAGE procedure.

Using HTML Expression to Display an Image

A lot is going to happen in this next section, so be patient as the details are presented.

The information on the HTML Expression section explained that it could be used to modify how the report column is displayed to the user. What is about to happen here will show the great flexibility of this column attribute. It will actually cause the HTML DB Engine to execute a stored procedure on our behalf and return the necessary HTML to display an image in the browser. This is made possible by the mod_plsql module.

1. Navigate to the Page Definition page for application page 1091. If the page is still running, click on the Edit Page 1091 link in the developer toolbar.

2. Click on the Report link next to the Easy Images region.

3. Click on the ▣ icon next to the IMAGE_ID column.

4. Enter the following text in the HTML Expression text area and click on the Apply Changes button.

    ```
    <img src="#OWNER#.display_easy_image?p_id=#IMAGE_ID#" />
    ```

Ok, this needs some explaining. It took me some time to learn and understand what was happening here so I hope I can explain it well so you do not have the same pain I had.

The HTML Expression is going to override the way the report column is rendered to the user. An image tag, <img>, is being created in order to display the image.

The src part of the tag is calling the stored procedure created earlier.

Previously, it was mentioned that the value from a column in the SQL select statement could be used here by using the substitution string. This is exactly what is being done here by using the #IMAGE_ID# substitution string. The value returned in the query will be substituted in by the HTML DB Engine. The results to the HTML DB Engine will look something similar to the following:

```
<img src="#OWNER#.display_easy_image?p_id=2739007729974300" />
```

This calls the DISPLAY_EASY_IMAGE PL/SQL procedure. The text after the question mark is the name of the parameter declared in the PL/SQL procedure as indicated below.

```
create or replace procedure display_easy_image( p_id number ) as
   ...
```

This is the syntax used in HTML DB in order to send parameters to stored procedures and functions. When HTML DB renders the page, it calls the PL/SQL procedure and sets the p_id parameter with the #IMAGE_ID# value for each row in the report. It will then return each of the images in a different row in the report.

> 🔔 To call multiple parameters for a procedure the ampersand (&) would be used to separate the parameter as shown in the following statement
>
> display_easy_image?p_id=#IMAGE_ID#&p_fname=Michael

As an exercise, navigate back to the Easy Image Upload page, load another image, and view the loaded image in the Easy Image Display report.

Uploading and Downloading Documents

Loading documents is very similar to loading images. Anyone who has ever surfed the Internet has been to a web site and downloaded a file. The online code depot for this book is a good example. This section describes the steps necessary to provide a document storage system in the database and two methods of providing download links in application pages.

The authors built an application to serve as the document storage repository for each of the chapters of the book, and it also served as a version control system. Since everything is stored in Oracle, there was an added benefit of nightly backups to insure none of their work was lost.

Up to this point, the f?p= syntax has been present on the URL which is used when accessing pages in HTML DB. This is an indication of the format used to call stored procedures in HTML DB. Actually, it is the syntax used by the modplsql module. The F part of f?p= is a stored procedure in the FLOWS_020000 schema of HTML DB. So, every page rendered in HTML DB is done by calling the f procedure and passing values into the P parameter. For downloading files, the P procedure is used. It then changes the URL to include p?n=. The P procedure receives the N parameter which is the value of the ID column in WWV_FLOW_FILES. Using this syntax in the URL will allow the file to be downloaded from WWV_FLOW_FILES.

This lesson will create a single page used to upload and download documents. It is a simplified version of what was used when writing the book. We will create a region for uploading the document and a report to show the documents available for download. We will also create a table named EASY_DOCUMENT so the name of the document and an abstract of what the document is about can be stored. The EASY_DOCUMENT table is also used to join to the WWV_FLOW_FILES view to limit the records returned from WWV_FLOW_FILES. Otherwise we would see a lot of records in the report that had nothing to do with documents.

Create the EASY_DOCUMENT table by running the following script in a SQL Command window.

□ create_easy_document_table.sql

```
create table easy_document(
    name       varchar2(90),
    abstract   varchar2(250)
)
/
```

Create the Document Upload Page

From the Easy HTML DB Book application home page click on the Create Page button.

1. Choose the Blank Page option and click Next.

2. On the Page Attributes page, enter 1092 for the Page and click Next.

3. On the Page Name page, enter Easy Documents for both Name and Title and click Next.

4. Tabs: NO, then click Next.

5. Click Finish.

When the Success page is displayed, click on the Edit Page so items can be added to the new page.

1. Click on the ⊞ icon in the Regions area.

2. Choose HTML and click Next.

3. For Title, enter Easy Document Upload and click Next.

4. Click the Create Region button.

5. Back on the Page Definition page, click the ⊞ icon in the Buttons area.

6. On the Button Region page, choose the Easy Document Upload option and click Next.

7. Choose Create a button in a region position and click Next.

8. On the Button Attributes page, enter UPLOAD for the Button Name and click Next.

9. On the Image Attributes page, click Next.

10. On the Display Properties page, click Next.

11. For Branch to Page enter &APP_PAGE_ID. complete with the ending period and click Create Button.

12. Back on the Page Definition page, click the ⊞ icon in the Items area.

13. Choose the File Browse option and click Next.

14. For Item Name enter P1092_NAME and click Next.

15. On the Item Attributes page:
    - Label: Document Name
    - Field Width: 80
    - Click Next.

16. On the next page, click Create Item.

17. Back on the Page Attributes page, click the ⊞ icon in the Items area.

18. Choose the Text Area option and click Next.

19. For Item Type, choose Textarea w/Character Counter and click Next.

20. For Item Name, enter P1092_ABSTRACT and click Next.

21. On the Item Attributes page:
    - Label: Abstract
    - Label Alignment: Top right
    - Field Width: 80
    - Click Next.

22. Click the Create Item button.

Run the application page as it is now. With the page running, notice the numbers below the Abstract text area (0 of 2000). This is called the character counter. It reads 2000 because the maximum length of the text area is set to 2000 by default. This must be changed to 250 to prevent too many characters from being entered and causing SQL errors when trying to perform the insert. The following example includes another way to edit items without too much navigation between pages.

While the application page is running, click on the Show Edit Links link in the developer toolbar. A bunch of little icons will show up in the Easy Document Upload region. Figure 9.2 shows this. Click on the Edit link below the 0 - 2000 character counter, as shown in Figure 9.2.

Figure 9.2: *Using the Edit link.*

Clicking on the Edit link as shown will display a popup window. When the popup window displays, locate the maxWidth page item in the Element region and change it to a value of 250. Then, click the Apply Changes button. When the changes have been processed, close the popup window.

Now that you are back on the running application page, click on the Hide Edit Links link in the developer toolbar. Refresh the application page. This is accomplished in Internet Explorer by pressing the F5 key. When the page refreshes, the character counter will change to 0 - 250.

The process created in the following example will insert information into the EASY_DOCUMENT table when a document is uploaded. Click on the Edit Page 1092 link in the developer toolbar.

1. Click on the ⊞ icon in the Processes area of the Page Processing region.

2. Choose the PL/SQL option and click Next.

3. On the Process Attributes, enter Insert Document for the Name and click Next.

4. On the Process page, enter the following for the text and click Next.

💾 insert_document_process.sql

```
begin
    insert into easy_document( name, abstract )
    values( :P1092_NAME, :P1092_ABSTRACT );
end;
```

5. On the Messages page:

   ▪ Success Message: Document successfully loaded.

   ▪ Failure Message: Document successfully loaded.

   ▪ Click Next.

6. On the Process Conditions page:

   ▪ When Button Pressed: Select the UPLOAD item.

   ▪ Click Create Process.

Now, it is time to upload a document. Run the application page.

Click on the Browse button and navigate to the online code depot. Select the file name EasyHTMLDB.pdf. Enter "A sample upload document" for the abstract text area, and click the Upload button. The success message will display once the document has successfully loaded.

Now that a document has been loaded, create a report to show the documents available in the repository.

Creating a Report to Display the Documents

Use the link in the developer toolbar to edit the page. Then, create a report region on the page using the SQL Report type. Make the Title Easy Documents and use the following for the SQL Query.

💾 easy_documents_report.sql

```
select
    wff.id, htf.anchor( 'p?n=' || wff.id, wff.filename ) filename_1,
    wff.filename filename_2, ed.abstract abstract
from
    wwv_flow_files wff, easy_document ed
where
    wff.name = ed.name;
```

The following will outline two ways to provide links in a report column, which is why the FILENAME column is selected twice. In the SQL Query, the id and FILENAME columns have been selected, the p?n= has been concatenated with the ID, and the htf.anchor function included. The htf.anchor function will return the proper html syntax to build the anchor tag. What you will see above are two columns being selected: FILENAME_1 and FILENAME_2. The query syntax for the column FILENAME_1 will return the following to be displayed in the browser.

```
<A HREF="p?n=2860904562035412">EasyHTMLDB.pdf</A>
```

The second method is to modify the HTML Expression. Edit the attributes for the report column named FILENAME_2. Enter the following text for the HTML Expression:

```
<A HREF="p?n=#ID#">#FILENAME_2#</A>
```

Apply the changes and run the application page. There will be two columns, FILENAME_1 and FILENAME_2, which look exactly the same. One was done within the SQL statement and one by modifying the HTML Expression.

There is one final method that can be used to provide a link to download the document. That is to modify the Column Link properties for the column. To try this, remove the text in the HTML Expression for the FILENAME_2 column and make the following changes to the Column Link property of the column attributes.

- Link Text: #FILENAME_2#

- Target: URL

- URL: p?n=#ID#

Apply the changes and run the page to try it out.

This section has shown three methods for providing a link to download a document. The truth is, I have not found any compelling reasons to use one or the other. My personal preference is to keep it out of the SQL if possible. Either way, developers now have three ways and can choose their favorite.

Downloading a PDF into the Browser

Although this chapter has shown how to provide document download capability to the audience, there is also the desire to permit a document, such as a PDF, to be downloaded directly into the browser. This is a common way to provide online documents to users and is much like what can be obtained from the Oracle web site.

This feature is also provided for by HTML DB and is as simple as adding another parameter in the call to the P procedure in the URL. To make the change for the HTML Expression method described above, change the text to the following:

```
<A HREF="p?n=#ID#&p_inline=YES">#FILENAME_2#</A>
```

To do the same thing using the Column Link method described above, change the URL text to the following:

```
p?n=#ID#&p_inline=YES
```

Now clicking on the link EasyHTMLDB.pdf will display the document directly in the browser. The Back button will return to the running application page.

Conclusion

This chapter has shown how to store images in a table named EASY_IMAGE and how to store documents into the HTML DB repository, WWV_FLOW_FILES. However, developers may want to simply store their images in the WWV_FLOW_FILES view and forego the creation of their own table to store the images. Even if the developers do allow the images to be stored in WWV_FLOW_FILES, they may still want to create a table to record which images have been stored. This is similar to what was done for EASY_DOCUMENT. If the decision is to just store the images in the WWV_FLOW_FILES view, it is also possible to do without the DISPLAY_EASY_IMAGE procedure. In this case, the images could be displayed using the P procedure (p?n=) as shown for the document section. Adding the following to the HTML Expression for a report column would then display the image in the report from WWV_FLOW_FILES.

```
<img src="p?n=#ID#" />
```

Likewise, documents can be stored in a custom table as was done with the images earlier in this chapter. Accomplishing this requires a custom procedure similar to the one used for the images in DISPLAY_EASY_IMAGE. Either way, it is the developer's choice, and new developers should have an idea of how to perform either method.

There are two advantages to putting images and documents in the user's own table as opposed to WWV_FLOW_FILES. One is that an export of the developer's schema would also export the images and documents. The other is that if there are other applications that need access to the stored images or documents, other than those written in HTML DB, the developer would definitely want to have their own table so they would be accessible to the other application.

The next chapter shows how to build several types of page components not already covered in the book. Using those components in an application will give it a professional look and feel.

Creating Other Components in HTML DB

This is a long chapter because it is jammed with information about creating page components. Each section is designed to serve as a reference for how to create page components in HTML DB.

Checkboxes

Checkboxes are a rather tricky feature to grasp in HTML DB. As with most components in HTML DB, creating them is relatively easy; however, updating the database with the values selected is another story.

For the explanation of the use of Checkboxes, a many-to-many database relationship involving three tables will be used. This is a simple three table example for explanation purposes only. The script file that can be used to create the data model and sample data is in the code depot with the file name create_checkbox_data.sql. To try the samples provided below, load the script into the SQL Workshop and run it.

The following information includes two examples of the use of checkboxes. One will be placing checkboxes in an HTML region, and the other will be putting checkboxes in a report which requires the HTML DB API for rendering the checkboxes.

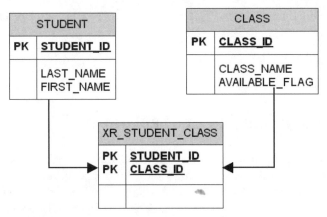

Figure 10.1: *Many-to-many sample data model to illustrate checkboxes.*

Working with Checkbox Data

This is an example of working with checkboxes in an HTML region. HTML region types are used for Forms. The region created for the purposes of this example looks similar to Figure 10.2.

Figure 10.2: *Working with Checkboxes.*

The region created was a Form region. While creating the page, the Form on a Table or View option was selected for which type of Form page to create. A Form Pagination process was then created to get the Next/Previous navigation through the records in the STUDENT table. Finally, the checkboxes were added using an LOV named Classes. The Classes LOV can be created using the following select statement.

```
select class_name d, class_id r
from  class
order by 1
```

Format of Data in Relation to Checkboxes

The checkbox item created above is named P2501_CLASS_ID. The session state for Checkboxes needs to be understood before a developer can effectively work with them. In Figure 10.2 above, there are three items selected: History; Programming; and Spanish. The data in the CLASS table looks like Figure 10.3:

CLASS_ID	CLASS_NAME	AVAILABLE_FLAG
1	Spanish	Y
2	History	Y
3	Programming	Y
4	Speling	Y
5	Calculus	Y

Figure 10.3: *Data in the class table.*

The session state of checkboxes is set to a colon delimited list of values. Based on the selections in Figure 10.2 and the data in the class table, the session state for the P2501_CLASS_ID page item is set to 2:3:1. This is how HTML DB sets the session state for checkboxes.

Armed with the knowledge presented so far it is time to learn how to use some of the HTML DB API language to construct and destruct the session state for checkboxes. This depends on whether the page is being rendered or processed after submit.

- During page rendering, it will be necessary to query the data out of the XR_STUDENT_CLASS table, construct a colon delimited string, and set the session state for the P2501_CLASS_ID page item.

- During page processing, it will be necessary to destruct the colon delimited string and insert each of the items into the XR_STUDENT_CLASS table.

Populating Form Checkboxes during Page Rendering

To set the checked value, ON or OFF, of checkboxes, the session state of a checkbox page item is set to a colon delimited string, such as 2:3:1. However, data is not stored in a database table in that format. Instead, the data may be stored in several rows of a table. For this example, the table is XR_STUDENT_CLASS. The next step is to loop through the records and construct the string. The code to do this is displayed in file ch10_1.sql.

🖫 ch10_1.sql

```
declare
  as_check_box  htmldb_application_global.vc_arr2;
  i           integer := 1;
begin
  for r in( select class_id
       from  xr_student_class
       where  student_id = :P2501_STUDENT_ID ) loop
    as_check_box(i) := r.class_id;
    i := i + 1;
  end loop;

  :P2501_CLASS_ID := htmldb_util.table_to_string( as_check_box, ':'
);
end;
```

This code is used in an After Header process named Populate Class ID. The PL/SQL above uses some of the HTML API to convert tabular data to a colon delimited string. A subsequent chapter in this book provides more detail into using the HTML DB API's.

It should be clear that the Populate Class ID process must be executed after any process that sets the P2501_STUDENT_ID session state. At that point, the code will loop through all the classes the student is signed up for and populate an array. The htmldb_util.table_to_string function then converts the array to a colon delimited string and sets the session state for the P2501_CLASS_ID page item.

Updating the Database from Form Checkboxes

The session state for a checkbox item is formatted as a colon delimited string. In order to update the database with the checkbox data, it is necessary to destruct the colon delimited string into an array. It can then be looped through the array and the data placed into a database table.

The code in file ch10_2.sql is stored in an On Submit – After Computations and Validations page process.

💾 ch10_2.sql

```
declare
  as_check_box  htmldb_application_global.vc_arr2;
begin
  delete from xr_student_class where student_id = :P2501_STUDENT_ID;

  as_check_box := htmldb_util.string_to_table( :P2501_CLASS_ID, ':'
);

  for i in 1..as_check_box.count
  loop
    insert into xr_student_class( student_id, class_id )
    values( :P2501_STUDENT_ID, as_check_box(i) );
  end loop;
end;
```

There is something very important to understand with checkboxes. Figure 10.2 shows five checkboxes. If the user selects three of the checkboxes and submits, the session state would look something like 2:3:1. Assume the session state for the P2501_CLASS_ID page item was set to 5:2:3:1 during page rendering and the user un-selected the Calculus item. Now, the problem is how to remove the data from the XR_STUDENT_CLASS table indicating the student has withdrawn from the Calculus class? The common practice is to delete all data in the XR_STUDENT_CLASS table for the student and re-insert the data from the P2501_CLASS_ID session state.

Listing 10.2 shows a DELETE statement which deletes all the current data in the XR_STUDENT_CLASS table. The session state for the P2501_CLASS_ID checkbox is then converted into an array. At that point, the process loops through the array and inserts records to the XR_STUDENT_CLASS table indicating the class the student is enrolled in. This will probably seem like an unnecessary task at first, but this is the usual method in HTML DB.

Working with Checkboxes in Reports and Tabular Forms

Working with checkboxes on a form is one thing, but working with checkboxes in reports or tabular forms is totally different. How to add checkboxes to reports and tabular forms is the sort of question often asked on the Oracle HTLM DB forum.

For this exercise, the report in Figure 10.4 was created:

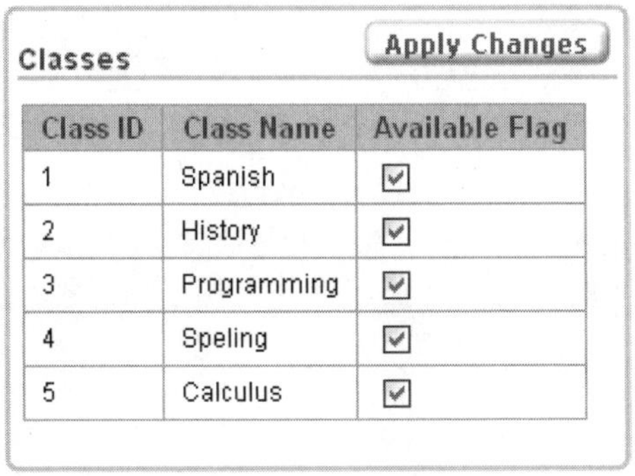

Figure 10.4: *Report with checkboxes.*

Populating Checkboxes in a Report Region

The code used to populate the report in Figure 10.4 is shown in ch10_3.sql. The key to populating a report with a checkbox is to use the htmldb_item.checkbox API function. The parameters used are a subset of the available parameters, but an explanation of them is necessary for a full understanding of what is happening. Table 10.1 explains some of the parameters for the htmldb_time.checkbox API function.

🖫 ch10_3.sql

```
select
  class_id, class_name,
  htmldb_item.checkbox( 10, class_id,
    decode( available_flag, 'Y', 'CHECKED', NULL)) available_flag
from
  class
```

Parameter	Description
p_idx	This is the form element name. In HTML DB this will be translated into f01, f02, etc. In the example, it will be translated to f10. It is important to know what number to use for the *p_idx*. A number higher than the number of columns in the report should be chosed. If there are five columns in the report, a number of six or higher should be chosen. There are only two other columns in our report, and a *p_idx* value of three could

Parameter	Description
	have been chosen. However, it is good practice to use a higher number in case more columns are added later. It will prevent further modification of the code for the checkbox *p_idx* to a higher value later.
p_value	This is the value to be returned if the item is checked. This is normally the value of a primary or unique column, so it can be used for updating data. Our example is using the value of the *class_id* column.
p_attributes	This is an attribute to be added to the HTML input tag. In the current case, if the value in the *available_flag* column is equal to Y, the *p_attributes* parameter should be set to CHECKED. This will cause the checkbox to be displayed as checked. If the value in the *available_flag* is anything other than Y, the checkbox will be displayed unchecked.

Table 10.1: *Some of the parameters for the htmldb_item.checkbox API function.*

Running the SQL statement from ch10_3.sql in an SQL Command window will result in what is shown in Figure 10.5. The htmldb_item.checkbox function returns the HTML syntax for an input of type checkbox. Also, take note of the name. It is set to f10 because the P_IDX parameter was set to ten. The value of each of the checkboxes is determined from the CLASS_ID column. Finally, all checkboxes will be displayed as checked.

CLASS_ID	CLASS_NAME	AVAILABLE_FLAG
1	Spanish	<input type="checkbox" name="f10" value="1" CHECKED />
2	History	<input type="checkbox" name="f10" value="2" CHECKED />
3	Programming	<input type="checkbox" name="f10" value="3" CHECKED />
4	Speling	<input type="checkbox" name="f10" value="4" CHECKED />
5	Calculus	<input type="checkbox" name="f10" value="5" CHECKED />

Figure 10.5: *Results of using htmldb_item.checkbox.*

Updating the Database from Report Checkboxes

Updating the database from checkboxes in a report is similar to that of checkboxes on a form. A separate On Submit page process will be used to handle the data from the checkboxes. Our example shows a report region. However, when using a tabular form, it should be allowed to perform its database updates, and then run the process to handle the checkboxes. Either way, a separate process will be created.

```
begin
  --
  -- Because Check Boxes are only posted if they are CHECKED we
won't have
  -- all the values in the g_fXX array.  So, first set them all to
'N'.
  -- Then we will set the available_flag with the check box array
items
  -- to 'Y'.  The idea is: if they are in the array they are
CHECKED, so
  -- set the value to 'Y'.
  --
  update class
  set  available_flag = 'N';


  --
  -- Now loop through the array updating the inspection items to
'Y'.
  --
  for i in 1..htmldb_application.g_f10.count loop
  update class
  set  available_flag = 'Y'
  where  class_id = htmldb_application.g_f10(i);
  end loop;
end;
```

The code in file ch10_4.sql is stored in an On Submit – After Computations and Validations page process. It will be executed when the page is submitted by pressing the Apply Changes button shown in Figure 10.2.

When the page is submitted, the values from the checkboxes are submitted in an array. Referencing the array is done by using the htmldb_application package. The g_f10 item is an array defined in the package. As with the checkboxes in forms, the report checkboxes are only submitted in the g_f10 array. Therefore, if there are four checkboxes checked, there will be four values in the array. In the PL/SQL code in ch10_4.sql, the first step is to update the AVAILABLE_FLAG in all the records of the CLASS table. Then the appropriate records are updated with a value of Y where the value in the g_f10 array item is equal to that of the CLASS_ID.

As I said in the beginning, "Checkboxes are rather tricky." Using the examples described in the preceding pages, it should be possible to do most of what a developer will ever need to do in HTML DB in regards to checkboxes.

Buttons

Buttons are used to submit or post the application page to the HTML DB engine. They can also be used to redirect one page to another page or a URL without submitting the application page. The differences between the two are:

- Submit Page and Redirect to URL: This type of button will submit the page to the HTML DB engine and save page item data in session state. When creating a button with this action, a page Branch will be used to determine where the navigation will go from here.

- Redirect to URL without submitting page: This type of button will simply navigate the browser to another application page or URL without posting the page and no page item data will be saved in session state. This type of button does not utilize a Branch to know where to navigate; that information is stored as properties of the button.

When creating buttons, the developer is asked to provide a button position. The location of the button in the region is the determining factor when deciding the button position. There are two positions from which to choose:

- Create a button in a region position
- Create a button displayed among this region's items

Create a Button in a Region Position

When a button is created in a region position, HTML DB is being told the button is to be rendered in a position defined in the region templates. This is the more common position to put buttons. The available positions are shown in Figure 10.6.

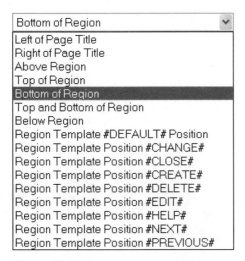

Figure 10.6: *Available button positions.*

Figure 10.7 below shows the region positions as indicated by the button labels. This Figure is of the upper right corner of a sample region created by the author in order to determine where each of the positions is located.

Figure 10.7: *The region positions enclosed with # from figure 10.6.*

Figure 10.8 below shows the remaining positions for buttons created in a region position. Notice the buttons that are aligned to the left side of the region. These have the alignment set to left. The default alignment when creating buttons is to the right.

Figures 10.7 and 10.8 can be used as a reference when buttons are added to application pages to a region position.

Figure 10.8: *Positions of buttons when created in a region position.*

When a button created in a region position submits a request to the HTML DB engine, the REQUEST is set to the name of the button unless specifically set in the Optional URL Redirect section of the button. The Optional URL Redirect will be covered later. Once the REQUEST is set to the button name, it can be used in conditions for other page components for conditional processing.

Create a Button Displayed Among This Region's Items

Creating a button as Create a button displayed among this region's items will result in both a button and a page item being created. This means it can be positioned in the middle of other page items by using the Displayed region for the button attributes. The button is then positioned in the region using Sequence, Begin on New Line, Begin on New Field, ColSpan and Display properties.

Notice in Figure 10.9, the buttons P2903_AMONG_ITEM_1 and P2903_AMONG_ITEM_1 are shown in the Buttons section and the Items section. This is an indication the button is created among a region's items.

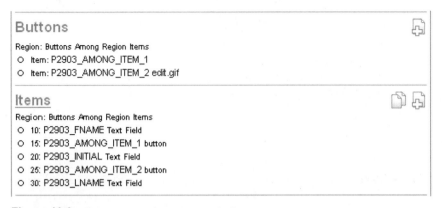

Figure 10.9: *Buttons created among a region's items.*

Buttons created among the region's items have some properties that are not available in a button created in a region position.

- Display Location: The position of the button among the other page items in the region is controlled by using the Displayed region on the Button Attributes page. This means the button can be positioned anywhere within the other page items.

- Button Request: Since a button among region items is treated just like another page item, it can have its label set via an SQL statement, database column, etc. When this is done, the value of the Label becomes the value of the REQUEST when the button is pressed.

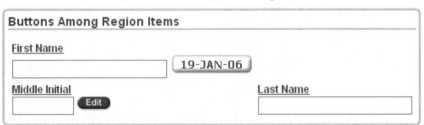

Figure 10.10: *Buttons among a region's items.*

In Figure 10.10, the button showing 19-JAN-06 had the label set with a SQL statement selecting SYSDATE. This shows the button label can be set just like any other page item such as a text field. The buttons are in positions in which other page items would normally appear.

Button Attributes

There are several attributes available to buttons, and they are different depending on how the button is created. Figures 10.11 and 10.12 show some of the subtle differences between the two.

Figure 10.11 shows the attributes page for a button created in a region position and the attributes are explained below.

Button Attributes for Buttons in a Region Position

- **Sequence:** The order in which the button will be rendered. If there are two buttons with the same button position, the sequence determines in which order they are rendered. The sequence attribute is used to control the form layout.

- **Button Name:** The name of the button.

- **Text Label / Alt:** If the button style is set to HTML Button or Template based button, this is the text displayed in the button. If the button is an image, this is the text for the HTML ALT tag.

- **Display in Region:** This is the region in which the button will be rendered and displayed.

- **Button Position:** This was explained in detail in previous sections in this chapter. See Figures 10.7 and 10.8.

- **Button Alignment:** This designates whether the button should align to the left or the right. The default setting is to align to the right. Figure 10.8 shows how the buttons will display if the alignment is set to the left.

- **Button Style:** There are three options: HTML Button; Template Based Button; and Image.

  - **HTML Button:** Displays as a standard HTML button. When this style is chosen, the Button Attributes field is enabled. There, CSS code can be entered to modify the look of the button (i.e. style="width:100;"). CSS is explained in a later chapter.

  - **Template Based Button:** The look for this style will be determined by the templates in the active theme.

  - **Image:** This style of button expects an image file such as edit.gif. The button can either be stored in the HTML DB repository or as a file on disk. Image Attributes, such as title="Press to search for a Customer.", may also be set.

- **Database Action:** The database action is used together with the Automatic Row Processing (DML) process types to issue dynamic database INSERT, UPDATE, and DELETE statements. This attribute is only available for a button in a region position.

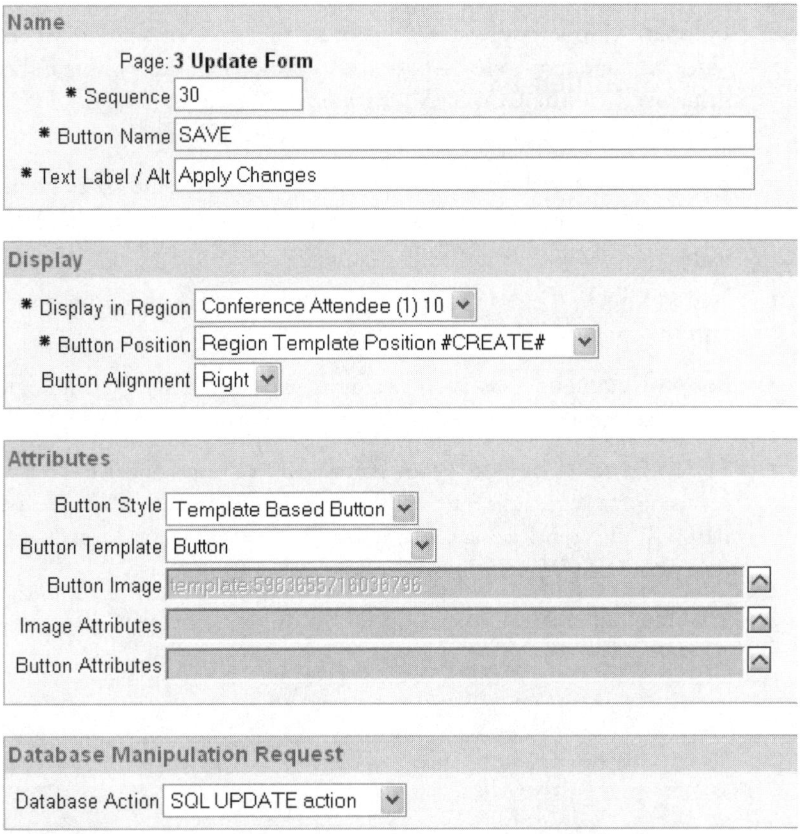

Figure 10.11: *Button attributes for button created in a region position.*

Button Attributes for Buttons Created Among a Region's Items

- **Name:** The name of the button.

- **Begin on New Line:** This works the same as other page items. If set to YES, the item will be displayed on a new line and will be the first page item on the new line. The default is YES.

- **Begin on New Field:** Indicates whether or not HTML DB will create a new table cell (<td>) to put the button in. If set to NO, the button will be displayed in the same table cell as the previous page item. The default is YES.

- **ColSpan:** Hopefully you have some knowledge of the HTML language. Since all page items are displayed in a table cell (<td>), this indicates the value used for the COLSPAN property. This item is ignored if Begin on New Line and Begin on New Field are set to NO.

- **Display**: This really should read Row Span like other page items. This value is used for the ROWSPAN property for the table cell. This item is ignored if Begin on New Line and Begin on New Field are set to NO.

- **Button Label**: This is the text that will be displayed on the button if the button type is not Image.

- **Button Request**: This is the value to which the REQUEST will be set when the button is pressed.

- **Button Request Source Type**: Figure 10.12 shows the REQUEST being set using static text, and this is the most common method. However, the REQUEST could be set using any of the other types such as a SQL query or PL/SQL function.

- **Post Element Text**: Use this option to display more text after the button.

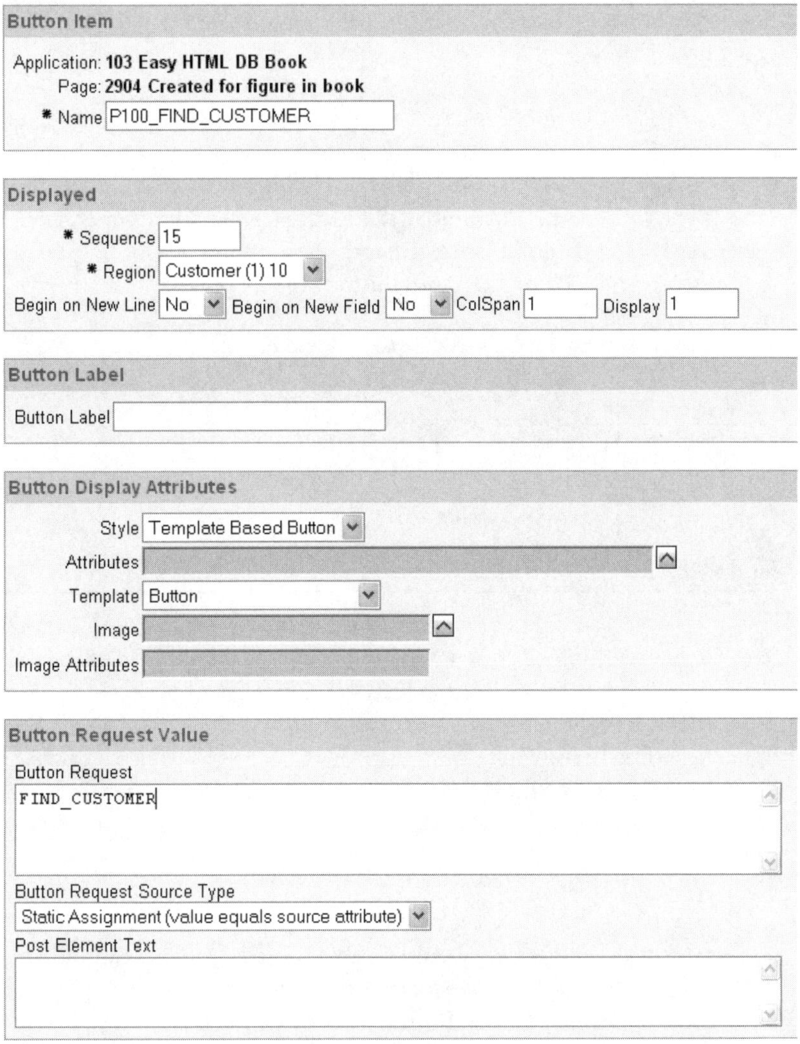

Button Item

Application: **103 Easy HTML DB Book**
Page: **2904 Created for figure in book**
* Name P100_FIND_CUSTOMER

Displayed

* Sequence 15
* Region Customer (1) 10
Begin on New Line No Begin on New Field No ColSpan 1 Display 1

Button Label

Button Label

Button Display Attributes

Style Template Based Button
Attributes
Template Button
Image
Image Attributes

Button Request Value

Button Request
FIND_CUSTOMER

Button Request Source Type
Static Assignment (value equals source attribute)
Post Element Text

Figure 10.12: *Button attributes for a button created among region's items.*

Creating Multiple Buttons

HTML DB provides a method for the creation of many buttons at one time. This method can be used to quickly define a number of buttons in a region all with the same button template. This will make consistent looking buttons throughout the page. Using this method can be a real time-saver if the developer knows what they want in their region. The following example will show how.

The first step is to click on the Create button in the Page Rendering section of a Page Definition screen. As before, this will begin the Button Wizard with the first page of the wizard shown in Figure 10.13. The difference this time is the link at the bottom of this page, Create Multiple Buttons, will be selected. But first, it will be necessary to specify the region in which to place the buttons by choosing the radio button for the region.

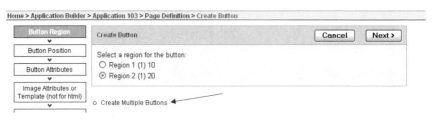

Figure 10.13: *Specifying the Region for the buttons.*

The Create Multiple Buttons link will display a new page that is shown in Figure 10.14. Up to 12 buttons can be defined at once. At the top of the page, there are two drop down boxes: one for the region; and one for the template. The region may be changed. The template drop down box only provides choices for the HTML DB button templates. There is another box, HTML Attributes, that is used to specify any additional attributes for the buttons.

In Figure 10.14, the creation of five different buttons using different labels and different positions has been specified. These buttons can only be created in the Region positions and not among the pages items. All that is left to do now is to click on the Create Buttons button. Quick and easy!

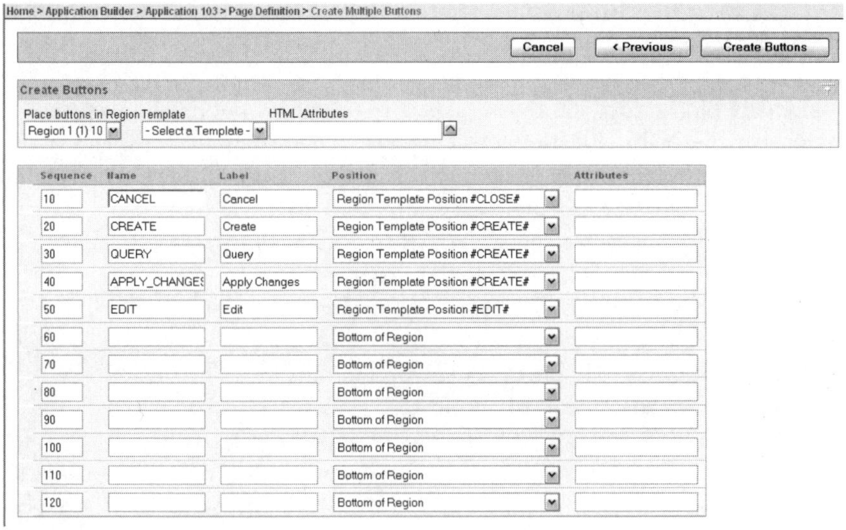

| | | | Cancel | ‹ Previous | Create Buttons |

Create Buttons

Place buttons in Region Template   HTML Attributes
Region 1 (1) 10 ▾   - Select a Template - ▾ [   ] ▲

Sequence	Name	Label	Position		Attributes
10	CANCEL	Cancel	Region Template Position #CLOSE#	▾	
20	CREATE	Create	Region Template Position #CREATE#	▾	
30	QUERY	Query	Region Template Position #CREATE#	▾	
40	APPLY_CHANGES	Apply Changes	Region Template Position #CREATE#	▾	
50	EDIT	Edit	Region Template Position #EDIT#	▾	
60			Bottom of Region	▾	
70			Bottom of Region	▾	
80			Bottom of Region	▾	
90			Bottom of Region	▾	
100			Bottom of Region	▾	
110			Bottom of Region	▾	
120			Bottom of Region	▾	

Figure 10.14: *Create Multiple Buttons.*

To make it even easier, something else that HTML DB provides is a list of Quick Buttons. This list is located on the right side of the Create Multiple Button page and is depicted in Figure 10.15. When one of the links from this list is chosen, the next empty slot will be filled with the corresponding required values. For example, if the Submit link in chosen, the Name of the button will be filled in with SUBMIT, the label value will be Submit, and the position will be #CREATE#.

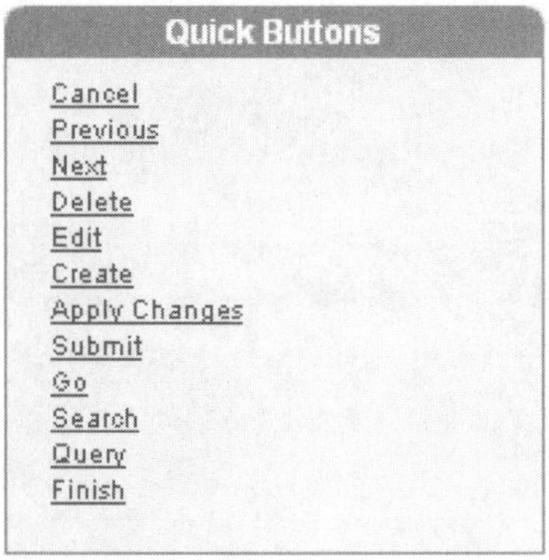

Quick Buttons

Cancel
Previous
Next
Delete
Edit
Create
Apply Changes
Submit
Go
Search
Query
Finish

Figure 10.15: *Quick Buttons*

Date Picker

The date picker page item type is used for dates, of course, but it provides an icon on the right side of the data picker page item that displays a popup window with a calendar. The icon is visible in the Date Pickers region in Figure 10.16. The popup allows the user to click on a date which will populate the data picker page item. Depending on the date format that has been set for the date picker, the calendar popup will display different information available for selection by the user.

Figure 10.16 shows the images of two data pickers. The one on the left has the format set to use the PICK_DATE_FORMAT_MASK which has been set to MM/DD/YYYY and the one on the right has the format set to MM/DD/YYYY HH:MI. Notice the image on the right. It has included select lists for hour, minute, and AM/PM. As a bonus, the date shown below the select lists is updated each time a piece of the date is selected.

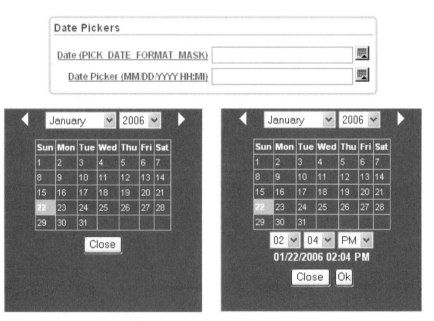

Figure 10.16: *Date pickers without and with time included in format.*

PICK_DATE_FORMAT_MASK

This is a user defined substitution string at the application level. This is the best way to keep the dates consistent throughout an application. The one caveat would be if the developer wants to use a combination of date only formats and date/time formats. In that case, it would make sense to choose the format most often used and set the PICK_DATE_FORMAT_MASK accordingly.

Creating the PICK_DATE_FORMAT_MASK is done on the edit application attributes page described in a previous chapter. For the information that follows, the following PICK_DATE_FORMAT_MASK was setup.

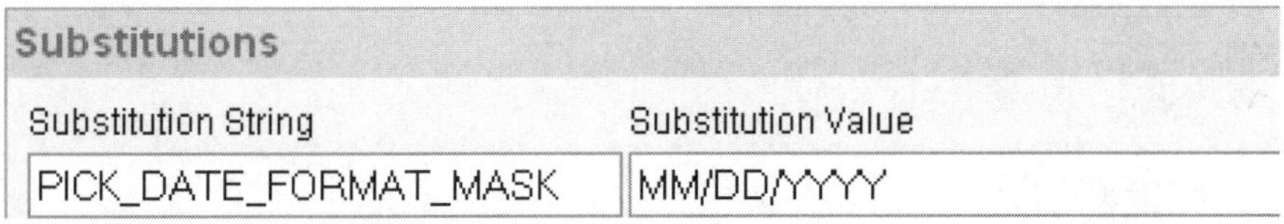

Substitutions

Substitution String	Substitution Value
PICK_DATE_FORMAT_MASK	MM/DD/YYYY

Figure 10.17: *Setting up the substitution string.*

Using the PICK_DATE_FORMAT_MASK in report columns is as easy as using the substitution string for the Date Format attribute of a column. See Figure 10.18 for an example.

Column Formatting

Number / Date Format &PICK_DATE_FORMAT_MASK.

Figure 10.18: *Using PICK_DATE_FORMAT_MASK for a column.*

Data in a web page is displayed as text and working with dates can be tricky at times. Using the PICK_DATE_FORMAT_MASK, as shown in the next two examples, can make working with dates easier.

Formatting data while selecting it from the database can be performed by including the PICK_DATE_FORMAT_MASK in a TO_CHAR function as shown here:

```
TO_CHAR( order_timestamp, :PICK_DATE_FORMAT_MASK )
```

Updating data in a database column from a page item also requires a conversion for the text representation of a date to the date format the database column is expecting. This can be done by using the PICK_DATE_FORMAT_MASK in a TO_DATE function as shown here:

```
TO_DATE( :P100_ORDER_DATE, :PICK_DATE_FORMAT_MASK )
```

SINCE

Have you noticed in HTML DB that there are reports showing information such as "2 weeks ago," "22 hours ago," or "35 minutes ago?" This is a date format known as SINCE. Putting the string SINCE into the Date Format of a page item will cause the date to be formatted in this manner. The ago time is rounded, but this is a simple way to provide this kind of date formatting. Figure 10.19 shows the date format setting and a sample of what it produces.

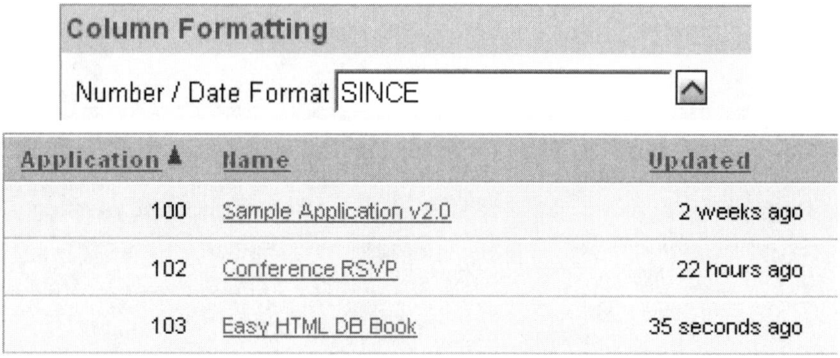
Column Formatting
Number / Date Format
SINCE
Application
Name
Updated
100
Sample Application v2.0
2 weeks ago
102
Conference RSVP
22 hours ago
103
Easy HTML DB Book
35 seconds ago

Figure 10.19: *Using the since date format.*

Lists of Values

A List of Values (LOV) is a reusable list that can be built dynamically with a SQL select statement or with a static set of values typed in by the developer. The two types of LOV's are Static and Dynamic.

Static LOV

To create a static LOV, navigate to the Shared Components page.

1. On the Shared Components page, click the Lists of Values link.

2. Click the Create button.

3. On the Source page, choose the From Scratch option.

4. On the Name and Type page:

    ▪ Enter the name for the LOV. The example is named GENDER.

    ▪ Type: Choose Dynamic or Static. The example is Static.

    ▪ Click Next.

5. On the Query or Static Values page, enter values for the LOV. The Display Value can be whatever the developer decides, but the Return Value should match any referential integrity in the database. Figure 10.20 shows the values entered for the example.

6. Finally, click the Create List of Values button.

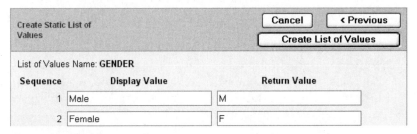

Figure 10.20: *Entering values for a static LOV.*

Dynamic LOV

The values in a dynamic LOV are populated using a SQL select statement.

To create a dynamic LOV, navigate to the Shared Components page.

1. On the Shared Components page, click the Lists of Values link.

2. Click the Create button.

3. On the Source page, choose the From Scratch option.

4. On the Name and Type page:

    ▪ Enter the name for the LOV. Our example is named PAYMENT_TYPE.

    ▪ Type: Choose Dynamic.

- Click Next.

5. On the Query or Static Values page, enter the query to select the data from a database table and then click the Create List of Values button. Our example has the query below.

```
select distinct payment d, upper( payment ) r
from  conference_rsvp
where  payment is not null
order by 1
```

Publish and Subscribe

The publish and subscribe feature of HTML DB allows components from one application to be shared with other applications. What this provides is a single point of maintenance for the LOV. Any changes made to the LOV would be updated in the master LOV and published to the applications that have subscribed to it. A common use for this is to have a Global application where shared components such as Lists of Values are maintained so other applications can subscribe to them.

The example below will create a List of Values with the As a Copy of an Existing List of Values option. The steps outlined are going to use the PRODUCTS list of values in the Sample Application installed with the creation of a new workspace in HTML DB.

1. On the Shared Components page, click the Lists of Values link.

2. Click the Create button.

3. On the Source page, choose the As a Copy of an Existing List of Values option and then click Next.

4. On the Copy From page, for Copy From Application, choose the Sample Application item and then click Next.

5. On the New Lists of Values page:

   - For the PRODUCTS item, the To Name can be left set to Copy of PRODUCTS.

   - In the Copy column, select the Copy and Subscribe option next to the Copy of PRODUCTS item.

   - Click the Copy List of Values button.

At this point, the program returns to the Lists of Values page. From there, click on the link for Copy of PRODUCTS. On the Edit List of Values page, the Subscription region will be visible as shown in Figure 10.21. This shows the LOV is subscribed to the PRODUCTS LOV in application 100. Anytime the LOV changes, the Refresh LOV button can be used to refresh the data from the master LOV.

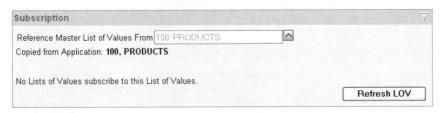

Figure 10.21: *Subscribing to an LOV in another application.*

Select Lists

Select Lists can exist in a region as a selectable page item or can be used in a tabular form region.

To create a Select List in a region click on the 🔲 icon in the Items region on the Page Definition page:

1. On the Item Type page, select the type of list from table 10.2 to create and click Next.

TYPE OF LIST	DESCRIPTION
Select List	This is the standard type of select list and just displays the text and provides a return value.
Select List Returning URL redirect	This type allows the developer to provide a list of web sites or links to other application pages. When the select list item is selected, the browser will redirect to the URL provided.
Select List with Branch to Page	This type has page IDs as the return values. When the item is clicked, HTML DB will branch to the application page.
Select List with Redirect	This type of select list will not submit the page for processing, but it will redirect the page back to itself. This can be used when the developer wants to set the session state for the item but not submit. It is commonly used when there are two select lists that work together in a parent child relationship. An example of this type of select list is shown later.

TYPE OF LIST	DESCRIPTION
Select List	This is the standard type of select list and just displays the text and provides a return value.
Select List with Submit	This type of select list will submit the page when an item in the select list is selected.

Table 10.2: *The types of Select Lists*

2. On the Display Position and Name page.

   ▪ Item Name: Enter the name of the item.

   ▪ Sequence: Enter the sequence based on where the page item is to be displayed in the region.

   ▪ Region: Select the region in which this page item should be displayed.

   ▪ Click Next.

3. On the Identify List of Values page:

   ▪ Named LOV: Enter the name of the LOV that will provide the values for this select list.

   ▪ Display Null Option: Choose whether or not to display the fact that the session state for the item is null.

   Answering YES here will cause the select list to be rendered with an extra item indicating null. The default text that will be displayed in the select list to indicate null is %.

   ▪ Null Text: Enter the text to be displayed in the event the session state for the select list is NULL. In Figure 10.22, the text – Select Payment – will be displayed in the select list when a value has not been selected from the list.

   ▪ Null Value: Enter a value to be used in session state if no item is selected in the select list. This item can be used in page validations to check if an item has been selected. It is common to use a -1 for numeric data and an X for character data.

   ▪ Click Next.

4. On the Item Attributes page:

   ▪ Label: Enter the text to display next to the select list.

- Label Alignment: Choose the position to place the label.

- Field Width: This is not used for select lists.

- Field Alignment: Select the position to display the select list in relation to the table cell in which it will be rendered.

- Label Template: Choose the template to be used for the label.

- Click Next.

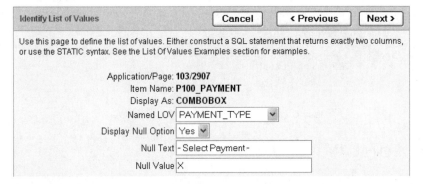

Figure 10.22: *Setting LOV properties for a select list.*

5. On the Source page:

- Item Source: Choose the source for where the value is being set from. It is normal to leave this set to Static Assignment where the value equals source attribute. What that means is when the page is rendered, the selected item will be set to the value corresponding with the session state for the page item.

- Default: Enter the value that the select list will default to. If NULL is displayed, this should be the same as the Null Value explained above.

- Click the Create Item button to not set any conditions, or click Next to set conditions.

6. On the Caching page, select the desired Derive Item Source option. The default is Only when the value is NULL.

7. Click the Create Item button.

Parent Child Select Lists

There have been several questions on how to do this on the HTML DB forum, so I figure I'd better cover the topic. A Parent/Child select list is two select lists working together. The child select list is populated based on the selection from the parent select list. So, if there are stores and departments, it would be desirable to select a store and then have the child select list populate with all the departments in that store. Furthermore, it would not be desirable to have the departments select list populated if there were no selection in the store select list.

Figure 10.23: *Parent / Child select lists.*

Figure 10.23 shows a region having two select lists. The following exercise shows how to create these two select lists. To follow along, create a page in the Easy HTML DB Book application with the page ID equal to 2908. To create the tables and data use the file name parent_child_tables.sql in the online code depot.

Creating the Store Select List

1. Click on the create item button in the Items area of the Page Rendering region.

2. Choose the Select List option and click Next.

3. Choose the Select List with Redirect option and click Next.

   Use of this option is not desirable in all cases. The reason is if the values in page items have not been saved in session state, the values will be lost performing a submit when the page is rendered again from the redirect. When page item values are to be saved in session state, the Select List with Submit option should be chosen.

4. On the Display Position and Name page:

   - Item Name: P2908_STORE_ID

- The rest can stay with the defaults and then click Next.

5. On the List of Values page:

   - Display Null Option: YES

   - Null Text: - Select a Store -

   - Null Value: -1

   - List of Values Query:

     ```
     select name d, store_id r
     from  store
     order by 1
     ```

   - Click Next.

   This case uses a query, as opposed to an LOV, to keep it simple. In reality it is better to use an LOV.

6. On the Item Attributes page, fill in the desired information and click Next. There is nothing special here pertaining to the parent / child relationship.

7. On the source page, enter -1 as the text for the Default value and click the Create Item button. A numeric value is used here since the STORE_ID column is numeric.

Creating the Department Select List

1. Click on the create item button in the Items area of the Page Rendering region.

2. Choose the Select List option and click Next.

3. Choose the Select List option again and click Next.

   This time there is no special action needed from the Select List when an item is selected.

4. Enter the Item Name, Sequence, and Region information and click Next.

5. On the List of Values page:

   - Named LOV: leave this alone

   - Display Null Option: YES.

   - Null Text: - Select a Department -

- Null Value: -1 because the column return value is numeric.

- List of Values Query: Enter the text shown in Figure 10.24

- Click Next.

This time something special must be done for the List of Values page. It is not desirable to create an LOV with a WHERE clause for this, so the select statement for the LOV will be provided right in the item definition as shown in Figure 10.18. The query uses the page item name from the parent select list, P2908_STORE_ID, to only select the departments associated with the store selected.

Figure 10.24: *Setting up the child LOV select statement.*

6. Again, the Item Attributes are not important for the outcome of the parent / child select list. Leave the default values and click Next.

7. On the Source page, enter X for the Default value and click the Create Item button.

8. Run the report and see the Parent / Child select lists in action.

Multiple Select Lists

Multiple Select Lists are much like select lists but allow the user to select more than one value at a time. Just like Select Lists, this is based on a LOV to populate the list. An example of a multiple select could be something like shown in Figure 10.25.

Figure 10.25: *Multiple Select List with Blue, Green and Red selected*

Notice in Figure 10.25, that there is a scroll bar for the box. This is another feature of the multiple select lists. There can be more values than are shown on the page. The length of the list can be controlled.

This type of item is good to use whenever the developer needs someone to select one or more items from a list. Some examples might include a pizza web site with a list of toppings or a maybe a new car purchasing website with a list of available options. The user selects each item by holding down the CTRL key as they select the item or use the SHIFT key and select.

To create a Multiple Select List in a region, click on the ⊞ icon in the Items region on the Page Definition page:

1. On the Item Type page, select the type Multiselect List and click Next.

2. On the Display Position and Name page.

  ▪ Item Name: Enter the name of the item.

  ▪ Sequence: Enter the sequence based on where the page item is to be displayed in the region.

  ▪ Region: Select the region in which this page item should be displayed.

  ▪ Click Next.

This is the most important part of the wizard. This is where the display values and the results are defined for the list. On this page, a LOV that has already be created and named will be chosen, type in a new SELECT statement or make a Static list. For the example in Figure 10.25, a static select list was used.

```
STATIC:Red;R,White;W,Blue;B,Green;G,Purple;P,Yellow;Y
```

The following is the explanation for some of fields on this page.

- **Named LOV:** Enter the name of the LOV that will provide the values for this select list.

- **Display Null** - Option: Choose whether or not to display the fact that the session state for the item is null.

  Answering YES here will cause the select list to be rendered with an extra item indicating null. The default text that will be displayed in the select list to indicate null is %.

- **Null Text**: Enter the text to be displayed in the event the session state for the select list is null. In Figure 10.24, the text Select a Department will be displayed in the select list when a value has not been selected from the list.

- **Null Value**: Enter a value to be used in session state if no item is selected in the select list. This item can be used in page validations to check if an item has been selected. It is common to use a -1 for numeric data and an X for character data.

3. On the Item Attributes page:

   - Label: Enter the text to display next to the select list.

   - Label Alignment: Choose the position to place the label.

   - Field Width: This is not used for select lists.

   - Field Alignment: Select the position to display the select list in relation to the table cell in which it will be rendered.

   - Label Template: Choose the template to be used for the label.

   - Click Next.

4. On the Source page:

- Item Source: Choose the source for where the value is being set from. It is normal to leave this set to Static Assignment where value equals source attribute. What that means is when the page is rendered, the selected item will be set to the value corresponding with the session state for the page item.

- Default: Enter the value that for the select list. This should be the same as the Null Value explained above.

- Click the Create Item button to not set any conditions, or click Next to set them.

5. On the Caching page, select the desired Derive Item Source option. The default is only when the value is NULL.

6. Click the Create Item button.

After the item is created, the list may only display that it has one value in size and shown in Figure 10.26. The reason that it displays this way is because the wizard does not give the option of making it larger. Thus, the page item should be edited.

Figure 10.26: *Multiple Select List after item creation from wizard*

First, edit the item by clicking on the item name in the Page definition. In the definition, there is a section called Element. This is where the height of the list can be defined. The height needs to be set to the number of values to show up on the page. As noted before, if there are more items than what is shown, a scroll bar will be provided so it is not necessary to show all the values at one time. The width is taken care of automatically, so there is no reason to worry about that.

Working with Multiple Select Lists

When a page is submitted, the value of a Multiple Select List page item will become a list of values separated by colons. For example, in Figure 10.25, the Blue, Green and Red values have been chosen. The page item will be set to the value B:G:R since those are the corresponding results from the LOV.

There are three ways to now process the value in the page item.

1. The string can be kept as a colon-delimited string and stored in the database.

2. The INSTR function can be used to process the information.

```
--  Search to see if Blue is part of the string
if instr(:P1_MLIST,'B') > 0 then
  -- process Blue
else
  If instr(:P1_MLIST,'R') > 0 then
    -- process Red
else
  ...
end if;
```

3. The list can be processed by utilizing the HTML DB API function called HTMLDB_UTIL.STRING_TO_TABLE. This function takes the result string and turns it into a PL/SQL array. The array can be processed in any manner. The following is an example of use:

```
declare
  selected_items htmldb_application_global.vc_arr2;
begin
  --
  -- convert the colon separated string of values into
  -- a pl/sql array
  selected_items := htmldb_util.string_to_table( :P1_MLIST );
  --
  -- loop over array to insert items into a table
  for i in 1..selected_items.count
  loop
    insert into colors_table
    values ( selected_items(i) );
  end loop;
end;
```

The reverse of this PL/SQL code can be performed in order to reassemble the value for the page item.

```
declare
  selected_list  htmldb_application_global.vc_arr2;
  i           integer := 1;
begin
  for r in( select color
       from  color_table ) loop
    selected_list(i) := r.class_id;
    i := i + 1;
  end loop;

  :P1_MLIST := htmldb_util.table_to_string( selected_list, ':' );
end;
```

List Manager

The List Manager page item is a interesting type of item. This type allows the user to enter values which will be added to a list. Values can also be selected from a designated LOV to populate the list. This type of item is good for information for which the user may not have direct knowledge. For example, a person who is providing a list of email addresses to email something. Since email addresses change all the time, it would be hard to keep up with a list. With this item, the user can supply any unknown email addresses and also provide them with a list of known email addresses. The next example will create a List Manager item just for this purpose.

Figure 10.27 shows an example of what this List Manager item will look like. The top horizontal box is the entry box where the user will enter any unknown addresses. After entering the address, the user will click on the Add button to add the entry to the list. The lower vertical box will contain the entered items. The user can remove items from the list by selecting the item in the list and pressing the Remove button.

There is a small icon next to the entry box. This box will invoke the Popup LOV. The LOV will provide a list of values to select. The return value will be placed in the list. The normal List Manager will convert everything to uppercase. Use the type with preserve case to allow upper or lower case.

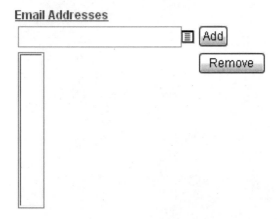

Figure 10.27: *Example of a List Manager item*

To create a List Manager in a region, click on the ⊡ icon in the Items region on the Page Definition page:

1. On the Item Type page, select the type of List Manager that you would like and click Next. The List Manager, based on Popup LOV, which preserves case, was chosen for the demonstration. Table 10.3 shows the different type of List Managers available.

LIST MANAGER	DESCRIPTION
List Manager (view only)	This will provide a list that is set to the page item. No entry will be allowed.
List Manager (based on Popup LOV)	This type will allow for the entry of items and the adding and removal of items from the list. The user can press on the LOV icon to see the list of values.
List Manager (based on Popup LOV, no fetch)	This type will allow for the entry of items and the adding and removal of items from the list. The PopUp LOV will not prefetch any values in to the LOV list. The user will be able to search in the LOV for values.
List Manager (based on Popup LOV, preserves case)	This type will allow for the entry of items and the adding and removal of items from the list. The PopUp LOV will not prefetch any values in to the LOV list. The user will be able to search in the LOV for values. This type will also preserve the case of the letters, upper or lower case.

Table 10.3: *The types of List Managers*

2. On the Display Position and Name page.

   - Item Name: Enter the name of the item, P1_EMAIL_ADDRESS.

   - Sequence: Enter the sequence based on where the page item is to be displayed in the region.

   - Region: Select the region in which this page item should be displayed.

   - Click Next.

3. This is the most important part of the wizard. This is where the display values and the results are defined for the list. On this page, the developer will choose a LOV that has already be created and named, type

in a new Select statement or make a Static list. For this example, a named LOV which was previously created was chosen. The SELECT statement for the LOV is:

```
select cust_last_name||', '||cust_first_name d, cust_email r
from  demo_customers
order by 1
```

The PopUp LOV will show the customers name and when selected will return the customers email address back to the list.

The following are the explanations for some of fields on this page:

- **Named LOV:** Enter the name of the LOV that will provide the values for this select list.

- **Display Null Option**: Choose whether or not to display the fact that the session state for the item is NULL.

  Answering YES here will cause the select list to be rendered with an extra item indicating NULL. The default text that will be displayed in the select list to indicate NULL is %.

- **Null Text:** Enter the text to be displayed in the event the session state for the select list is NULL. In Figure 10.24, the text Select a Department will be displayed in the select list when a value has not been selected from the list.

- **Null Value**: Enter a value to be used in session state if no item is selected in the select list. This item can be used in page validations to check if an item has been selected. It is common to use a -1 for numeric data and an X for character data.

- Click Next.

4. On the Item Attributes page:

- Label: Enter the text to display next to the select list, Email Addresses.

- Label Alignment: Choose the position to place the label.

- Field Alignment: Select the position to display the select list in relation to the table cell in which it will be rendered.

- Label Template: Choose the template to be used for the label.

- Click Next.

5. On the Source page:

- Item Source: Choose the source for where the value is being set from. It is normal to leave this set to Static Assignment where value equals source attribute. What that means is when the page is rendered, the selected item will be set to the value corresponding with the session state for the page item.

- Default: For a certain value to be selected as the default, the value of the display item will be entered here. This should be the same as the Null Value explained above.

- Click the Create Item button to not set any conditions, or click Next to set conditions.

6. On the Caching page, select the desired Derive Item Source option. The default is Only when the value is NULL.

7. Click the Create Item button.

When the page is run, the List Manager item will start out empty. Figure 10.28 gives an example of how the list looks after a few entries including an entry that is about to be added to the list. The list box will expand and collapse based on the entries.

Email Addresses

| Michael@dba.com | ▤ | Add |

| kent@yahoo.com |
| JohnDulles@aol.com |
| Eugene_Bradley@msn.com |

| Remove |

Figure 10.28: *Example of a List Manager item with entries*

When the page is submitted, like the Multiple Select Lists, the page item will be set to the list values delimited by colons. In this example, the page item will be equal to:

```
kent@yahoo.com:JohnDulles@aol.com:Eugene_Bradley@msn.com:Michael@dba
.com
```

Working with List Manager Items

There are two ways of handling the values. The use of INSTR for this item type is impracticable since the values entered would be unknown.

1. The string can be kept as a colon-delimited string and stored in the database.

2. The list can be processed by utilizing the HTML DB API function called HTMLDB_UTIL.STRING_TO_TABLE. This function takes the result string and turns it into a PL/SQL array. The array can be processed in any manner. The following is an example of use:

```
declare
  list_items htmldb_application_global.vc_arr2;
begin
  --
  -- convert the colon separated string of values into
  -- a pl/sql array
  list_items := htmldb_util.string_to_table( :P1_EMAIL_ADDRESS );
  --
  -- loop over array to insert items into a table
  for i in 1..list_items.count
  loop
    insert into email_addresses_table
    values (list_items(i));
  end loop;
end;
```

The reverse of this PL/SQL code can be performed in order to reassemble the value for the page item.

```
declare
  item_list     htmldb_application_global.vc_arr2;
  i            integer := 1;
begin
  for r in( select customer_email_address
        from  email_address_table) loop
    item_list(i) := r.class_id;
    i := i + 1;
  end loop;

  :P1_EMAIL_ADDRESS := htmldb_util.table_to_string( item_list,
  ':' );
end;
```

Radio Buttons

Radio buttons are used to give the user a list of choices where they can only pick one value from the list. Unlike a Select List, all the choices for the radio button are given on the page when rendered. Because of this, it is a best practice to limit the number of choices to only a few. An example of a Radio Button group is shown in Figure 10.29.

Colors

○ Blue ○ Green ○ Purple ○ Red ○ White ○ Yellow

Figure 10.29: *Radio Button group of Colors.*

The user will only be allowed to select one of the colors which will then specify the value for the page item.

Radio button page items are based on a LOV. In the LOV, the display values are specified and the value the page item will be set to when the radio button is selected. The Color example above will be created in the following exercise.

To create a Select List in a region, click on the ⬚ icon in the Items region on the Page Definition page:

1. On the Item Type page, select the type of list to create. This case will just use the standard type Radiogroup and click Next. Table 10.4 shows the different types of Radiogroups available.

RADIOGROUP	DESCRIPTION
Radiogroup	This is the standard type of radio group and just displays the text and provides a return value.
Radiogroup with Redirect	This type of radio group will not submit the page for processing, but it will redirect the page back to itself. This can be used to set the session state for the item, but not submit. It is commonly used when something else on the page may depend on the value for the radio group in a condition.
Radiogroup (with Submit)	This type of radio group will submit the page when an item in the radio group is selected.

Table 10.4: *The types of Radiogroups*

2. On the Display Position and Name page.

- Item Name: Enter the name of the item.

- Sequence: Enter the sequence based on where the page item is to be displayed in the region.

- Region: Select the region in which this page item should be displayed.

- Click Next.

3. This is the important page. This is where the display values are defined and the result which will be set to the page item. There are some options to fill in which are explained below. For this example, the Display Null has been set to NO. A simple static LOV will be used for this example. The List of Values definition is:

```
STATIC:Red;R,White;W,Blue;B,Green;G,Purple;P,Yellow;Y
```

If the values were saved in a table, a Select statement could be used to also populate the LOV. The Select statement might look like:

```
select  color_name  display_value, color_code result
from  color_table
order by color_name;
```

- **Named LOV**: Enter the name of the LOV that will provide the values for this select list.

- **Display Null Option**: Choose whether or not to display the fact that the session state for the item is null.

  Answering YES here will cause the select list to be rendered with an extra item indicating null. The default text that will be displayed in the select list to indicate null is %.

- **Null Text**: Enter the text to be displayed in the event the session state for the select list is null. In Figure 10.24, the text Select a Department will be displayed in the select list when a value has not been selected from the list.

- **Null Value**: Enter a value to be used in session state if no item is selected in the select list. This item can be used in page validations to check if an item has been selected. It is common to use a -1 for numeric data and an X for character data.

- Click Next.

4. On the Item Attributes page:

   - **Label**: Enter the text to display next to the select list. Enter Colors.

   - **Label Alignment**: Choose the position to place the label. Choose Above.

   - **Field Width**: This is not used for radio buttons.

   - **Field Alignment**: Select the position to display the Radio button in relation to the table cell in which it will be rendered.

   - **Label Template**: Choose the template to be used for the label.

   - Click Next.

5. On the Source page:

   - **Item Source**: Choose the source for where the value is being set from. It is normal to leave this set to Static Assignment where value equals source attribute. What that means is when the page is rendered the selected item will be set to the value corresponding with the session state for the page item.

   - **Default**: Enter the value that for the radio group. This value could be any of the values but make sure to use the result and not the display value.

   - Click the Create Item button to not set any conditions, or click Next to set conditions.

6. On the Caching page, select the desired Derive Item Source option. The default is Only when the value is NULL.

7. Click the Create Item button.

At this point, the radio group is not quite finished. Running the page will show that the radio group displays in a single column shown in Figure 10.30, which is not quite the desired result. The reason that it is in a single column is because the item creation wizard did not give the option necessary to have the values in a single line. The item will have to be edited and a value changed.

Colors
- ◯ Blue
- ◯ Green
- ◯ Purple
- ◯ Red
- ◯ White
- ◯ Yellow

Figure 10.30: *Radio Button group in a single column.*

First, edit the page item, P3_COLORS, or whatever you named it. A change needs to be made in the LOV definition for the COLUMNS field. This field specifies in how many columns across the display values should appear. In this case, the goal is to have a single line, so the value will be changed to six. For two lines of values, three columns would be used.

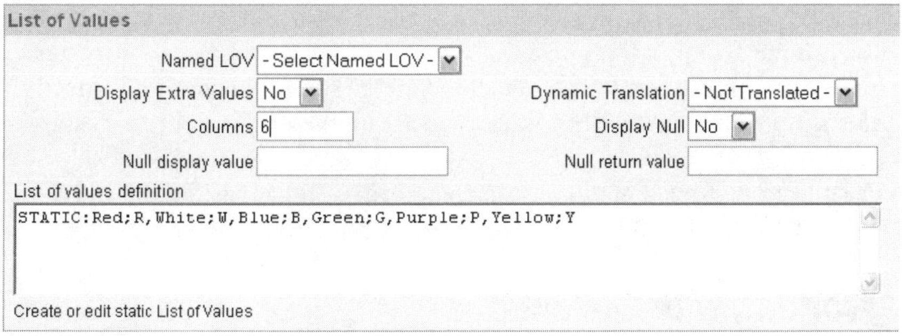

List of Values

Named LOV	- Select Named LOV - ▾	
Display Extra Values	No ▾	Dynamic Translation - Not Translated - ▾
Columns	6	Display Null No ▾
Null display value		Null return value

List of values definition

```
STATIC:Red;R,White;W,Blue;B,Green;G,Purple;P,Yellow;Y
```

Create or edit static List of Values

Figure 10.31: *Changing the Columns value for the Radio group.*

On display, the page item can be set to equal a value. When the page is rendered, the display value corresponding to the item value will be shown as chosen. For example, if P3_COLORS have the value of W, when the page is rendered, White will be chosen.

Radio groups are great way to display a full list to the user and have them select only a single value. Remember, to limit the choices to only a few because it may take up quite a bit of space on the page.

Collections

A collection is a way to work with a set of data without committing it to the base database tables. The concept is very much like a shopping cart. The data is collected, then, when all the necessary data has been collected, it can be inserted into a table, or tables, from the collection. Another way to put it is a collection works like persistent session state for a multi-dimensional array of data.

The data in a collection can only be seen by the session that created it. Also, a session can have many collections. For example, there may be one collection for books and another collection for music CDs.

If you have downloaded and installed the EASY Samples application from the code depot, you will be able reference it with the explanations that follow. The collections page ID is 1132.

The explanation provided here will be a departure from the way things have been done so far. The normal process walks through the steps to create all the components, but since collections are an intermediate to advanced topic, it is assumed you already know how to create the components necessary.

A collection stores data in a character format. It can store up to 50 elements plus a CLOB. The 50 columns are of data type varchar2(4000).

Working with Collections

The use of collections utilizes some of the HTML DB API. The package for this process is htmldb_collection. This package has several procedures and functions.

Creating a Collection

The collection being created here is a subset of the CONFERENCE_RSVP table. The code is in the Create Collection process on page 1132 of the EASY Samples application.

```
if htmldb_collection.collection_exists( 'CONF') = TRUE then

  htmldb_collection.delete_collection( 'CONF' );

end if;
```

```
htmldb_collection.create_collection_from_query(
  p_collection_name => 'CONF',
  p_query          => 'select id, last_name, first_name, rsvp_date,
                  company, ''O''
               from  conference_rsvp
               where  payment = ''Check''',
  p_generate_md5  => 'YES');

htmldb_collection.reset_collection_changed( 'CONF' );
```

While creating the collection above, the first step is to check to see if the collection exists. If it does, it is deleted. Then, the CONF collection can be created using a query to populate it.

Sorting a Collection

A button was provided to sort the collection by the LAST_NAME column in the collection. In reality, the data from the LAST_NAME column is stored in the collection in a column or element named C002, but that will be covered a little later.

The procedure to sort by the LAST_NAME, aka C002, column is:

```
htmldb_collection.sort_members( 'CONF', 2 );
```

Updating a Collection Member

A member in a collection is the same as a record in a table. However, an UPDATE command cannot be issued because it is a collection and not a table. Updating a collection member is done in the EASY Samples application with the following process.

```
htmldb_collection.update_member(
  p_collection_name => 'CONF',
  p_seq          => :P1133_SEQ_ID,
  p_c002         => :P1133_LAST_NAME,
  p_c003         => :P1133_FIRST_NAME,
  p_c004         => :P1133_RSVP_DATE,
  p_c005         => :P1133_COMPANY,
  p_c006         => 'U' );
```

The C006 element of the collection is being used as a place holder for actions performed on the collection. This idea was learned by looking at the Collections Showcase application included with HTML DB. The U indicated the member in the collection has been updated. Looping through the members in the collection can be done later to issue update statements on the CONFERENCE_RSVP table.

Saving Changes from a Collection to a Table

Although one cannot issue INSERT, UPDATE, or DELETE statements against collections, it is possible to issue SELECT statements. The htmldb_collections is a view into the data stored as a collection. The code that follows selects the C001…C006 columns from the htmldb_collections view. Then, looping through the collection starts to check the C006 column for any changes that have taken place. Members where C006 = 'I' indicates a new record and it needs to be INSERTed into the conference_rsvp table. The U means the member was updated and an UPDATE is performed. The D is a member that was deleted, and the record will be deleted from the table. Once the data has been updated, the collection is deleted and re-created so it can be displayed in a report.

This code is located in the Save Changes to CONFERENCE_RSVP process on page 1132 in the EASY Samples application.

```
--
-- Loop through the collection and update the CONFERNCE_RSVP
-- table according to the c006 column.
--
for r in (
    select c001, c002, c003, c004, c005, c006
    from  htmldb_collections
    where  collection_name = 'CONF' )
loop
  if r.c006 = 'I' then
    insert into conference_rsvp(
      id, last_name, first_name,
      rsvp_date, company )
    values(
      r.c001, r.c002, r.c003,
      r.c004, r.c005 );
  elsif r.c006 = 'U' then
    update conference_rsvp
    set  last_name  = r.c002,
        first_name = r.c003,
        rsvp_date  = to_date( r.c004, :PICK_DATE_FORMAT_MASK ),
        company  = r.c005
    where id = to_number( r.c001 );
  elsif r.c006 = 'D' then
    -- don't do the delete while testing for the book.
    -- delete from conference_rsvp where id = r.c001;
    null;
  end if;
end loop;
```

```
--
-- Repopulate the collection
--
htmldb_collection.delete_collection( 'CONF' );

htmldb_collection.create_collection_from_query(
  p_collection_name => 'CONF',
  p_query          => 'select id, last_name, first_name, rsvp_date,
company, ''O'' from  conference_rsvp where payment = ''Check''',
  p_generate_md5  => 'YES');

htmldb_collection.reset_collection_changed( 'CONF' );
```

Displaying Data from a Collection in a Report

Again on page 1132 there is a report that is populated with the following
query. This is an example of being able to query the members from the
htmldb_collections view. The query is using aliases to make it easier to know
what each column is doing. This is not necessary, but if looking at this code
six months after it was originally written, it would be easier figuring out what
is what.

```
select seq_id, c002 last_name, c003 first_name,
    c004 rsvp_date, c005 company, c006 mod
from  htmldb_collections
where  collection_name = 'CONF'
and  c006 <> 'D'
```

There is more information about the collections API in the HTML DB
documentation.

Charts

There are two types of charts from HTML DB.

- **HTML Chart**: This is a simple chart provided for in the HTML language.
  This type of chart is rendered using HTML table tags.

- **Chart (SVG)**: This is a more powerful type of chart using the Adobe
  Scalable Vector Graphics (SVG) standard.

The HTML DB is limited because it has to be drawn in the browser using
HTML table tags as mentioned. Therefore, only a bar chart can be created
with HTML table tags. However, SVG chart provides several options such
as Bar, Stacked Bar, Line, Pie, and Dial charts.

For the examples, the CONFERENCE_RSVP table will be used. The scenario is the promoters of the conference would like to see a chart on how many people made donations. Of those donating, they would like to see how many paid by which payment type.

Creating a Page with a Chart

The explanation is done in tutorial fashion. Two charts will be created on a single page.

1. Navigate to the Application home page for the Easy HTML DB Book application.

2. Click the Create Page button.

3. Choose the Chart option and click Next.

4. Choose the Bar (HTML) option and click Next.

5. On the Page Attributes page:

   - Page: 1134

   - Page Name: Charts

   - Region Template: Chart Region

   - Region Name: HTML Chart

6. No tabs and click Next.

7. On the Chart Definition page:

   - Chart SQL: Use the query in ch10_5.sql.

   - Uncheck the Average Value checkbox but leave the rest to see what they provide.

   - Click Next.

8. Click Finish.

Run the page to see the chart in action. There will be links next the bars that can be clicked on.

🖫 ch10_5.sql

```
select 'f?p=102:11:&SESSION.:::::P11_PAYMENT:' || payment l,
    NVL( payment, 'No Donation' ) payment, count(*) c
```

```
from conference_rsvp
group by payment
```

The query in ch10_5.sql assumes that when the CONFERENCE_RSVP application was created, it had an application ID of 102. If it is different, it will be necessary to modify the query accordingly. The URL links being created here are going to navigate back to the report page created in an earlier chapter. It is going to set the session state for the P11_PAYMENT page item to the value the user clicks on and filter the results of the report.

Creating a SVG Chart

Navigate to the page definition for page 1134.

1. Click on the Create region icon.
2. Choose the Chart option and click Next.
3. Choose the Pie option and click Next.
4. On the Display Attributes page enter SVG Pie Chart for the Title and click Next.
5. On the Source page, enter the query from above in ch10_5.sql and click the Create Region button.

The chart may have a default name of Chart 1. Since the chart building wizard did not allow this to be set during the creation of the chart, it must be changed. To do this, navigate to the page definition for page 1134.

1. Click on the Chart link for the SVG Pie Chart region. This will navigate to the Chart Attributes tab for the chart.
2. Enter the text Easy Pie Chart into the Chart Title field.
3. Scroll down and change the Font Size for the Legend to 12.
4. Click on Apply Changes.

Run the report. Use of the SVG chart allows users to click on the pieces in the pie chart to drill down to the Conference Attendees report, or the text in the chart legend can also be clicked to access the information.

Calendars

Calendars can be built two ways in HTML DB: the Easy Calendar; and the SQL Calendar.

- **Easy Calendar**: Using the Easy Calendar wizard prompts for the table or view to use, and then asks what column to use as the source for the date, and another column for what to display in the calendar.

- **SQL Calendar**: This wizard asks the developer to provide a query in which to populate the calendar. The query must select at least two columns and one of them must be a date. To display aggregated data, such as a count of records for a date, this wizard will be used to build the query.

The methods for creating both calendars are similar, so creating the Easy Calendar will not be included in detail. The following example will create a calendar to display the count of conference attendees who responded via RSVP on a date. The query is simple.

```
select rsvp_date, count(*) rsvp_count
from   conference_rsvp
group by rsvp_date
```

Creating a Calendar

1. Navigate to the Easy HTML DB Book application and click on the Create Page button.

2. Choose the Calendar option and click Next.

3. Choose the SQL Calendar option and click Next.

4. On the Page Attributes screen:

   - Page: 1135.

   - Page Name: Calendar Sample.

   - Region Name: Count of RSVPs by date.

   - Click Next.

5. No tabs and click Next.

6. On the Table / View Owner page, enter the following query and click Next:

   ```
   select rsvp_date, count(*) rsvp_count
   from   conference_rsvp
   group by rsvp_date
   ```

7. On the Date / Display Columns page:

- Date Column: RSVP_DATE.

- Display Column: RSVP_COUNT.

- Click Next.

8. Click Finish.

Run the report. Pressing the Previous button on the calendar several times will get to the month of September 2005. That is where the data can be found.

Customizing a Calendar

The calendar from above does not contain much data on the page, and it does not appear to offer much. However, if links are added to the page that will navigate to a report where all the RSVPs for that date can be seen, then it would be useful. This example will modify the calendar attributes to add links.

1. Edit the calendar. If the page is still running, click on the Edit Page 1135 link in the developer toolbar.

2. Click on the CAL link next to the Count of RSVPs by date region.

3. In the Column Link region, select URL for the Target and enter the following into the URL Target and click Next.

```
f?p=102:11:&SESSION.::::11:P11_RSVP_DATE:#RSVP_DATE#
```

The Column Link and Day Link operate as a branch. It is possible to either branch to pages in the current application or to a URL. The URL Target is being used to branch to another application.

For this branch to work, the P11_RSVP_DATE will have to be added to page 11 in the Conference RSVP application. Then, the query on the report would be changed to add the following at the end of the WHERE clause.

```
and ( rsvp_date = :P11_RSVP_DATE or :P11_RSVP_DATE is null )
```

Other Customizable Attributes of the Calendar

A few of the other attributes that can be set on the calendar are also located on the Calendar Attributes page.

- **Calendar Template**: There are three built in calendar templates from which to choose: Calendar; Calendar Alternative; and Small Calendar.

- **Display Type**: Setting this to Custom will allow the Column Format to be treated similarly to the HTML Expression attribute on reports. Using the Custom display type, an image could be displayed in the calendar column like this:

```
<img src="#IMAGE_PREFIX#24find.gif" />
```

Stop and Start Table

A Stop and Start Table page item is used to help control the layout of page items in a region. What it does is closes the table tags with </table> and then it restarts a new table. In effect, it is resetting the column widths for the table cells.

Figure 10.32 shows a region without using the start and stop table page item. The first two page items have the label alignment set to Right. What this does is cause two table cells (<td>) to be created, one for the label, and one for the field. Then the History text area has the label alignment set to Above. What this does is put the history page item in the first table cell which aligns it vertically with the labels from the other page items.

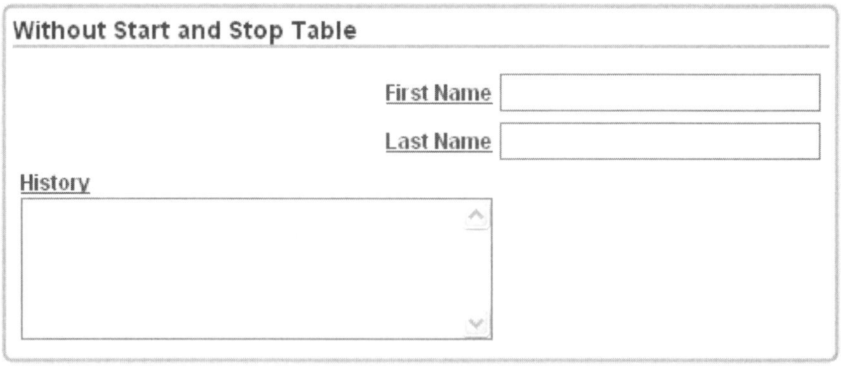

Figure 10.32: *Region without using the Start and Stop Table.*

Really, the goal is to move the first and last name fields to the left. To accomplish this, a Stop and Start Table is added after the last name page item. Figure 10.33 shows the same region with the stop and start table page item. The sequence for the stop and start page item is set to a value between the last name and history page items. Also, the Label attribute of the stop and start table page item should be set to NULL.

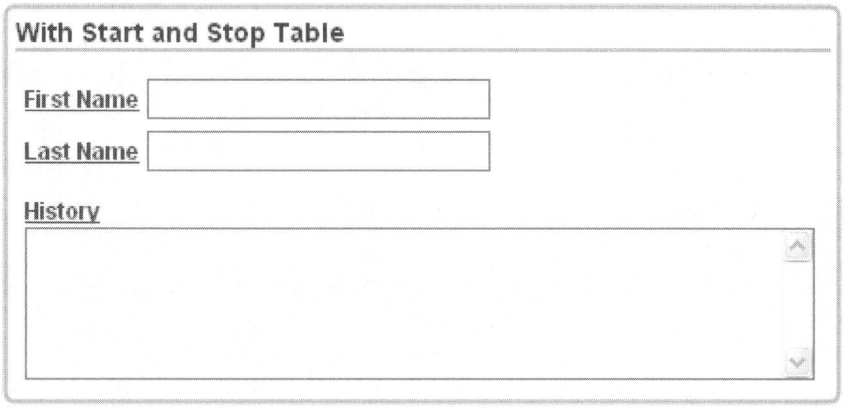

Figure 10.33: *Region using the Start and Stop Table.*

Text Fields

Text items are the most basic and most commonly used items in HTML DB. They are the item used for entry and display of values to and from the user. There have been many examples of text items already in this chapter, for example, the First Name and Last Name items of Figure 10.33 are text items.

A Text field is used for the normal data entry from the user. It will accept any characters typed into it and will save the value to the session state when the page is submitted. The values then can be inserted into the database or used in any other fashion during processing. There can be up to a maximum of 30,000 characters entered into a text field.

There are a few different types of Text items:

- **Text Field**: This type renders as a text field. The value entered into the text field will be saved in the session state when the page is submitted.

- **Text Field (Disabled, does not save state)**: This type of text field is read only. The user will not be able to type into the field. It will display the value of the item in a subdued color, grayed out. The value will not be saved to the session state upon page submission.

- **Text Field (Disable, saves state)**: This type of text field is much like the Text Field (Disabled, does not save state) but as the name implies, it does save the value to the session state upon page submission. The value display will be more normal.

- **Text Field (always submits page when Enter pressed)**: This type is the same as the normal text field. The distinction is that if the Enter button is pressed on the keyboard, the page will automatically submit. This is a good option to use if the goal is to let the user have quick data entry while keeping their hands on the keyboard instead of having to click a button with the mouse.

- **Text Field with Calculator Popup**: This is another specialized version of the text field. This field is like a normal text field, but it will have a small calculator icon next to the field. When the icon is clicked, a calculator will popup. The user can use the calculator to compute a value. When Done, the value will be copied into the field. Figure 10.34 shows the field with the calculator popup.

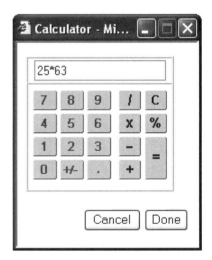

Figure 10.34: *Text with calculator popup and the Calculator Popup.*

Text Field Attributes

Like other item types in HTML DB, the text field also has attributes:

- **Sequence**: The order in which the text field will be rendered. If there are two text field items with the same sequence number, the order will be when they were created. The sequence attribute is used to control the form layout.

- **Label**: Specifies the label which will be associated with the text field. This label can be displayed in many different positions, such as Above, Right, Left, or Below the item depending on the choice.

- **Template**: This specifies the template of the label. Choices can be No Label, Optional, Optional with Help, Required, and Required with Help. If the template is Optional or Required, the label will be bolded. If either with Help option is selected, the label will be underlined and it will be a link to the help text for the field. Additionally, if the option is Required, a icon will appear before the label to indicate that the user must enter information in the field. How the label is shown depends on the Application theme used.

No Label   **Optional with Help**   ● **Required with Help**

- **Display in Region**: This is the region in which the button will be rendered and displayed.

- **Post Element Text**: This is additional text that can appear after the text field. A good use for this is to display the units for a particular value. For example, it might be useful to display pounds after a Weight field or inches after a Height field.

Weight   **Height**
[   ] Pounds   [   ] inches

- **Width, Maximum Width**: The width is the number of characters that will be displayed in the field. The maximum width is the largest number of characters that can be entered into the field. If the maximum width is greater than the display width, the value will scroll in the field up to the maximum width. Text fields can only be one character in height.

- **Help Text**: The help text is used in conjunction with the Template described above. The text entered into this attribute will be displayed when a user clicks on a label that has been defined with the template of with Help. Upon clicking the label, a popup box will appear showing the help text. Figure 10.35 shows an example of what the popup box for height might look like:

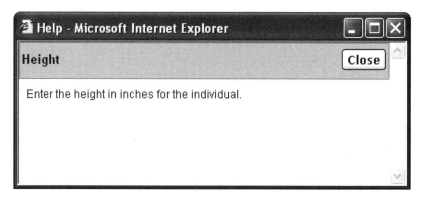

Figure 10.35: *Help text popup.*

Text Area Fields

Text Area fields are much like the Text fields described in the previous section. The feature of the text area fields is that it can accept multiple lines of entry. The field has automatic word wrap and scrolling built-in. Text Area fields have no maximum amount that can be entered into the field. An example of a text field might look like:

History

Alexander the Great, born in Pella, Macedonia on July, 356 BC, died in Babylon, on June 10, 323 BC. King of Macedon 336–323 BC, is arguably the most successful military commander in world history, conquering most of the known world before his death. Alexander is also known in the Zoroastrian Middle Persian work Arda Wiraz Nāmag as "the

There are a few different types of Text Area Field definitions:

- **Text Area (auto height):** This type attempts to vary the size of the text area depending on the amount of data. If the amount of data being shown is large, the area will be larger. The reverse is true for a small amount of data.

- **Text Area with Counter:** This type of text area comes with a counter. It will provide the user with a real-time counter of the number of character they have entered into the text area.

98 of 4000

- **Text Area with Spell Checker**: This text area integrates a Spell Checker with the text area. For now, it is only configured for the English language. An icon will be next to the text area. The user can click that to spell check what is entered. Figure 10.36 shows the spell checker results.

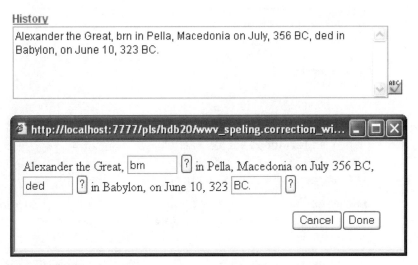

Figure 10.36: *Spell Checker*

- **Text Area with Spell Checker and Counter**: The type combines the Spell Checker and the text counter.

- **Text Area with HTML Editor**: This text area provides the user will some basic editing controls for the text. The user can do formatting such as bold, italics, underline, fonts, size, colors and so forth. The controls are simple but do help the user provide some formatting to the data. The formatting will converted to the HTML equivalent tags: Bold will convert to <strong>, italics to <em> and underline to <u>. This must be taken into consideration because these new tags will take up space.

The attributes for the Text Area are all the same as a Text Field but the height will now have to be configured. This will create the text area for the number of lines specified.

Display Only Fields

Display Only fields are used just to display information in a simple format. The following is an example of a Display Only field:

Display Field Label
The display value.

Like all items fields, the Display Only fields can be conditional for display.

- **Display as Text (does not save state)**: The value of the page item will be displayed as text on the screen. The value of the page item will not be saved to the session state when the page is submitted.

- **Display as Text (does save state)**: Same as Display as Text (does not save state) but the value is saved to the session state when the page is submitted.

- **Display as Text (escape special characters, does not save state)**: The value of the page item will be displayed without any conversions. Normally if the value contains HTML tags, the tags will be translated and rendered. With this type of item, the tags will not be translated.

    Display Field - Escape
    The display value.

- **Display as Text (based on LOV, does not save state)**: This type of display field will be based on the results from a LOV. Remember, each LOV has a display value and a result. If the item is equal to the result, the display values will appear on the screen. For example: A LOV has the following display values and results:

    STATIC:Red;R,Blue;B,Green:G,White;W

If the value of the page item is W from a SELECT statement, computation, process, etc., the display will be White. The value of the page item will not be saved to the session state when the page is submitted.

- **Display as Text (based on LOV, does save state)**: This is the same as the Display as Text (based on LOV, does not save state), but the value is saved to the session state when the page is submitted.

- **Display as Text (based on PLSQL, does not save state)**: This is the more complicated type of the Display as Text fields. This field is based on the results of an anonymous PL/SQL block. When this field is rendered, the PL/SQL block will be evaluated and the result is displayed. The PL/SQL block must set the page item to the value to be displayed. The source of the item must be anonymous PL/SQL block.

Hidden Fields

Hidden fields are page items which are not displayed when the page is rendered. These fields still exist in the background and are able to hold a value. There is no size limit to the value in a hidden item. Frequent uses of hidden fields include holding temporary values, primary keys, and values that are passed to the page. Any values set to the hidden field will be saved to the session state when the page is submitted.

Password Fields

Password fields are rendered just like a text field which accepts entry. In this field, the characters entered are replaced by a dot as each character is entered. The following is an example of the password field:

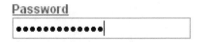

The value entered into the field is saved to the session state in its original form so the value can be processed. Password fields are not exclusively used for passwords. They can be used for any type of information that the developer may want to hide on the screen, such as Social Security Numbers or credit card numbers.

Conclusion

This chapter has shown the various types of items that can be presented on a web page. Each item performs a different task. Depending on what the web page is required to do, some items are preferable to others, such as when Radiogroups should be used instead of Select Lists. The reasoning behind this has been pointed out throughout this chapter. With all the various choices of items, any input situation can be handled. Plus some non-input items such as Display Only and Hidden have been included.

The next chapter will explain the various options for navigating through pages in HTML DB. After all, when a user has finished his input, the web page will need to perform some action and navigate to a new form.

Navigation in HTML DB CHAPTER

Another area of HTML DB which can be helpful to the users are the built-in Navigation facilities. Some of these methods, such as Lists and Tabs, should already be familiar; however, HTML DB also provides navigation through the use of Trees and Breadcrumbs. All or some of these methods can be combined in pages in order to make navigation of a site fast and efficient. Best of all, the methods are easy to create and use!

Lists and DHTML Lists

Multiple links can be collected into an object called a List. Lists can be displayed in different areas of the screen depending on the template used. Examples of lists have already appeared in HTML DB development. One example is on the login page, and is shown in Figure 11.1.

Tasks
○ Reset Password
○ Request a Workspace

Figure 11.1: *Example of a List*

Creating a List

This example will create a simple list to navigate to three different screens in the system. The process of starting a list can be accomplished in three ways:

- Go to the Shared Components, select Lists and click Create.

- From the Page Definition, click the Lists link in the third column

- From the Page Definition, click on the Create button in the Lists box

1. On the List creation screen, the name of the list will be entered. This example will use Book List. On this page, the template for the list will

also be specified. This screen is shown in Figure 11.2. After entering the Name of the list and choosing the type of template desired, click on the Create button. This will create the list but without any entries as shown in Figure 11.3.

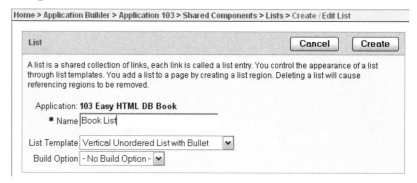

Figure 11.2: *List creation screen*

Figure 11.3: *List entries screen*

2. To create a list entry, click on the Create List Entry button. In this screen, the actual item is being created. Although there are only two required entries, the label and the target page number, this is like any other page item where the item is conditional. An example of a simple entry is shown in Figure 11.4.

   The label on the list will be Documents. When that link is clicked, it will navigate to the 1092 screen.

3. Optional items are:

   ▪ **Parent List Item**: Specifies a parent item for the link in order to create a hierarchal structure such as a tree. Not all templates support this structure.

   ▪ **Sequence**: Specify the order within which the link appears in the list.

- **Image**: Name of an image file to use as the link. The template must be able to support the images which are indicated in the template name.

- **Image Attributes**: Attributes to be applied to the image such as height=”10” and width=”10”.

4. The target branch can be a page or a URL.

5. Click on the Create or Create and Create Another button to create the link.

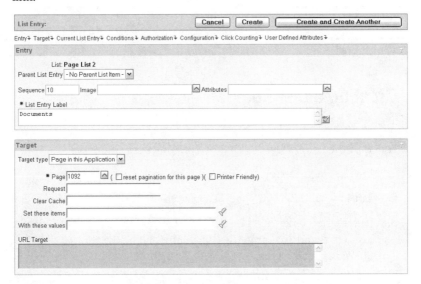

Figure 11.4: *List creation screen*

Depending on the list template that has been chosen, the list will be displayed in a certain way. Table 11.1 below is an explanation of each of the different types of list templates.

LIST TEMPLATE	EXPLANATION
Button List	The labels will appear as buttons.
Horizontal Image with Labels	Images will be display as the links including the label specified.
Horizontal Links List	Links will be displayed horizontally.
Tabbed Navigation List	Links appear to be tabs across a horizontal list.
Tree List	Vertical List of links in a tree fashion with sublists. Each item can be a link.

LIST TEMPLATE	EXPLANATION
Vertical Images List	Vertical List of images.
Vertical Ordered List	Vertical list of links which are ordered by the sequence number.
Vertical Sidebar List	Vertical list with bar which is highlighted as the cursor passes over.
Vertical Unordered List with Bullets	Vertical list that is displayed alphabetically with bullets.
Vertical Unordered List without Bullets	Vertical list that is displayed alphabetically without bullets.
Wizard Progress List	Used to show the progress of a wizard. Links will be conditionally displayed as the wizard progresses.

Table 11.1: *Templates and their descriptions*

Creating a List Region

After the list is created in the Shared Components area, the list must be added to the page. This is done by creating a region in which to put the list.

1. On the Page Definition for the page, create a new region.

2. In the Create Region page, select the type List, click Next.

3. Enter the Title of the region, the region Template, Display Point, Sequence and Column for the Region. These settings will control how the region will be displayed. Click Next.

4. The next page will provide a dropdown of all the lists. Choose the list to be shown in the region. Click Next.

5. Conditions can be entered on this page to conditionally display the region.

6. Click on Create Region.

Now the List will be available on the screen for the user to utilize. Lists are a great way of providing quick links for the various parts of the application or even external links. Figure 11.5 displays examples of many of the list templates.

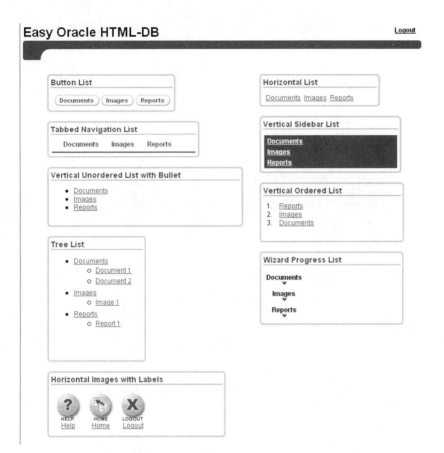

Figure 11.5: *Examples of List Templates*

DHTML Lists

A new type of list, the DHTML List, was added in Version 2.0 of HTML DB. This type of list creates a menu or tree type list. Many examples of the DHTML Image lists already exist and have likely been seen by the readers. The icon drop down lists are a DHTML Image list.

Figure 11.6: *Example of DHTML Buttons used in HTML DB*

DHMTL Lists are created just like any other list with entries and targets. DHTML menus also have sublists. The sublists will appear when the icons are pressed. Users have seen this action using the HTML DB DHMTL buttons.

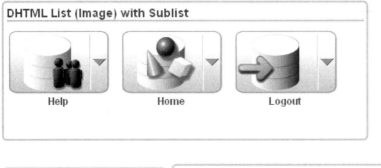

Figure 11.7: *Example of DHTML Menus*

If using images, the DHMTL List (Image) with Sublist option must be chosen. The images must be specified in the Lists that will be used as the source of the List region. The image can be any image the developer wants to use. The template has two image specifications: one for the button; and the other for the right side drop down menu. These specifications can be changed if necessary to add the developer's own graphics. It is not necessary to be limited to the button that Oracle has provided. If one wants to provide their own graphics, simply change the subtemplates in the Template Definition. The following subtemplates will have to be modified: The List Template Current, List Template Current with Sub List Items, List Template Noncurrent, and List Template Noncurrent with Sub List Items.

The following steps can be used to modify the template:

1. From the page definition, click on the DHTML List (Image) with Sublist in the Templates box or access this template through the Shared Components.

2. In the template, look for the Template Definition section as shown in Figure 11.8.

3. Now modify the templates as desired. For example, the List Template Current will be equal to the following when installed.

```
<div class="dhtmlMenuItem"><a href="#LINK#"><img
src="#IMAGE_PREFIX#themes/generic_list.gif" #IMAGE_ATTR#
/></a><img src="#IMAGE_PREFIX#themes/generic_open.gif" width="22"
height="75" /><a href="#LINK#"
class="dhtmlBottom">#TEXT#</a></div>
```

Careful examination of the HTML code will reveal two references to images. The first reference is to the left side of the icon drop down, generic_list.gif, the second is the right side of the button, generic_open.gif. These two images are plain gray boxes, but they do not have to be! The source of the button image can be changed to whatever the developer wants it to be! For instance, the src was changed to use the image specified in the List definition. The Template Definition could be changed to be like the following:

```
<div class="dhtmlMenuItem"><a href="#LINK#"><img src="#IMAGE#"
#IMAGE_ATTR# /></a><img src="#IMAGE_PREFIX#themes/generic_open.gif"
width="22" height="75" /><a href="#LINK#"
class="dhtmlBottom">#TEXT#</a></div>
```

The *src* of the image can be anywhere that you specify.

Figure 11.8: *Examples of List Templates*

Breadcrumbs

Breadcrumbs are used to provide a trail of links for the user. Depending on the template specified, the breadcrumbs can be a list of links or display as a breadcrumb path. An example of the breadcrumb menu is located at the top of most development screens. An example is displayed in Figure 11.9.

Home > Application Builder > Application 103 > Shared Components > Breadcrumbs

Figure 11.9: *Breadcrumb menu to the Breadcrumb creation*

Breadcrumbs are great to use for tracing a path to a particular screen. It will allow the user to see the path and if necessary they can back up to any point along the path.

Creating a Breadcrumb Menu

Creating a breadcrumb is very similar to creating a list. Again, there are three ways to create a breadcrumb:

- Go to the Shared Components, select Breadcrumbs, and click on the Create button.

- From the Page Definition, click the Breadcrumbs link under the Shared Components region.

- From the Page Definition, click on the Create button in the Breadcrumbs box under the Shared Components region and then follow the prompts.

The first page in the Breadcrumb wizard is shown in Figure 11.10.

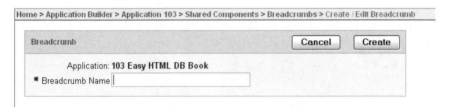

Figure 11.10: *Breadcrumb creation page*

1. Enter the name of the breadcrumb menu and click the Create button.

2. This will create the container in the Shared Components for the actual breadcrumb entries. After creating the container as shown in Figure 11.11, the breadcrumb entries will have to be created. In other words, the links that the user will click on will have to be created. From the Breadcrumb Entries screen, click the Create Breadcrumb Entry button. The Breadcrumb Entry screen will be displayed which is shown in Figure 11.12.

3. In the Breadcrumb entry screen, the Page number and the Name are required.

   - Page: This is the page number associated with this breadcrumb. The breadcrumb entry will highlight when the user is presently on this page number and navigated to it by another means. Also, the breadcrumb menu display will compensate depending on where the page is in the menu.

   - Sequence: The sequence where the entry will appear in the menu.

- Parent Bread Entry: Indicates the parent breadcrumb of this entry.

- Short Name: The text to display in the breadcrumb.

- Click on Create to create the entry.

4. In the Target section, the page or URL to branch to when the breadcrumb entry is selected must be identified.

5. In the Conditional Display, conditions can be specified for the entry display.

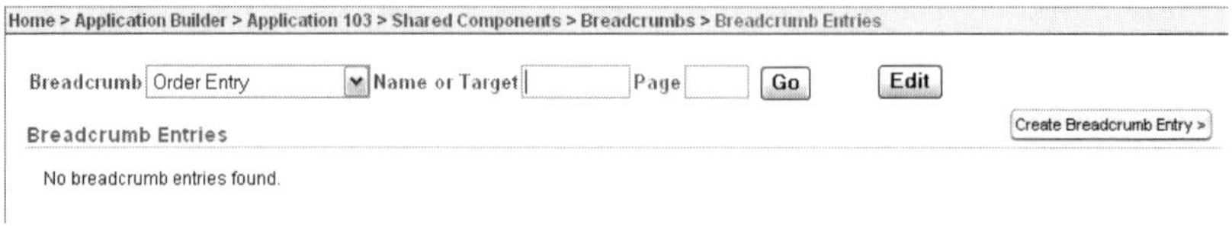

Figure 11.11: *Breadcrumb Entries screen*

Figure 11.12: *Breadcrumb Entry*

Creating a Breadcrumb Region

After the breadcrumb menu has been created, a region must be created to show the menu.

1. On the Page Definition for the page, create a new region.

2. In the Create Region page, select the Breadcrumb option, click Next.

3. Enter the Title of the region, the region Template, Display Point and Sequence for the Region. The region template should be set to Breadcrumb Region since that is defined in the template. These settings will control how the region will be displayed. Click Next.

4. The next page will provide a dropdown of all the breadcrumbs. Choose the breadcrumb that will be shown in the region. Also choose the Breadcrumb template. This will specify how the breadcrumb itself will appear in the region. Click Next.

5. On the next page, the Entry Label for the breadcrumb will be specified. Also, the parent entry to this entry can be specified. Click Next.

6. The next screen will summarize the choices. If all are correct, click on Finish; otherwise, the Previous button can be used to make changes.

Navigation Bar

Navigation bars are areas in the page template which can be used to provide links to other pages in the application or on the external website. The links will be displayed as a series of horizontal text or image links. The difference with the navigation bar and other types of link lists is that it is not necessary to define a separate region to contain the links. If the Navigation bar is part of the page template, the links will appear on every page. The navigation bar is global to all pages in an application.

HTML DB development pages have a navigation bar defined, and they have three entries.

Figure 11.13: *HTML DB Development Navigation Bar*

Although any type of link can be placed on the Navigation Bar, it is typically used to perform auxiliary functions such a Print, Help, Logout, Print Friendly View, About information, or Contact List.

Creating a Navigation Bar

Creating a Navigation Bar entry is very similar to creating a list. There are three ways to create an entry:

- Go to the Shared Components, select Navigation Bar and click Create.

- From the Page Definition, click the Navigation Bar link in the 3rd column.

- From the Page Definition, click on the Create button in the Navigation Bar box and then click Create.

1. The first screen in the wizard will ask the developer to specify the method they wish to use to create the Navigation Bar. A bar can be created from scratch, manually entering in each entry, or a bar can be copied from another application and modified as necessary. If a bar already exists, copying the navigation bar can speed up the development. In this example, one will be created from scratch. Click Next.

2. On the next page, the following fields can be filled out, as shown in Figure 11.14:

   - **Sequence**: The position of the entry on the bar.

   - **Alt Tag Text**: This will be text shown if the entry is an icon and the mouse hovers over it.

   - **Icon Image Name**: The name of the image file to use as the navigation bar icon. This is optional if the entry is only to be text.

   - **Image Height and Width**: Specify the height and width of the image when displayed. These should be entered if an icon is used.

   - **Text**: The text which will appear at the bottom of the entry. Either an Icon and/or Text need to be entered.

   - Click Next.

3. On this page, the target will be identified. The target can either be a page in the application or a URL to an external website.

4. The next page will allow the developer to specify conditions for the display of the navigation bar entry.

5. Click Create.

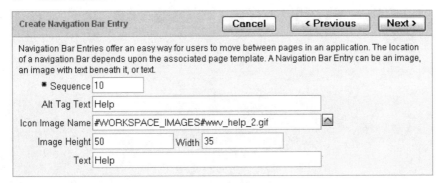

Figure 11.14: *Example of a Navigation Bar entry*

The following is the result of the navigation bar entry example. A Logout entry was also created to give a perspective of how they are displayed.

Figure 11.15: *Result of the Navigation Bar entry example*

Notice that the Text also appears in the bar. When using this type of icon, the additional text may not be desirable. The completed navigation bar is displayed in Figure 11.16.

Figure 11.16: *Result of the Navigation Bar entry example without Text*

Navigation Bars and Images in the Page Templates

It should be noted that when creating my first Navigation Bar, the icons would not display. When installed, HTML DB does not contain an entry in the Page Template for the image to be displayed. For help displaying the image, look at the Navigation Bar Entry subtemplate in the Page Template described below.

1. From the Page Definition page, click on the Page Template in the Templates box. In my case, it was No Tabs.

2. In the Page Template, scroll down to the Navigation Bar Entry section as shown in Figure 11.17.

Navigation Bar Entry

Figure 11.17: *Navigation Bar entry in the Page Template*

3. There is no reference to an image. The image tag was added to the entry in order to display the image.

```
<a href="#LINK#"><img src="#IMAGE#" title="#TEXT#" alt="#ALT#"
width="#WIDTH#" height="#HEIGHT#" /><class="t2navbar">#TEXT#</a>
```

Trees

Trees can be used to display hierarchal data. Trees are based on a base table. The table must have an ID column, a Parent ID column, and a display text item. The following example uses the information in the following CAR_PARTS table. A car is made up of parts and each part can have sub-parts. The records that make up the CAR_PARTS table are shown in Table 11.2 and Figure 11.18.

Column Name	Data Type	Nullable	Default	Primary Key
ID	NUMBER	Yes	-	-
PARENT_ID	NUMBER	Yes	-	-
ITEM	varchar2(20)	Yes	-	-

Table 11.2: *Car parts*

ID	PARENT_ID	ITEM
0	-	Easy Sedan
1	0	Engine
2	0	Wheels
3	0	Brake Lights
4	0	Transmission
5	0	Body
6	1	Pistons
7	1	O-Rings
9	1	Engine Block
8	1	Fuel Injectors
11	2	Hubs
12	2	Tires
14	3	Light Bulbs
15	3	Light Housing
17	3	Bulb Socket Assembly
16	5	Side Rails
17	5	Engine Rack
18	5	Cross Rails

Figure 11.18: *List of Records in the CAR_PARTS table.*

When a tree is created, a new page is created with all the information required to display the tree. A tree can be complicated to build. It is recommended that the tree be created first in order to create the page. Then, modify the page afterwards.

Creating a Tree

The first step to creating a tree is to navigate to the Shared Component area of the application. Choose the Trees link in the second column. This will start the Tree wizard.

1. On the first page of the wizard, as shown in Figure 11.19, the following information is required. All of these entries can be left at their default values.

   - **Page**: This is the number of that page which will be created

   - **Page Name**: Name of the page created.

   - **Region Template**: Template of the region which will display the tree.

   - **Region Name**: The name of the region. Click Next.

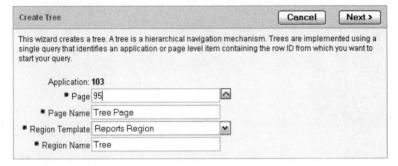

Figure 11.19: *Page one of the Tree creation wizard*

2. The next page, shown in Figure 11.20, will require:

   - **Tree Name**: The name of the tree. Enter in Car Parts.

   - **Default Expanded Levels**: This is how many levels the tree will show when first displayed.

   - **Start Tree**: The method to provide the starting point. A Static Value will be used for the example. Normally, this might be based on a LOV or other page item. Click Next.

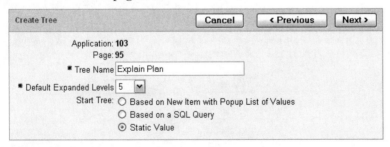

Figure 11.20: *Page two of the Tree creation wizard*

3. On the next page, as shown in Figure 11.21, the Tree template will be chosen. Each tree still performs in the same manner; they just vary in the graphics which are shown in the tree. The Standard Tree will be chosen for this example. Click Next.

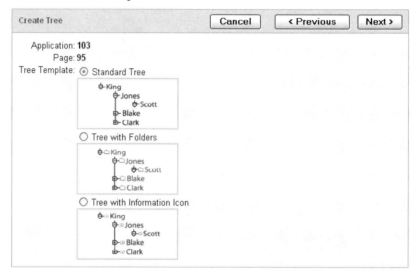

Figure 11.21: *Tree templates*

4. On this page, shown in Figure 11.22, the starting point for the Tree, the root, will be specified. This will be a static value, a query, or a popup value depending on what was selected on page two of the wizard, as was shown in Figure 11.20. Enter the number zero (0). Click Next.

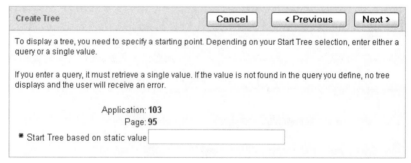

Figure 11.22: *Start point for the Tree.*

5. The next page of the wizard, shown in Figure 11.23, is to select which buttons to include with the Tree. There are three buttons from which to choose: one to Collapse All nodes of the tree; one to Expand All nodes of the tree; and, one to Reset the tree to when it was first rendered. Click Next.

Figure 11.23: *Buttons to include with the Tree.*

6. Using the next two pages, shown in Figure 11.24, of the wizard, the base table for the Tree will be chosen. In this case, this will be the CAR_PARTS table. The first page is where the Table Owner will be selected and the table itself will be selected on the second page. Click Next.

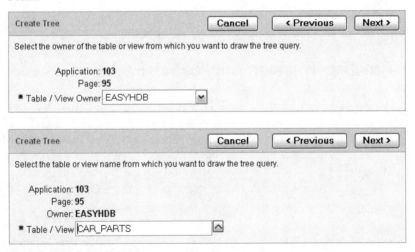

Figure 11.24: *Selecting the Owner and Table name.*

7. The next page, shown in Figure 11.25, is very important. This is where the three columns which are required for a Tree will be specified: the ID;

the PARENT ID; and, the LEAF NODE. The link can be additional information on the part such as a picture and details. In this example, a link will not be created. Click Next.

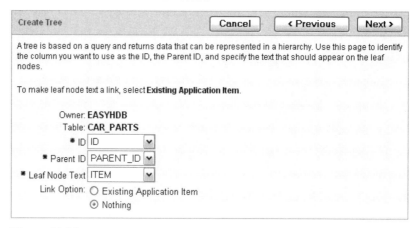

Figure 11.25: *Selecting the column names for tree nodes.*

8. The next page is where optional WHERE and ORDER BY clauses can be specified for the Query. Click Next.

9. The summary page is last. It will show all the options that were included in the wizard. If all looks good, click Finish.

Creating Trees on Application Pages

A page will now be created. When running the page, there will be a region with the tree. If links were specified for the leaf nodes, each link could navigate to a new page. The nodes can be collapsed or expanded by the user. To learn more about the trees, look over the page that was created, as shown in Figure 11.26.

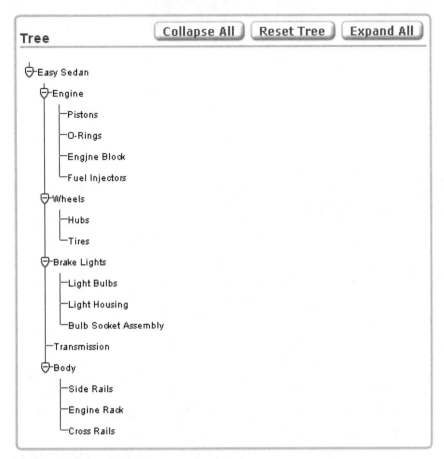

Figure 11.26: *A fully populated and expanded tree.*

Tabs

Tabs are an easy way to allow users to move between pages and even applications. Tabs are displayed on the page in the location defined by the page template. A good example of tabs is shown right in HTML DB, Figure 11.27. They have created three tabs which are displayed on every screen except for the login page. These are the Application Builder, SQL Workshop, and Administration tabs at the top right of each screen by putting them on Page of each application. These tabs actually tab between applications in HTML DB.

Figure 11.27: *HTML DB tabs.*

There are two types of tabs that can be defined in HTML DB. The first is the standard tab which is a typical setup of tabs such as that shown in Figure 11.27. The second type is the parent tab. A parent tab is used as a container for a number of standard tabs. The parent tab configuration can give the user a sense of where they are in the navigation.

Standard Tabs

Tabs are grouped into a collection called a tab set. Each tab set will contain one or more tabs. When a tab is created, it may also be necessary to create the tab set, much like creating a list with list entries.

There are three ways to create a tab:

- Navigate to the Shared Components and click Tabs

- From a page definition page, click on the Tabs and then click on Create

- On the page definition page, click the create icon in the Tabs box

Once the tabs have been selected, the Standard Tab creation wizard will begin.

1. On the first page of the Standard Tab creation, shown in Figure 11.28, the developer can specify whether to create a new tab and tab set or to just create a new tab in an existing tab set. This example will create a new tab and tab set. Click next.

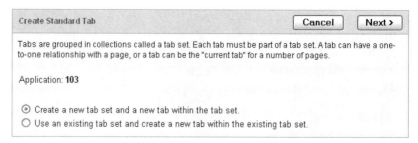

Figure 11.28: *Creating a tab set and tab.*

2. On this page, the name of the tab is specified. This name will not appear anywhere on the page. It is just used for reference.

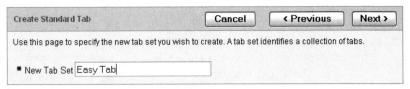

Figure 11.29: *Entering a name for the Tab Set.*

3. The next page is where one specifies if they want to put this new tab set into a parent tab set. Since a parent tab set has not been created, just click Next.

4. On the next wizard page, a tab will be created in this tab set. Remember, at this point there is only a container for the tabs; the tab itself must be added. Tabs will be created for the Easy Tab set which are Reports, Documents, and Images. The first tab, Reports, will be entered here.

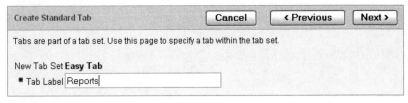

Figure 11.30: *Entering a name for the Tab.*

5. On the page show in Figure 11.31, the target for the tab will be defined. This is the page to which the application will branch when the tab is clicked. For this tab, the goal is to go to page 1070.

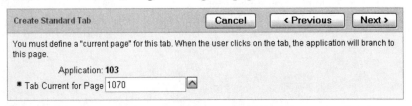

Figure 11.31: *Entering the target page number for the Tab.*

6. Next, the sequence of the tab is specified. This will be the sequence where the tab will fall in the tab set. An image to use as the tab can also be specified. The Current image will be displayed when the user is on the target page, which in this case is 1070. The Non Current Image will be displayed when the user is on another page. Image attributes are optional to apply to the images. The sequence number will remain ten (10) since this is the first tab in the tab set. For this example, images will not be used for the tabs, so the labels will be used.

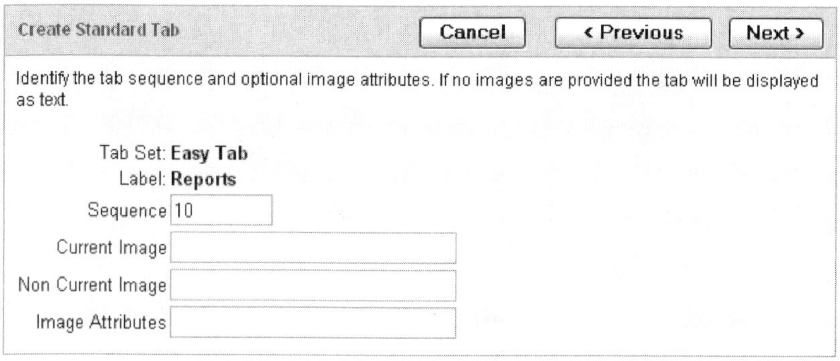

Figure 11.32: *Specifying the sequence for the tab in the tab set.*

7. The next page is the familiar conditional specification page. Here conditions for the display of this tab can be specified. This does not affect the display of the tab set.

8. The next page is the confirmation page. If all looks okay, click on Create Tab.

Editing Tabs

Once a tab is created, it can easily be edited. Now when the developer goes to the Tabs in the Shared Components, they will be presented with a graphical interface, shown in Figure 11.33, to create more tabs and tab sets.

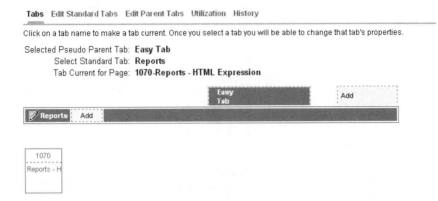

Figure 11.33: *Editing tabs and tab sets.*

Figure 11.33 has two Add links. The one on the long dark bar next to Reports is used to add more tabs to the Easy Tab tab set. When clicked, it will start the wizard at Step four outlined above. The Add on the upper right is to add new parent tab sets. The Documents and Images tabs have been added to the Reports tab set below.

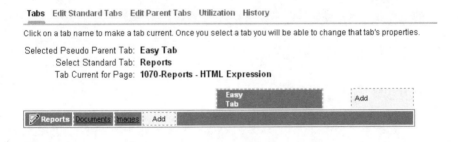

Figure 11.34: *New tabs.*

Adding Tabs to a Page

After a tab set is created, it has to be added to the page. The tab set can be added to the page during the page creation. One step of the page creation will ask if the developer wishes to use tabs and if so which tab to use on the page.

To add the tab set to an existing page, the developer must enter the Edit Attributes for the page. Once in Edit Attributes, scroll down to the Display Attributes section.

Figure 11.35: *Display Attributes for a Page.*

In the Display Attributes section, use the Standard Tab Set drop down list to specify which tab set to use. Also, a Page template that supports tabs must be selected; otherwise, the tabs will not appear. After the selections have been made, click on Apply Changes.

When running the form now, the tab set will be displayed. When the user clicks on the tabs, they will navigate to the specified pages.

Figure 11.36: *Example Tab Set.*

Parent Tabs

As noted before, parent tabs are containers for standard tabs. The parents tab will contain entries which, when selected, will show a standard tab. For example, one might create a Parent Tab called Library. The Library tab set will contain two tabs called Files and Data, respectively. When clicked, the Files tab will navigate to the Easy Tab that has already been created. The Data tab will navigate to another tab set that has been created.

Conclusion

This chapter covered several areas of HTML DB navigation. The topics covered were the creation and use of the following page components.

- Lists

- Breadcrumb menus

- Navigation Bar

- Trees

Other forms of navigation were also covered in other chapters where they could be discussed in their appropriate subject areas such as using links in HTML DB Reports, links in calendars, and buttons.

The next chapter dives into the area of logic controls and page processing. It will show how to take full control over the rendering of page data as well as the processing of the data when the page is submitted.

Page Processing

Introduction

Although this chapter is titled Page Processing, information regarding the logic controls included in the Page Processing alone is not enough, coverage of their use during Page Rendering is also necessary. There are also application level logic controls which execute when HTML DB sessions are created during login.

Using Page Rendering and Page Processing effectively can be somewhat confusing when learning to develop applications using HTML DB. When I first saw the Page Processing region, I was confused and did not know how to use it. After all, I've been used to having to write every line of code in other programming languages.

The fact is, Page Processing in HTML DB is a clever method of providing logic control to developers of web pages who do not have a programming background. The tricky part is understanding what is happening, why it is happening, and when it is happening. This chapter will help answer those questions.

The Page Processing region is shown in Figure 12.1. This example is taken from application page 29 of the Sample Application included with HTML DB.

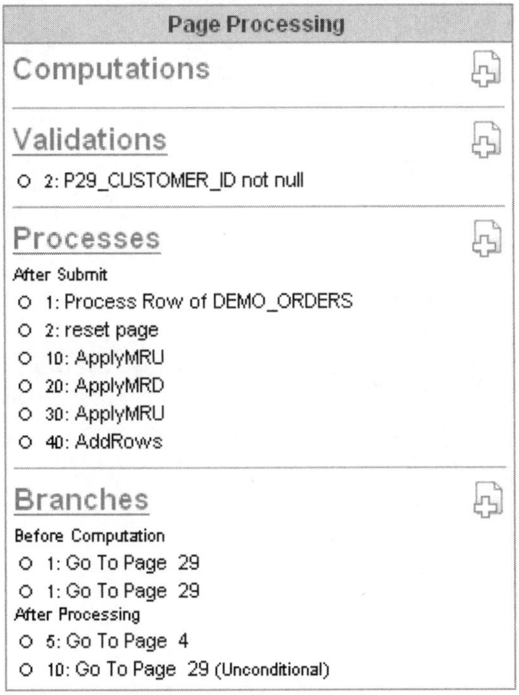

Figure 12.1: *The Page Processing region.*

The Page Processing region contains the logic that is to be executed when the page is submitted. The items in the Page Processing region are called Logic Controls. When the page is submitted, the HTML DB engine considers each of the logic controls in a specific order determined by the developer. The Conditions set on each of the logic controls is the deciding factor on whether they will be executed. It is just like a big IF … THEN statement for all the logic controls.

There is an exception to this rule. If one of the processes or branches navigates off the page before the logic control is considered by the HTML DB engine, it will be ignored. This navigation is usually performed in a Before Computation, Before Validation, or Before Processing branch. Branches will be covered later in the chapter.

Logic Controls

The Logic Controls included in Page Processing are:

- **Computations**: Used to set values of page items.

- **Validations**: Used to verify the accuracy of user input.

- **Processes**: Programming logic to make changes to data.

- **Branches**: Used to navigate to other application pages, other applications or a URL when the page is submitted.

Computations

A computation is used to set the value of a page item either during page rendering or during page processing. There is also the ability to create Application Computations to set page item values when a new session is created during login. When creating computations, properties are set to define what page item(s) will be set, when the computation will be executed, and how it will be done.

- Computation Location

- Computation Point

- Computation Type

- Conditions

Computation Locations

Computation locations identify where the page item is located that will be set by the computation.

- **Item on This Page**: This type of computation is used to set the value of a single item on the current application page.

- **Item on Another Page**: This type of computation is useful when navigating to another page and wanting to set page items on that page. Using this method, the values can be hidden by not having to send them in the URL. The limitation of using this method is the page will not provide a URL for the user to save in the browser as a Favorite. A common example would be saving a sale item on the web site.

- **Application Level Item**: This type of computation is used to set the value of an item defined at the Application Level. Application level items act as global items. A benefit of using an application level item is when the page cache is cleared, the application level items are not cleared. A disadvantage of using application level items as place holders for values is another page may overwrite the value.

Computation Points

A Computation Point defines when the logic control will be considered in the order of execution. This happens for both page rendering and page processing.

Application Level Computation Points

On New Instance is an application level computation and should be created as such. It can be a little confusing since this computation point is available when creating a computation at the page level. However, do not use the On New Instance display point on application pages. These should be defined as an Application Computation in Shared Components. When an On New Instance computation is created at the application level, it will be executed during login when the session is created in HTML DB. A good use of this type of computation would be to read a cookie from the user's browser to set some application level items.

Page Rendering Computations

The computation points covered in this section are executed during page rendering. This may be confusing when first starting to build web applications using HTML DB, but this chapter will show how they are used and reveal their inherent value.

- Before Header
- After Header
- Before Region(s)
- After Region(s)
- Before Footer
- After Footer

The explanation of these execution points will be delayed until the section on Computation and Processing Points in Detail is covered in this chapter. There, a thorough explanation of the execution points during page rendering will be presented.

Page Processing Computations

The final computation point is After Submit. An After Submit Computation Point is considered for execution during Page Processing.

An After Submit computation would be used to calculate a person's age based on a birth date page item, to calculate the number of days between two dates, or to set a page item with the total amount from a list of numbers. As mentioned earlier, it could also be used to set values on another page so as to not pass the values in the URL.

Computation Types

The following explanations include syntax samples for each computation type. The examples show text that could be entered into the Computation text area for the computation attributes.

- **Static Assignment**: This computation type will enter the text value for the page item to be set.

    Example:

    > Copyright 2006

    Example (with space between items):

    > &P100_FIRST_NAME. &P100_LAST_NAME.

- **PL/SQL Function Body**: This computation type allows a PL/SQL function to be written that returns a value. The page item will be set to the value returned from the PL/SQL function.

    Example:

```
declare
   s_full_name   varchar2(100);
begin
   for r in (
      select first_name, last_name
      from   conference_rsvp
      where  id = 8 )
   loop
      s_full_name :=
         r.first_name || ' ' || r.last_name;
   end loop;
   return s_full_name;
```

```
end;
```

- **SQL Query**: The value returned from the SQL query will be used to set the page item value.

    Example:

    ```
    select first_name || ' ' || last_name
    from   conference_rsvp
    where  id = 8;
    ```

- **SQL Expression and PLSQL Expression**: These two expressions produce the same results. They take the results of the expression and set the page item value.

    Example:

    :P100_FIRST_NAME || '' || :P100_LAST_NAME

- **Item Value**: This will set the value of one page item to the same value of another page item.

    Example:

    P100_FIRST_NAME

Creating Computations

Creating computations is done from the page definition page. The example shown below will create a computation to query the database for the full name of a customer. A condition is set to only execute this computation if the current value of the page item is null.

1. Click on the 🔳 in the Computations area under Page Processing.

2. On the Item Location page select the Computation Location and click Next.

3. On the Item page:

    - Select the Compute Item for which the computation is created.

    - Set the Sequence to the order in which the computation is to execute.

    - Select the Computation Point. For this example, After Submit was chosen, so it executes when the page is submitted.

- Select the Computation Type. For this example, PL/SQL Function Body was chosen.

- Click Next.

4. On the Computation page enter the source code for your computation and click Next. In this example, PL/SQL Function Body was chosen and the code is shown below.

```
declare
   s_full_name varchar2(100);
begin
   for r in (
      select salutation, first_name, last_name
      from   customer
      where  customer_id = :P100_CUSTOMER_ID )
   loop
      s_full_name := r.salutation
         || ' ' || r.first_name
         || ' ' || r.last_name;
   end loop;
   return s_full_name;
end;
```

5. On the Condition page select the Condition Type and enter the Expressions as necessary. The following example shows the information entered as:

- Condition Type: Value of Item in Expression 1 is NULL.

- Expression 1: P100_FULL_NAME.

- Finally, click the Create button.

Validations

Validations are used to check the validity of data entered into the page items. Validations are used to make sure a mandatory field has data; a number field, such as currency, actually has a numeric value; that dates fall into an acceptable range; and much more. When creating validations, properties are set to define what page item(s) will be set, when the computation will be executed, and how.

- Validation Level

- Validation Method

- Error Message and Display Location

- Conditions

Validation Levels

- **Item Level Validation**: A validation specific to a single item on an application page.

- **Page Level Validation**: A validation usually used to check multiple items on an application page. Often this is a PL/SQL function used to validate the data before an INSERT or UPDATE is attempted by a Process. HTML DB uses this kind of validation to make sure the query entered into a Report region is a valid query.

Validation Methods

Validations are written to return a TRUE or FALSE value. A return value of TRUE means the validation is successful. A return value of FALSE means there is as an error.

SQL

- **Exists**: Allows the creation of a SQL select statement that checks for the existence of data in the database. The validation will return TRUE if at least one row is returned from the query.

  Example:

  ```
  select 1 from inventory_items
  where  item_id = :P100_ITEM_ID
  and    qty_available >= :P100_QTY_ORDERED;
  ```

- **NOT Exists**: This is a good validation to use to prevent the insert of a record that already exists. If a row is found, the validation returns a false value indicating an error. The syntax is the same as for the Exists example above.

- **SQL Expression**: Evaluates a SQL or PL/SQL expression and returns a TRUE or FALSE value of the expression. This type of validation is valuable, for example, checking that a birth date is not some date in the future. It is also valuable for comparing numeric values since page items are displayed in alphanumeric format.

  Example:

  ```
  :P100_BIRTH_DATE <= SYSDATE
  ```

Example:

```
TO_NUMBER(:P100_AMOUNT_OWED)
      = TO_NUMBER(:P100_AMOUNT_PAID)
```

PL/SQL

These types of validations use the PL/SQL language to determine the outcome of the validation. Take note that while using the validation creation wizard to create this type of validation, text will appear below the main region on the Validation Method page as shown in Figure 12.2. Clicking on the links of the text in bold reveals the syntax examples. These are valuable and should be used when necessary. The following is a brief summary of help not found in the HTML DB documentation.

- **PL/SQL Expression**: Same at the SQL Expression above.

- **PL/SQL Error**: Used to raise an application error.

- **Function Returning Boolean**: A PL/SQL function returning the TRUE or FALSE validation status.

- **Function Returning Error Text**: This is useful if error messages are stored in a database table because the text could be queried and returned from the function. If this method is used, a value for the Error Message is not needed even though it still shows as a mandatory field.

```
⊙ PL/SQL Expression Syntax Example
to_char(sysdate,'D') = 1


⊙ PL/SQL Error Syntax Example
if to_char(sysdate,'D') > 5 then
   raise_application_error (-20001,'Supplied day is invalid.');
end if;


⊙ PL/SQL Function Returning Boolean Syntax Example
if to_char(sysdate,'D') = 1 then
   return true;
else
   return false;
end if;


⊙ PL/SQL Function Returning Error Text Example
if to_char(sysdate,'D') = 1 then
   return 'The first day of the week is not a valid day.';
else
   return null;
end if;
```

Figure 12.2: *PL/SQL Validation Syntax.*

Item Not Null

This is a simple validation to verify a page item must contain a value.

 When the create validation wizard is first started, a link appears below the main region named Create Multiple, not null validations. This link will navigate to a page where several not null validations can be created in a matter of seconds.

Item String Comparison

The Item String Comparison will compare string values and return true or false depending on the type of comparison chosen. If there are two numbers to compare, they must have the same string values. For example: comparing "100" and "100.00" will not return a status of being the same. The item string comparison types are pretty much self-explanatory, but where applicable, an example will be provided to help clarify it usefulness.

- Item in Expression 1 contains at least one of the characters in Expression 2: This is handy to enforce some type of password security. For example, an expression of !@#$%^&*()[]? may be entered to enforce that, at least, one of these characters appears in the password. To make sure a number is also included, a second validation with the expression of 0123456789 could be used. Some expressions require a comma separated list, but these are not like that, they simply require all the characters with no spaces or commas.

- Item in Expression 1 contains only characters in Expression 2

- Item in Expression 1 does NOT equal string literal in Expression2

- Item in Expression 1 does not contain any of the characters in Expression 2

- Item in Expression 1 equals string literal in Expression 2

- Item in Expression 1 is NOT contained in Expression 2

- Item in Expression 1 is contained in Expression 2

- Item specified is NOT zero

- Item specified contains no spaces: This can be a valuable string comparison. For example, have you ever created a NOT NULL validation and had users figure out that if they entered a space, they could avoid the NOT NULL error? Well, using this validation in conjunction with a NOT NULL validation will eliminate this loophole for those clever users.

- Item specified is NOT NULL or zero: This can be just as valuable as the previous item. One thing to keep in mind is another validation may be required to make sure it is a positive number if that is a required validation.

- Item specified is alphanumeric

- Item specified is numeric

- Item specified is a valid date

Regular Expression

These provide an extremely powerful method of validating that the text meets a particular format. Anyone who has ever tried to write code to validate the format of something such as a phone number will come to appreciate regular expressions. There are several default regular expression validations provided by HTML DB shown in Figure 12.3. Located at the top of this figure is a checkbox named Return error message. Leaving this checkbox on will cause an appropriate error message to be provided in the Error Message field.

☑ Return error message?
- URL: http(s)://domain/path/doc.(pdf)(html)(etc...)
- IP Address
- Phone Number, US: (999)-999-9999
- Phone Number, US: (999) 999-9999
- Phone Number, US: 999.999.9999
- Phone Number, US flexible: 999.999.9999, (999)-999-9999, 999 999 9999, etc...
- ZIP Code: 99999
- ZIP + 4: 99999-9999
- Date: MM/DD/YYYY
- Date: MM-DD-YYYY
- Date, flexible: MMDDYYYY with any separator
- Date: DD/MM/YYYY
- Date: DD-MM-YYYY
- Date, flexible: DDMMYYYY with any separator

Figure 12.3: *Regular Expressions supplied in HTML DB.*

Error Messages Display Location

For the following explanations, refer to Figure 12.7. Take note of the location of the #NOTIFICATION_MESSAGE# substitution string.

- **Inline with Field and in Notification**: When a validation produces an error, the error message text will be displayed on both; next to the page item label and in the notification area.

- **Inline with Field**: When a validation produces an error, the error message text will be displayed next to the page item label only.

- **Inline with Notification**: When a validation produces an error, the error message text will be displayed in the notification area only.

- **On Error Page**: This type of validation will result in the user being directed to a separate Error Page. The drawback of using this type of error message display is only the first error found on the page will have its error message displayed. That means the user would have to fix one error and try again to see the next error on the page. The other display locations above will display all errors found on the page.

Creating Validations

Creating validations is done from the page definition page. The example shown below will create a validation to check the format of a date.

1. Click on the ⬚ in the Validations area under Page Processing.

2. Select the Validation Level and click Next. The example uses Item level validation.

3. On the Item page, select the Item in the list of options, click Next.

4. On the Validation Method page, choose the method that will be used for the validation. The example uses Regular Expression.

5. On the Sequence and Name page:

   - Set the Sequence to the order in which the validation is to execute.

   - Enter a Validation Name. By default this is the name of the page item being validated.

   - Select the Error Display Location.

   - Click Next.

6. On the Validation page:

   - Enter a Validate Item. This should already be filled in with the page item selected in step three.

   - Enter the validation expression for the Regular Expression. This example will select the [Date MMDDYYYY] link as shown in Figure 12.4. Select the ✐ icon to see the popup window shown in Figure 12.3 for a larger selection of supplied regular expressions.

   - Enter an appropriate Error Message.

   - Click Next.

7. On the Conditions page, create conditions if desired and click Next.

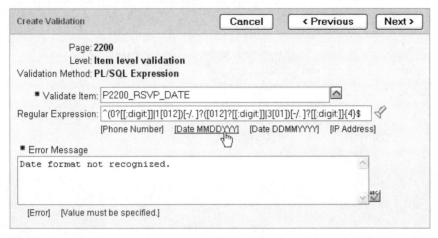

Figure 12.4: *Regular Expression validation.*

> 🔔 A link is available on the first page of the Validation wizard titled Create Multiple, not null validations. This link will navigate to a page where several not null validations can be created in a matter of seconds.

Processes

A Page Process is the control that executes programming logic in the form of SQL statements, PL/SQL, API calls in the HTML DB engine, and more. This is where data updates are performed to data in the database. There are application level processes, page rendering processes, and page level processes executed when the page is submitted. They are the same functionally, but differ in where they are defined with HTML DB.

Application Level processes are defined in Shared Components with the Application Processes link. An application level process can later be called by a page level On Demand process.

Process Types

When the wizard is first started to create a process, the developer will choose which kind of process to create. This depends largely on what the process needs to accomplish.

PL/SQL

The PL/SQL process is the most common type of process that will be used. Do not let the title PL/SQL deceive you because a simple select statement can also be written for this type of process. In fact, it is quite common to use a Before Region PL/SQL process to populate items on the page. This can be done using several SQL select statements in a single PL/SQL process. An entire Anonymous PL/SQL block can also be entered to be executed in this type of process.

A PL/SQL page process After Submit is common for inserting, updating, or deleting data from the database.

Reset Pagination

A Reset Pagination process is used to set the pagination of a report back to the beginning of the result set. This was presented in detail in a previous chapter of this book.

On Demand

An On Demand process is a special process that will execute an Application Level process from the page level. It provides a mechanism for sharing processes among pages, but it must be defined globally at the application level.

On Demand – at the Application Level is called by the On Demand page level process or through the URL.

The syntax to execute an On Demand process in the URL is:

```
f?p=APP_ID:PAGE_ID:SESSION:APPLICATION_PROCESS=process_name
```

Session State

The Session State process is used to modify values in the session state for applications, pages, or page items. They are also used to modify the session state for Preferences.

During normal use of an HTML DB application, it will become necessary to clear the session state for one reason or another. For example, if a four-page wizard is used to create an employee record, the session state for all page items on all four of the pages must be cleared.

- **Clear Cache For Applications** (removes all session state for listed applications): Will clear session state for all page items in all the applications listed in a comma separated list. If two applications that work together exist, like HTML DB does, and the cache in both apps needs to be cleared, this is the processes to use.

- **Clear Cache For Current Application** (removes all session state for current application): Same as the item above except this only clears the session state cache for the current application.

- **Clear Cache For Current Session**: Clears all session state for the current session id. This can be valuable if two HTML DB applications that navigate back-and-forth between each other exist. The same session id between both applications will be used. This process type can also be used to clear the cache for all applications this session id is using.

- **Clear Cache for Items**: One the most common session state processes used, it clears the session state for page items. The page items being cleared do not have to be on the page where this process exists. Since all page items are accessible on all application pages, this process can clear them. The page items are separated by commas to clear multiple items.

- **Clear Cache for all Items on Pages**: This option is useful when starting a wizard consisting of several pages. This option easily clears the session state for all the items on each of the pages listed.

- **Reset Preferences**: This process will not only clear the preferences, but it will remove them from persistent session state. This process should be used carefully. For example, if one logs in to HTML DB with username EASYDEV, and also logs into an application that is being developed with the same EASYDEV username, using Reset Preferences will remove all preferences. Therefore, all settings such as preferences for the View, either Icons or Details, or any sorting for HTML DB reports, such as in Application Builder, will be lost. This happens because the preferences are stored based on the username for the session.

- **Set Preference to Value of Item**: This type of process is what is used to set the user preference when the page is submitted. The default value can then be set to the select list to be based on the value of the Preference.

- **Set Preference to Value of Item if Item is Not Null** – This is almost the same as the item above. The difference is if the page item has a NULL value, the preference will not be changed.

More information regarding Preferences is included in an earlier chapter of this text.

Data Manipulation

Data Manipulation is the built-in process types designed to reduce the amount of manual programming. When wizards are used to build forms and tabular forms, these types of processes are built by the wizard to INSERT, UPDATE, and DELETE data from the database. Although they are a little tricky to learn to use and build manually, many benefits will be gained with their use.

These types of processes are dynamic in nature. What that means is, if after the web page form is initially built and another page item is added to the page, then the dynamic process will include that new field in the SQL, generated behind the scenes. The single most beneficial feature gained from using the dynamic processes is row level concurrency.

Row Level Concurrency is a built-in functionality with the dynamic processes that have not been seen in other development languages. It prevents two different users from updating the same row of data. For example, assume two users open an employee record for Jean Peters at the same time.

- User #1: Since Jean Peters has married Howard Hughes, user #1 is changing her last name to Hughes and her marital status to married.

- User #2: Jean Peters got a raise last week and is making the change to her employment record.

User #1 makes the changes and saves the data. At this point in time, User #2 is now looking at data on the screen that is not up to date. When user #2 attempts to update the data, she will get a checksum error. This is because HTML DB recognizes the data in the database has changed since the data was originally selected from the database. User #2 is prevented from updating the record, and it is a good thing because if it were allowed, the name would have been updated back to Jean Peters thereby erasing the work done by user #1.

Automatic Row Processing is covered in more detail in a previous chapter of this text.

The types of processes available in the Data Manipulation wizard are:

- **Automated Row Fetch**: When built by the HTML DB wizard, this type of process is created as an After Header page process which executes during page rendering. It dynamically builds the SQL select statement, executes the statement, and sets the session state for the appropriate page items. Even though this type of process is usually built by an HTLM DB wizard, it can also be created manually.

- **Automatic Row Processing (DML)**: This is the partner to the Automated Row Fetch process described above. When the wizard is used to build a form page, both of these processes will be created. This process, Automatic Row Processing (DML) process, will be created as an After Submit – After Computations and Validations process. It will dynamically build the SQL to perform INSERT, UPDATE and DELETE statements against the database.

- **Multi Row Update**: This type of process will update multiple rows of modified data from a Tabular Form. A tabular form is a report, but has the region type set to SQL Query (updateable report). The properties are set for each of the columns in the Column Attributes page, in the Tabular Form Element region.

- **Multi Row Delete**: This is similar to the Multi Row Update process described above, except it performs the SQL delete statement. This process needs to know the names of the primary key columns to know how to dynamically build the delete statement.

- **Add Rows to Tabular Form**: This type of process will cause the creation of an empty row at the bottom of the tabular form so that data can be entered for a new row. When using this type of process, a process should be available that would update any currently changed data prior to creating the empty row. Otherwise the changes would be lost. If the wizard is used to build the tabular form, this extra Multi Row Update process is created automatically.

Although the dynamic processes described in this section are powerful and beneficial, there is one drawback. They are limited to use on tables that have a maximum of a two-column unique index or primary key. If a table exists with three or more columns defined on the unique index, custom code in a PL/SQL type process will need to be written.

Web Services

A Web Service process enables users to make requests across the network or Internet to other servers; for example, web services available on the internet such as zip code lookup, Federal Express package tracking, Amazon book search, and many more. Creating web service processes is how data from those services is included within other applications. Web Services are covered in an earlier chapter in this text.

Form Pagination

This type of process is used in a Form region of an application page. A process of this type is created automatically if the wizard is used to create a Master/Detail form. However, the Form Pagination process wizard would also be used to provide users the ability to scroll forwards and backwards through records in the table being utilized on any other form. During the creation of this type of process, the developer will be asked the name(s) of the page item(s) containing the primary key value(s). The wizard for a Form Pagination process will then create other page items:

- 2 Buttons: Next and Previous.

- 2 Hidden Text Fields: To hold session state for the next and previous values of the primary key.

- A Get Next or Previous Primary Key Value Process: Dynamically obtains the next and previous values.

- 2 Branches: To set the page item(s) for the primary key.

This type of process was created automatically by the Create Application in an earlier chapter of this book. Figure 4.4 shows the buttons created, and the Page Definition is available to view the other objects for reference.

Close Popup Window

This type of process is used to close a popup window and will refresh the application page that opened the popup.

Process Points

A Process Point defines when, during the page rendering or page processing, the process will be considered for execution.

Application Level Process Points

On New Instance - After Authentication: This is an application level process and should be created as such. When creating an application level process in the shared components section, it is called On New Session - After Authentication. This can be confusing as it is for an application level computation. A technique that can be used for this type of process if the user logging in is listed as a developer is to set an application level item to a TRUE value. Then the application level item in the Conditions of other page level items can be used for debugging information.

Page Rendering Processes

The following is a listing of page rendering processes:

- On New Instance. After Authentication
- On Load – Before Header
- On Load – After Header
- On Load – Before Regions
- On Load – After Regions
- On Load – Before Footer
- On Load – After Footer
- On Submit – Before Computations and Validations
- On Submit – After Computations and Validations

The On New Instance and On Load will direct the process to be considered for execution during page rendering. These display points are commonly used for populating the page items of an application page.

When a Form page is created using the wizard, it will create an After Header process used to fetch the row from the database and populate the page items. This is the process point to choose when writing custom queries to populate page items. The Before Header and Before Regions process point could also be used for populating page items during page rendering.

On Submit – Before Computations and Validations

An On Submit - Before Computation and Validations process will execute before any computations or validations take place. Although this process point is seldom used, it is available. Some uses for this process point are:

- Update collections prior to performing a PL/SQL validation on the data. HTML DB uses this technique internally.

- Inserting records into an audit table to record values, since knowing what a user was trying to do even if the validations fail can be helpful.

On Submit – After Computations and Validations.

This process point is executed after all computations and validations have been executed. If validations fail, the On Submit – After Computations and Validations process will not be executed. In the normal flow of logic, computations and validations will verify the data on the page. This process point will then make the changes in the database. It may also be desirable to use other processes on the page after the database modifications, such as managing session state and reset pagination.

Creating Processes

Often when creating application pages, the wizard will be used to quickly create a form region on a page. However, most pages have more than one region on a page, and therefore creating other processes manually to deal with the other regions is needed. It may be a process that executes in the before region processing point for populating the page, or in the after submit processing point to update the database.

The exercise shown below follows the idea that an additional region on an application page has been created and some page items, to display a persons name and address, were added. The process to create will be a Before Regions process used to populate the page items. The same process would be followed for creating a process that would execute in the After Submit process point.

Creating processes is done from the page definition page.

1. Click on the 🗅 in the Processes area under Page Rendering.

---

2. On the Process Type page, select the process type and click Next. This example chose the PL/SQL option.

3. On the Process Attributes page:

   - Enter a Name for the process: Populate

   - Enter the Sequence in which it should execute the process point selected. For this example, it will be sequence ten (10).

   - Select the Process Point: On Load - Before Regions.

   - Click Next.

4. On the Process page, enter the SQL code necessary for the process and click Next. The code used to populate the example page items is shown here.

```
select
    first_name, last_name, address_id
into
    :P100_FIRST_NAME, :P100_LAST_NAME, :P100_ADDRESS_ID
from
    employee
where
    employee_id = :P100_EMPLOYEE_ID;

select
    address_line_1, city,
    state, zip
into
    :P100_ADDRESS_LINE_1, :P100_CITY,
    :P100_STATE, :P100_ZIP
from
    employee_address
where
    address_id = :P100_ADDRESS_ID;
```

5. On the Messages page:

   - Enter a Success Message if desired: Success messages are not commonly used in page population processes, but they are available.

   - Enter a Failure Message if desired: In the event there is an error, this message will be displayed to the user. It will be the same message regardless of where in the process the error occurred. For advanced programming I have seen the failure message not used, and the programmers often use raise_application_error in-line with the SQL code for the process, especially if there are multiple statements written in the process.

   - Click Next.

6. On the Process Conditions page, the conditions under which this process should execute can be entered. For example, the developer may only want this process to fire if the value of P100_EMPLOYEE_ID is NOT NULL.

7. Click the Create Process button to complete the wizard.

Creating the other types of processes is similar. Use the notes in the rest of the chapter to understand each type of process and the various attributes that need to be set for them.

Branching

A Branch is the logic control used to navigate to other application pages, either in the current application or another application or navigate to another URL such as www.rampant-books.com. When creating branches, properties are set to define when and how the branch behaves. The following are some of the properties.

- Branch Point
- Branch Type
- Branch Target
- Conditions

Branching Points

- **On Submit: Before Computation** (Before Computation, Validation, and Processing): A Before Computation branch will branch to another page without processing other logic controls on the page. Using a Before Computation branch is a handy way to provide a button that simply navigates to another page without performing any processing.

- **On Submit: Before Validation**: (After Computation and Before Validation and Processing): This branch point will execute after computations have taken place. A common use for this branch is to allow the computations to set the session state for page items on another page and then use that branch point to branch to the page.

- **On Submit: Before Processing**: (After Computation, Validation and Before Processing): This branch point will execute after computations and validations. Often this branch point is used for a Cancel, Back, or

Previous button. HTML DB often uses this branch point in wizards for the Back and Previous buttons.

- **On Submit: After Processing**: (After Computation, Validation, and Processing): This is the kind of branch point introduced in previous chapters and is the most common branch point used in HTML DB. It will be executed after all other page processing logic has been executed.

- **On Load: Before Header**: This branch point is actually executed prior to page rendering. A good use for this is to interrupt the rest of the page processing and branch to another application page or URL, and it is most commonly used with a condition. The condition being such that it would not be desirable to render the current page if the condition were TRUE.

Branch Type

- **Branch to Function Returning a Page**: With this branch type, a PL/SQL function is written that returns a numeric page id to branch to.

    Example:

    ```
    declare
       n_page_id integer;
    begin
       select 2205 into n_page_id from dual;
       return n_page_id;
    end;
    ```

- **Branch to Function Returning a URL**: Similar to the previous branch type, this type expects a character string returning a URL to branch to. Tip: Make sure to include the http:// part of the URL.

    Example:

    ```
    declare
       s_url varchar2(200);
    begin
       select ' http://www.rampant-books.com'
       into   s_url from dual;
       return s_url;
    end;
    ```

- **Branch to PL/SQL Procedure**: This branch type is very uncommon, but available. A procedure can be written that will do the branching using this branch type.

Example:

```
owa_util.redirect_url( 'http://www.google.com' );
```

- **Branch to Page**: It does just what it says.

- **Branch to Page Identified by Item** (Use Item Name): This branch will use the value of another page item to determine the application page id to branch to. This can be used if the user is provided with a select list of areas for them to branch to, such as Employee Management, Payroll, Billing, etc.

- **Branch to Page or URL**: This is the default branch type presented when creating a branch and is the most common. Using this type, it is possible to set many of the properties available in the other branch types. The reason it is the most common is because the page to branch to can be set, along with the page items to set, and with which values to set them. It is also possible to set the pages for which to clear the session state at the same time. This branch type allows this to be set in the create branch wizard. Even though it is manually possible to go back and edit the branch later to set these properties, it is convenient to do it in the wizard.

- **Branch to URL Identified by Item** (Use Item Name): This branch will use the value of another page item to determine the URL to branch to. This can be used if the user is provided with a select list of web sites for them to branch to, such as Google, Amazon, CNN, etc.

Creating a Branch

Creating branches is accomplished from the page definition page. The imaginary example shown below will create a branch to a page, clear the cache, and send two values to set page items.

1. Click on the in the Branches area under Page Processing.

2. On the Point and Type page:

   - Select the Branch Point: this example uses On Submit After Processing.

   - Select the Branch Type: this example uses Branch to Page or URL.

   - Click Next.

3. On the Target page enter the appropriate information and click Next. Figure 12.5 shows the Target page for this example. Notice the use of the &ITEM. notation in the With these values field.

4. On the Branch Conditions page:

    ▪ Set the Sequence for the order in which the branches are to execute.

    ▪ Select the correct item for When Button Pressed if this branch should only execute when a particular button is pressed.

    ▪ Select a Condition Type, if appropriate, and fill in the proper Expressions

    ▪ Click Next.

🔔 If there are two or more buttons that the branch should respond to, the When Button Pressed option cannot be used. Instead, use a Request Is Contained within Expression 1 condition type and enter the names of the buttons in Expression 1, such as CREATE or EDIT. Then the branch will be executed for either of the two buttons.

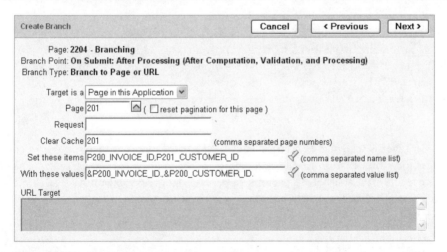

Figure 12.5: *Branch Target properties.*

Computation and Processing Points in Detail

Instead of explaining, earlier in the chapter, when each of the processing points was executed, I decided to wait until this section so the explanation could be condensed into one section. Otherwise the information would have been spread throughout the sections above.

When I was first starting out, I found it difficult to know when to use which execution point and why one should be chosen over the other. The following description helped me, and it should remove some of the confusion for you as well.

A review of where the regions are laid out in respect to the page rendering of each region is in order. Figure 12.7 does not represent the layout for every page template in HTML DB, but is useful for the descriptions soon to be given. For reference, this is the No Tabs page template.

There is a region named After Header that displays at the top of the page. Then, located at the beginning of the HTML Body (the <body> tag), is an area named Region Pos 1. Next in line is what HTML DB calls the Box Body. The box body is surrounded by the Before Regions and After Regions execution points. Following those regions are the remaining Region Positions and finally the Before Footer region.

During page rendering it is important to create processes in the proper execution point depending on what is to be accomplished. There may come a time when page items being set in one computation or process need to be referred to in another computation or process. They must be processed by the HTML DB engine in the proper order. This can cause hours of frustration if the developer does not have a solid understanding of the order of things being executed during page rendering.

In regards to which is being executed first, the Computation or the Process, it is the Computation that is executed first. In other words, if a Computation is executing in the before regions point and a Process executing in the before regions execution point, it is the Computation that will be executed first by the HTML DB engine.

Before Header Computations

Before Header computations are the first pieces of logic to be executed by the HTML DB engine. A Before Header computation can set the values of any page item regardless of its position on the page or which region it is in. It can also reference a page item set by another before header computation that has a lower execution sequence.

As shown in Figure 12.6, the P2300_AFTER_HEADER computation would be able to use the value set in P2300_REGION_1, but P2300_REGION_1 would not be able to reference the value set in P2300_AFTER_HEADER. That is because P2300_AFTER_REGION has a higher sequence (20) and is executed after the other computation (10).

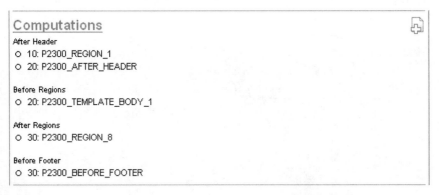

Figure 12.6: *Page Rendering Computations.*

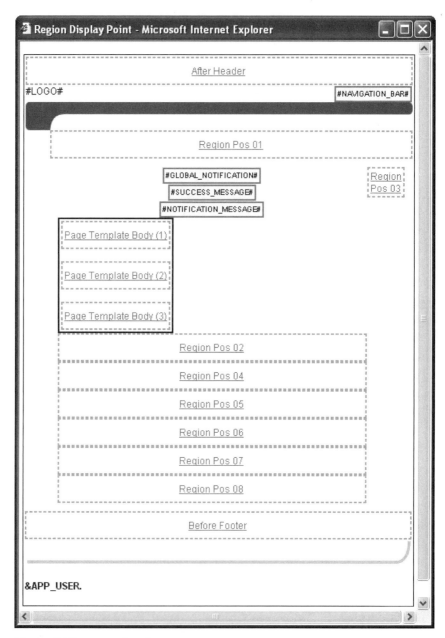

Figure 12.7: *Region Display Points.*

Before Header Processes

Not only is this execution point performed first, but it is also executed before any HTML is rendered. Reviewing the HTML code below shows that a Before Header process writes HTML code before the HTML engine renders the <html> tag. See the example below. A common use for the before header process is to populate page items on the application page.

```
BeforeHeader Process Point
<html lang="en-us" xmlns:htmldb="http://htmldb.oracle.com">
<head>
```

The text BeforeHeader Process Point at the top of Figure 12.8 was written using this type of process.

After Header Computations

An After Header computation can reference page item values set in prior execution points. The only prior execution points happen to be the before header computations and before header processes. After header computations can be used to set page item values in the after header region and below. In Figure 12.8, the after header page item was set using an after header computation. It could not have been set with any execution point later than the after header computation or after header process.

After Header Processes

As shown in Figure 12.8, the After Header process is actually executed prior to the after header region. For that reason the after header process can still be used to set page item values in the after header region. It can also reference any page item values set by an earlier execution point.

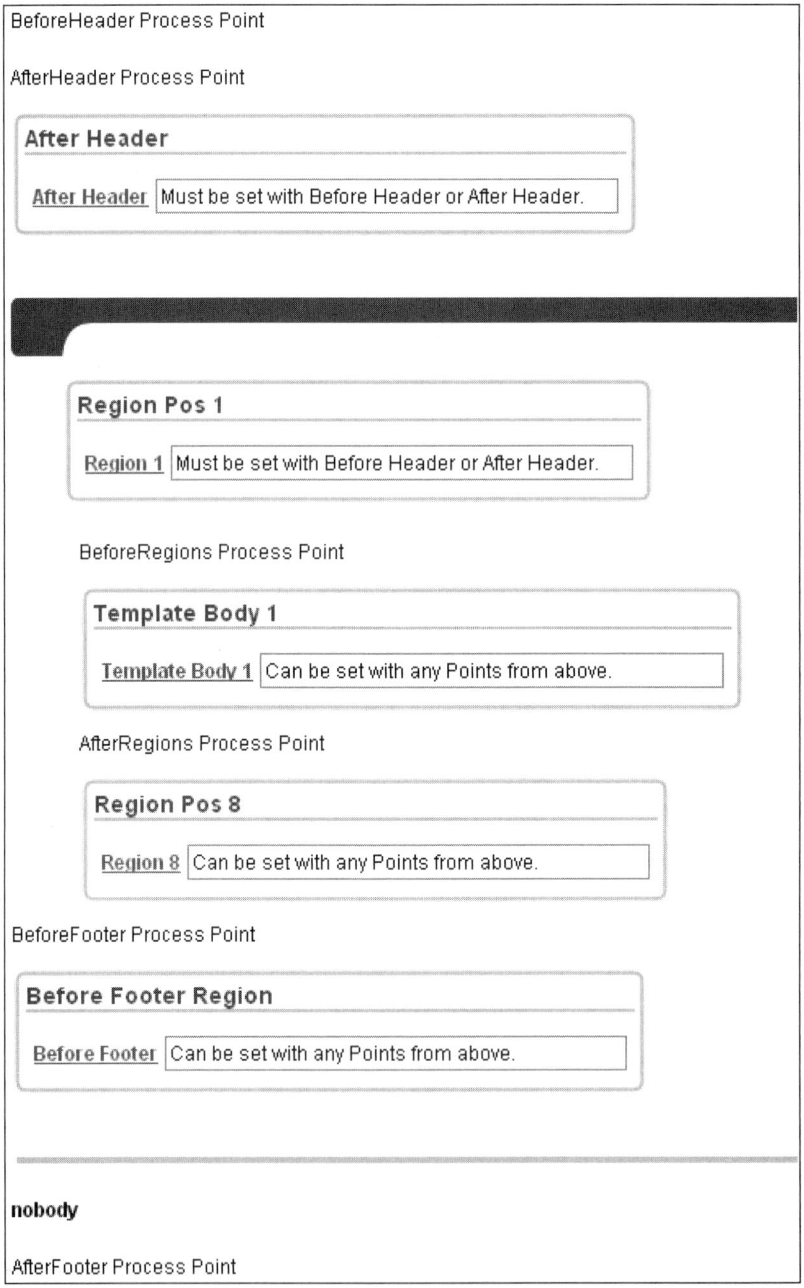

BeforeHeader Process Point

AfterHeader Process Point

After Header

| After Header | Must be set with Before Header or After Header. |

Region Pos 1

| Region 1 | Must be set with Before Header or After Header. |

BeforeRegions Process Point

Template Body 1

| Template Body 1 | Can be set with any Points from above. |

AfterRegions Process Point

Region Pos 8

| Region 8 | Can be set with any Points from above. |

BeforeFooter Process Point

Before Footer Region

| Before Footer | Can be set with any Points from above. |

nobody

AfterFooter Process Point

Figure 12.8: *Page Rendering Execution Points.*

Region Pos 1

Notice in Figure 12.8 that the Region Pos 1 region is rendered above the text BeforeRegions Process Point. This is significant because to use computations or processes to set a page item in the Region Pos 1 region, execution points of before header or after header must be used. Trying to set page items in the Region Pos 1 region with any other execution points would fail.

Before Regions Computations and Processes

Keeping an eye on Figure 12.8, notice that the Template Body 1 region is rendered after the text BeforeRegions Process Point. Therefore, computations and processes can be used in the before regions execution point to set page item values in the Template Body 1 region.

After Regions Computations and Processes

Throughout this book, many regions were created in the same position as Template Body 1. This is because this position is the default location when a new location is created, and most often it is simply accepted. Actually the default is Template Body 3, but they are both part of the box body, the #BOX_BODY# substitution string in page templates.

There will come a time when a developer will create a region in this location or execution point and try to set page item values with an After Regions computation or process. This would be in error, but it happens. What will happen is that when the web page is refreshed, the page item will then have a value. This is because when the page is rendered the first time, the session state of the page item in the Template Body 1 region was set to after the region was rendered.

However, when the page refreshed, the page item was populated with the value from session state. This could give a false indication that the change is working. What really needs to be done is to either move the computation or process to a before regions execution point or move the region down to be after the after regions execution point.

The after regions execution point is used to set page item values rendered after this execution point. It can reference any page item that is rendered prior to this execution point.

Before Footer Computations and Processes

Many web sites display information in the after footer region that may be dynamic in nature and not a candidate to be hard coded onto a web page. Therefore, it would be best to store it in the database and select it during page rendering. The before footer process is just the place to put this. Of course, this could also be done with a computation or process that executed at an earlier point, but the preference is to execute them closest to the point where they are going to be used.

After Footer Computations and Processes

There is not too much use putting computations or processes here because by the time they are executed, the page has finished being rendered. However, to write a record to the database to keep track of the number of times a page was viewed or the ending time of when the page finished being rendered, this is a good place for it. The HTML code below will show the after footer process is executed after all HTML has been rendered.

```
</script>
</body>
</html>AfterFooter Process Point
```

Page Processing Events

There is a way to view the page rendering and page processing events graphically. The graphical view shows the order in which computations, processes, region rendering, validations, and branches are executed by the HTML DB engine. This is called the Events page. To view the events page, navigate to the page definition page for any application page. Select the Events item in the View select list as shown in Figure 12.9 and click the Go button.

Figure 12.9: *Selection to view the Events page.*

Due to space constraints, only the Page Processing region of the Events page is shown in Figure 12.10. This is a great page to help developers understand the order of things. Figure 12.10 shows the order of execution for logic controls executed when a page is submitted.

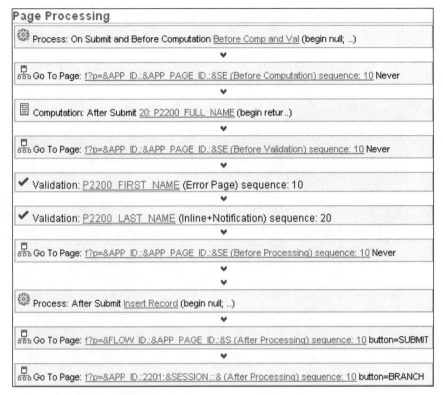

Figure 12.10: *Page Processing region for Events page.*

Conclusion

This chapter introduced the logic controls within HTML DB.

- Computations
- Validations
- Processes
- Branches

A good understanding of where, when, and how each of these are used will remove a lot of the confusion often encountered when beginning with HTML DB. There are computations and processes executed during page rendering and during page processing. Additionally, validations can occur during page processing.

Branching, which is the most common method of providing navigation between the pages in an HTML DB application, was covered in this chapter.

Finally, the processing points were explained in detail. Here is another area where a thorough understanding will make development much more efficient.

The next chapter will cover the customization of an HTML DB application to allow each developer to add their own favorite touches to their projects.

Customizing HTML DB CHAPTER

13

Introduction

As one gains experience using HTML DB, there is no doubt they will want to start expanding the default functionality provided with HTML DB. This involves customizing the functionality and look and feel of their web applications. There are four areas that warrant explanation such that developers gain an understanding of how to customize HTML DB.

- **Themes**: A theme is a group of templates all combined together to create a consistent look and feel throughout application pages and components. Themes are designed using a standard that makes it easy to switch a theme for an application. Changing a theme takes only a minute or two and changes the entire look of an application.

- **JavaScript**: JavaScript is used for adding functionality to a web page. Although teaching JavaScript is beyond the scope of this book, it is something a developer will need to know how to incorporate into their HTML DB applications.

- **Cascading Style Sheets**: Controlling the look and feel of an application is done by using Cascading Style Sheets (CSS). A popular way to manipulate the width of page items is to use CSS.

- **Templates**: Templates are used to control the look and feel of various components such as regions, buttons, calendars, pages, etc. A template may incorporate the use of JavaScript and CSS to accomplish this.

Themes

An HTML DB Theme is a group of templates, JavaScript, and CSS's. The JavaScript provides custom functionality; the templates provide the layout of pages, regions and page items; and the CSS's customize the look of the pages, regions and page items.

Hierarchically, a theme contains several templates. The templates contain several CSS's and JavaScripts. They all work together to provide the look and feel of an application. There are 12 themes included with HTML DB. Throughout this book, theme 2 – Blue and Tan has been used.

The important thing to understand about themes is it is really the templates and CSS that change the look of the application pages. A theme just groups the templates and CSS together to provide consistency for all the components that make up the application.

Changing the Theme for an Application

To change from one theme to another, a new theme must be created in the application. Once a new theme is created, it is possible to switch from one theme to the other in a minute or two.

Creating a New Theme

1. .Navigate to the Shared Components page in the Easy HTML DB Book application.
2. Click on the Themes link.
3. Click on the Create button.
4. Choose the From the HTML DB Repository option and click Next.
5. Choose Theme 10 and click Next.
6. Click the Create button.

This action just created a copy of a theme into the example application. That way all the templates in the theme can be modified and it will not affect any other application using the same theme.

Switching to a Different Theme

1. Navigate to the Shared Components page.
2. Click on the Themes link.
3. Click on the Switch Theme button.
4. Choose the Sand theme and click Next.

The following page is the Verify Compatibility page. When templates are built, they are assigned a Class. The Verify Compatibility page checks to make sure the template classes from the current theme have matching template classes in the new theme. If there is no template class in the new theme that matches, it is not possible to switch the theme.

5. If the verification passes, then click Next.

6. Finally, click the Switch Theme button.

Run the application to see the new theme being used.

Default Templates for a Theme

A default template is part of the definition of a theme. When creating page components, a template is selected to use for the look of the component. However, there is always a template selected as the default. Each theme allows the developer to set what that default template is. To set the default templates:

1. Navigate to the Shared Components page.

2. Click on the Themes link.

 For this example, verify the Themes page is available with the View set to Details.

3. Click on the Switch Theme button.

4. Click on the Blue and Tan link. This brings up the Edit Theme page.

   This page will show the default templates. Any of the default templates can be changed, but there are a few that warrant more description.

   Figure 13.1 shows the default templates for three components.

   - **Page**: This is a very useful default template setting. The reason is because when pages are created, their Page Template setting gets set to - Use Application Level Default Template -. Figure 13.1 shows it set to No Tabs. If all pages have the page template attribute set as indicated, the template for every page in the application could be changed by modifying this default setting.

   - **Error Page**: This is the template that will be used by any page displayed as an error page. An earlier chapter covered validations and how the Error Display Location could be set to On Error Page. This is the template that will be used to display those errors. A new error page template could be created and selected here and all error pages would then use the new template.

- **Printer Friendly Page**: This is the template that will be used when a page in rendered in Print Friendly mode.

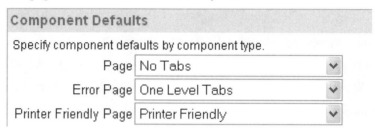

Figure 13.1: *Theme defaults.*

5. Once the defaults are set, click the Apply Changes button. Otherwise click the Cancel button.

The explanation above mentioned the error page and the printer friendly page. There can be only one active template of this kind for an application. More templates can be defined, but only one will be used and this is where that selection is made.

A common practice would be to create a custom error page template that might give a contact phone number or an email for the user to send trouble information.

Using the *www_flow.show_error_message* procedure from the HTML DB API, HTML DB can be directed to render the error page. This is covered more in a later chapter of this text.

JavaScript

JavaScript is a scripting language created by Netscape that can be embedded into the HTML of a web page to add functionality. HTML is the language that tells the browser what to render, where to put it on the screen, etc. However, to add some functionality such as responding to an event such as the selection of a select list, JavaScript will be required. For the most part, this is handled by HTML DB in the built-in templates, cascading style sheets, and the JavaScript provided, but eventually aspiring developers will want to add their own functionality.

The goal of this chapter is not to teach JavaScript. This section will illustrate the what, where, why, and how of adding JavaScript to an HTML DB application. An excellent on-line tutorial for JavaScript can be found at: http://www.w3schools.com.

JavaScript can be embedded into HTML; however, the developer needs to know where to add it within the HTML DB development environment in order to benefit from its use. It is easier to define the use of JavaScript in HTML DB if it is broken down into two main areas:

- The JavaScript source code.

- The call to a JavaScript function.

JavaScript Source Code

Although JavaScript can be embedded almost anywhere within the HTML source code, it is most commonly embedded between the <head> and </head> tags of an HTML Document. In HTML DB this area is identified in each application page in the HTML Header region of the Page Attributes page. This is illustrated in Figure 13.2.

Embedding JavaScript source code in HTML DB can be accomplished in any of three ways:

- As In-Line source code in the HTML Header section of the page attributes for an application page.

- As a Static File in Shared Components → Static Files.

- As a file in a directory on the machine hosting the HTTP Server.

By this point in the book, you should be familiar with creating the various objects so this will not be included in detail. To exercise the steps in this section, a new application page would be created with a region including two page items: 1) a USERNAME page item of type Text Field; and, 2) a PASSWORD page item of type Password. Do not use the Password (submits when Enter pressed) option. Also, create a button with the name SUBMIT in the region as Create a button in a region position.

The JavaScript used in this section is shown below and can be found in the on-line code depot so it does not have to be typed in manually.

🖫 set_focus.txt

```
<script language="JavaScript1.1" type="text/javascript">
   function setFocus(PageItem) {
      document.getElementById(PageItem).focus();
   }

   function validateLogin(User,Pwd) {
      if (document.getElementById(User).value == "") {
         alert("Login ID must have a value provided.");
         document.getElementById(User).focus();
      }
      else if (document.getElementById(Pwd).value == "") {
         alert("Password must have a value provided.");
         document.getElementById(Pwd).focus();
         document.getElementById(Pwd).select();
      }
      else {
         doSubmit('SUBMIT');
      }
   }
</script>
```

The code above performs two functions. One is to set the focus of the page item, and the other is to validate the USERNAME and PASSWORD page items are not null before the page is submitted for processing.

In HTML DB, page items are referenced using the HTML tag ID Attribute – not the Name Attribute.

The button that was just created is going to be used to execute the validateLogin function. If the validation is ok, the function will then perform the SUBMIT for the page.

Adding JavaScript to an Application Page

This section will show how to create a JavaScript script and add it to the page in the HTML Header section. Then code will be added to the submit button to call the JavaScript function – validateLogin when the button is clicked.

When first developing the JavaScript code, it is common to put it into the HTML Header section as indicated in Figure 13.2. Putting it here in the first place is for development purposes. During developing, changes will be made to the code and keeping it here makes it easy to make those changes. Later, after the code is finished being tested, it can be moved to a JavaScript file where it can be reusable on many application pages. This will be covered later in this chapter.

```
HTML Header

HTML Header
<script language="JavaScript1.1" type="text/javascript">
    function setFocus(PageItem) {
        document.getElementById(PageItem).focus();
    }

    function validateLogin(User,Pwd) {
        if (document.getElementById(User).value == "") {
          alert("Login ID must have a value provided.");
          document.getElementById(User).focus();
        }
        else if (document.getElementById(Pwd).value == "") {
          alert("Password must have a value provided.");
          document.getElementById(Pwd).focus();
          document.getElementById(Pwd).select();
        }
        else {
           doSubmit('SUBMIT');
        }
    }
</script>
```

Figure 13.2: *JavaScript in HTML Header section of page attributes.*

Before a JavaScript function can be called, it first must be accessible to components on the application page. This is done by adding it to the HTML Header region of the Edit Attributes page. Navigating to the Edit Attributes page is performed by clicking on the Edit Attributes button on the Page Definition page.

After navigating to the HTML Header region, type the code into the HTML Header text area as shown, or the code can be copied and pasted from the code depot file set_focus.txt.

When the code is in the HTML Header text area, click on the Apply Changes button.

Calling JavaScript on Page Loading

The JavaScript source code shown above has a handy function, called setFocus, that may warrant reuse. This function accepts a parameter of the page item name to set focus to. The code will be called from the Page

Attributes page in the On Load region. Navigate to the Page Attributes page for the Java Script application page and enter the text shown in Figure 13.3. Then, apply changes.

 Although the page attributes has a property named Cursor Focus that can be set to First item on page, it may not be desirable to set focus to the first item on the page. For this reason, the setFocus( ) function may be the best option to use.

You will likely need to change the name of the page item to match the name you have. Now when the page is rendered, the focus will be placed on the Username text field.

Figure 13.3: *Calling JavaScript on Page Loading.*

Using the Page HTML Body Attribute will modify the <body> tag as shown here:

```
<body onLoad="javascript:setFocus('P4_USERNAME');">
```

Creating a Button to Call JavaScript

Now the JavaScript code has been set in an application page, it can be called from other page components on that page. For example, the call to the JavaScript code can be added to the Submit button created earlier.

Previous chapters covered the creation of a button and how to set properties to branch to another page, set the HTML Request, clear the page cache, and set item values. In those sections, the button performed the Submit by default; however, this section will show how to override the default submit behavior of a button and cause it to call the JavaScript. This is accomplished by editing the button attributes for the Submit button and setting the target URL to the code shown here.

```
<a href="javascript:validateLogin('P4_USERNAME','P4_PASSWORD');">
```

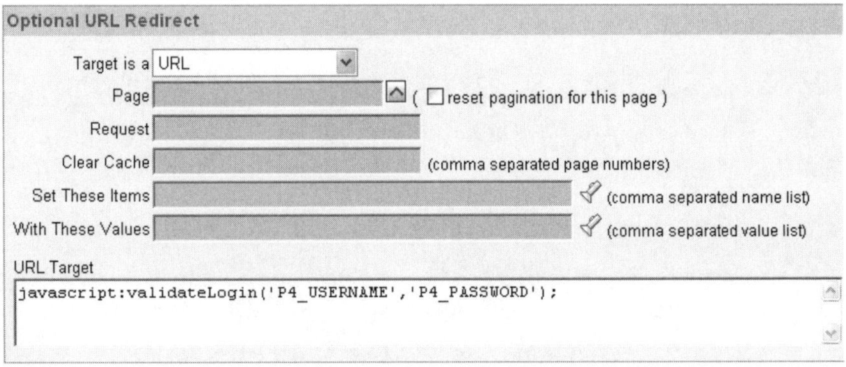

Figure 13.4: *Calling JavaScript from a Button.*

Even though the target is being set to URL, it is not a traditional looking URL. Instead, it is a call to the JavaScript.

Edit the attributes of the Submit button and enter the text from above in the URL Target text area as shown in Figure 13.4. When the Submit button is clicked, it will execute the JavaScript.

> The reader's page items will likely have different names than those of the author, so make the necessary changes before saving changes.

JavaScript file in the static file repository

Putting JavaScript in the HTML Header works just fine, but after the JavaScript function has been developed as described above, it should be put into a script so it can be made reusable on several web pages. If you already have a previously created JavaScript file or have downloaded reusable code from the internet, the same steps mentioned here can be followed to add the file to the script repository.

First, create the JavaScript file named *easy_java.js* using the code in the file *set_focus.txt*. However, when converting the inline code from the HTML Header section, it will be necessary to remove the <script> and </script> tags. These tags are necessary in the HTML Header section, but are not

---

permitted when the code is in a JavaScript file. The file named *easy_java.js* in the code depot can also be used or used as a reference.

To upload the *easy_java.js* script into the script repository:

1. Navigate to Shared Components for the Easy Samples application.

2. Click on the Static Files link.

3. Click the Create button.

4. Application: select the Easy Samples option.

5. Filename: click the Browse button, navigate to the Code Depot and select the easy_java.js file.

6. Click the Upload button.

Now that the *easy_java.js* script has been added to the script repository, it is available for all application pages to take advantage of. Navigate back to the page attributes page for the JavaScript page and edit the HTML Header text area to include the text as shown in Figure 13.5.

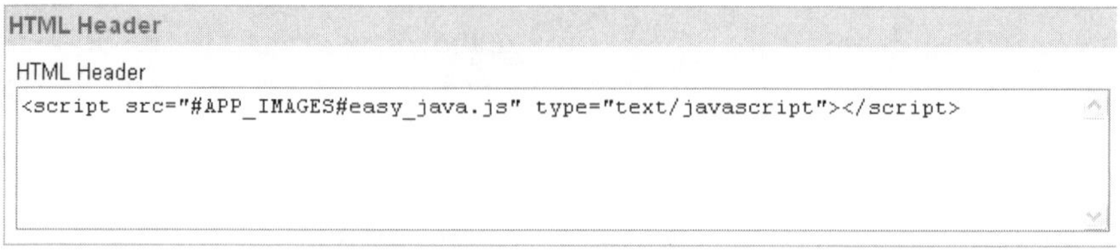

HTML Header

HTML Header

```
<script src="#APP_IMAGES#easy_java.js" type="text/javascript"></script>
```

Figure 13.5: *Using JavaScript from Script Repository.*

JavaScript in the Directory Hierarchy on the HTTP Server

Putting the JavaScript source code in the script repository makes it reusable, and it is easy to deploy in this manner. However, it can still be done better. This next step is better because it allows the users web browser to cache the *easy_java.js* script locally. That way the next time the same script is referenced it does not need to be downloaded to the users' browser since it was downloaded previously.

The following explanation assumes the user has the appropriate privileges to create files in the directories described below. The directories mentioned are on the machine running the HTTP Server. This also assumes the readers' images directory is the same as the path shown here:

Windows:

```
C:\oracle\product\10.2.0\ohs\Apache\Apache\images
```

Unix/Linux:

```
/u01/app/oracle/product/10.2.0/ohs/Apache/Apache/images
```

At this point, a new directory named *easy_htmldb* should be created under the images directory.

```
C:\oracle\product\10.2.0\ohs\Apache\Apache\images\easy_htmldb
```

Then, copy the *easy_java.js* script from the code depot directory to the new *easy_htmldb* directory. This places the file in the correct location from which it can be referenced on each of the application pages. It also makes it available to all applications in all workspaces running from this HTTP Server.

To change the reference in the HTML Header region of the Java Script page navigate back to the page attributes page and make the changes as shown in figure 13.6.

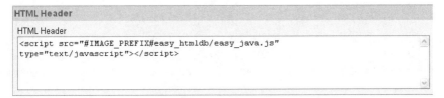

Figure 13.6: *Using Java Script from the File System*

The changes in figure 13.6 involve the substitution string and a reference to the new *easy_htmldb* directory.

```
<script src="#IMAGE_PREFIX#easy_htmldb/easy_java.js"
type="text/javascript"></script>
```

> 🔔 The easy_java.js script can be referenced directly from a browser with the following URL. What this shows is the URL path to the file on the file system:
> http://localhost:7777/i/easy_htmldb/easy_java.js

Cascading Style Sheets

Cascading Style Sheets (CSS) provide a way to control the look and feel of HTML pages in an organized and efficient manner. Teaching how to design and write the code for CSS is beyond the scope of this book, but it does warrant some explanation. Methods for creating templates for use in HTML DB will be covered later in this text, and there will likely come a time when developers will want to use their own CSS to change the CSS provided by HTML DB.

Including CSS in HTML DB is accomplished in the same manner as JavaScript as covered in the Adding JavaScript to an Application Page section earlier in this chapter. For the HTML DB developer, it will be important to understand there are three ways to reference CSS in HTML code. These are referred to as internal, external, and inline. Internal and external CSS are included at the application page level between the <head> and </head> tags. Inline is used directly within an html tag such as the paragraph (<p>) tag. In HTML DB, it is valuable to know how to use inline CSS with page level items.

Another important factor to understand is that CSS has a pecking order. That is, it has a priority based on where it is included in the HTML code. Inline CSS has the highest priority and will override any previously defined, internal or external, CSS code. In terms of the internally and externally defined CSS, the pecking order is dependent upon its location in the <head> tag. Since HTML is rendered from top-down, the latest CSS will override something defined above it. What this means is that if one CSS statement defines a CSS property for a page item such as setting the font color to red and the next CSS statement defines the color as blue, the second definition will override the first and the resulting color will be blue. This is a handy little piece of information because it allows a CSS style to be overridden in the HTML DB themes by simply redefining it. An example will be included later in this book.

Internal CSS

Internal CSS is where the CSS code is typed directly into a <style> tag and included in the <head> tag as shown below:

```
<head>
    <style type="text/css">
            p {color: blue; }
    </style>
</head>
```

Inline CSS code is included by adding it to the HTML Header section of an application page. Just like JavaScript, it is a great way to include CSS in the application page while developing the CSS code. However, if the developer has any plans to reuse the CSS code, it would be better to convert the code into a file and use it as external CSS.

External CSS

External CSS is where there is CSS code in a file and it is included by linking it in to the HTML Document using the <link> tag.

When putting the CSS code into a file, the <style> tag is not needed. In fact, it is not allowed.

External CSS files can be included in one of two ways: 1) by adding them to the HTML DB repository and referencing them there; or, 2) by putting them in a directory and referencing them there.

To include a CSS file from the repository use the following syntax:

```
<link rel="stylesheet" href="#APP_IMAGES#custom.css" type="text/css"
/>
```

To include CSS from a file on the file system, use the following syntax:

```
<link rel="stylesheet" href="#IMAGE_PREFIX#easy_htmldb/custom.css"
type="text/css" />
```

The <link> tags above would be placed in the HTML Header section for an application page.

Inline CSS

The most practical use for inline CSS in HTML DB is to modify the look of a single page item with regards to things like the width, color, etc. It is very common to use a <style> tag in the properties of various page components to modify their size, color, case of the text, width, and other attributes. The

---

following example, Figure 13.7, illustrates setting a tabular form element to UPPERCASE and setting the width to 200 pixels.

Tabular Form Element	
Display As	Text Field
Date Picker Format Mask	- Select Date Format -
Element Width	16 Number of Rows
Element Attributes	style="text-transform:uppercase;width:200px;"

Figure 13.7: *Using CSS to modify the look of a tabular form element.*

There are several examples of this technique used to modify properties of page items in a later chapter on Best Practices and Techniques.

HTML DB Cascading Style Sheets

To get a good understanding of how templates and cascading style sheets can be modified and overridden, the developer should know where the CSS files are that are used by the themes and templates.

The 12 themes that come with HTML DB are located in the Oracle HTTP Server directory tree at:

```
C:\oracle\product\10.2.0\ohs\Apache\Apache\images\themes
```

In this directory, there are 12 directories representing the themes. The cascading style sheet used for theme 2, which has been used throughout the book, is named:

```
C:\oracle\...\themes\theme_2\theme\theme_V2.css
```

This information will be useful in later sections.

Overriding Properties Defined in the HTML DB Style Sheets

The following assumes that readers have some knowledge about CSS syntax.

Earlier it was mentioned that Inline CSS could be used to override the CSS in the HTML DB templates. One such template that I've been asked to override is the calendar template. I was asked if I could make the calendar a little bit shorter so it would fit onto a web page without having to scroll to see the whole calendar.

What I did was look at the Calendar template by navigating to Shared Components → Templates → then clicking the Calendar template. From there, I could see in the Month Open Format attribute the template was using the t2Calendar CSS class.

Next, I looked in the *theme_V2.css* file introduced earlier and saw that the cells for the calendar were defined as shown here:

```
.t2Calendar td{
   width:14%;
   height:75px;
   background-color:#f7f7e7;
   border:1px inset #cccc99;
}
```

From there, I could see the task was to change the height to a lower number. Since I did not want to change the height for all calendars and I only needed to do this on the one page, I decided to use inline CSS to override the settings in the *theme_V2.css* file.

To do that, all I needed to do was to add the following code to the page definition attribute HTML Header:

```
<style type="text/css">
  .t2Calendar td{ height:60px; }
</style>
```

Since my definition was later in the pecking order than the definition provided by the *themes_V2.css* file, my setting was now in control of the height of the calendar cells.

Creating and Adding Your Own CSS

This brief tutorial is on how to add CSS to an application so it can be used in all application pages and templates. The JavaScript tutorial showed how to add files to the repository and to the file system. It also showed how to put the JavaScript directly into the HTML Header section for a page. This tutorial will put custom CSS into the repository and reference from there. The information in the JavaScript section can be used to put it into the file system. CSS can be included in the HTML Header just as was done with JavaScript.

Adding CSS to the Repository

1. Navigate to the Shared Components for your application.

2. Click on the Cascading Style Sheets.

3. Click the Create button.

4. On the Create Cascading Style Sheet page:

   ▪ Stylesheet filename:

     ```
     C:\htmldb_book\CodeDepot\easy_region.css.
     ```

5. Click Upload.

The CSS was added to the workspace so all applications could take advantage of it. The code in the easy_region.css file is shown below.

Now that the CSS file is loaded, it can be linked into the application by including the following text in the HTML Header attribute on an application page. The save text could be entered into a page template so that all pages using the page template can use the styles in the uploaded style sheet.

```
<link rel="stylesheet" href="#WORKSPACE_IMAGES#easy_region.css"
type="text/css" />
```

🖫 easy_region.css

```css
table.easyRegion{
  width:200px;
  margin:0 0 10px 0;
  table-layout:fixed;
}

table.easyRegion th{
  background-color:#900000;
  font-weight:bold;
  height:20;
  font-size:12px;
  color:#ffffff
}

table.easyRegion th.left{
  text-align:left;
```

```
}

table.easyRegion th.center{
  text-align:center;
}

table.easyRegion td.bodytext{
  background-color:#ffffff;
  border:1px #aaaaaa solid;
  border-top:none;
  font-size:12px;
  padding:6px;
}

table.easyRegion p{
  font-size:12px;
  color:#CC0000
}
```

Templates

Templates play a vital role in how page components are rendered on application pages. Throughout the book, several application pages have been created using the various templates.

The following tutorials will create a custom region that will use the CSS loaded in the previous section. You will be guided through two tutorials: One on creating a region template from scratch, and one on copying a page template and modifying it.

Creating a Region Template

The region template to be created here will use the style classes from the easy_region.css file that were loaded earlier.

1. To create the region template, navigate to Shared Components.

2. Click on the Templates link.

3. Click on the Create button.

4. Choose the Region option and click Next.

5. Choose the From Scratch option and click Next.

6. On the Name page:

   - Name: easyRegion.

- Theme: leave the default of Blue and Tan.

- Template Class: Custom 1.

Template classes are assigned to templates to indicate a particular use for the template. They are mostly important when switching themes for an application. The classes used in the current theme must exist in the new theme or it will not be possible to switch the theme. Since this template will not have anything else like it, it should not be assigned to a class that exists. That is the reason for assigning it to the Custom 1 class.

7. Click the Create button.

8. On the Templates page, find the new *easyRegion* and click on the link to edit the region.

9. For the Template attribute, enter the text from the file *easy_region_template.txt* in the code depot. What this is doing is creating a region based on the classes defined in the easy_region.css file.

10. Click Apply Changes.

🖫 easy_region_template.txt

```
<table cellspacing="0" cellpadding="0" border="0" class="easyRegion"
summary="" id="#REGION_ID#">
  <tbody>
    <tr>
      <th class="center">#TITLE#</th>
    </tr>
    <tr>
      <td class="bodytext">#BODY#</td>
    </tr>
  </tbody>
</table>
```

Creating a Page Template

Using page templates allows total customization of the page layout. This section will show how to create a new template by copying an existing one and describe some of the substitution strings used in page templates.

The scenario used for demonstration is that an application contains groups of pages: Order Entry; Billing; and Inventory Management. For each group, the developer wants to have a different banner across the top of the page. It will be further assumed that the pages are to be similar to the No Tabs page template, so that is the one that will be copied and modified.

1. Navigate to Shared Components.

2. Click on the Templates link.

3. Click on the Create button.

4. Choose the Page option and click Next.

5. Choose As a Copy of an Existing Template and click Next.

6. On the Copy From Application page leave the default and click Next.

   This is where a template could be copied from another application. This is handy if the developer has templates in other applications they want to use. For this case, a template will be copied from the example application.

7. On the Identify Theme page, leave both selections set to Blue and Tan and then click Next.

8. On the New Templates page, modify the To Name field for the No Tabs page template and enter Inventory Management. Change the Copy option to YES and click the Copy Page Templates button. See Figure 13.8.

   Also, several templates can be copied at a time.

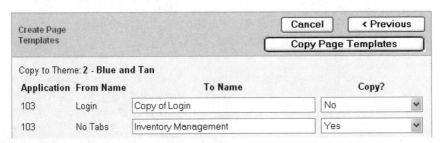

Figure 13.8: *Copying a page region.*

Modifying the New Inventory Management Page Template

After the new template has been created, it must be modified so it can be used on the group of Inventory Management pages. You will already be on the Templates page, so click on the link for the new Inventory Management template.

1. Scroll down to the section where the Body is defined. That is where the #LOGO# substitution string will be found. Figure 13.9 shows how it looks before any modifications.

```
* Body
<table width="100%" cellpadding="0" cellspacing="0" border="0" summary="">
<tr>
<td valign="top" class="t2Logo" width="100%">#LOGO#</td>
<td valign="top" align="right">#NAVIGATION_BAR#</td>
```

Figure 13.9: *Before modifications.*

2. The next step is to modify the <td> containing #LOGO# and add a custom banner. Since the global Logo from the application should not display on this page, the #LOGO# substitution string will no longer be included.

3. Figure 13.10 shows the Body of the template after modifications. The height of the <tr> tag has been modified, a font tag with Inline CSS has been added as has the text Inventory Management. This will now display in the banner of every application that uses the new Inventory Management template.

```
* Body
<table width="100%" cellpadding="0" cellspacing="0" border="0" summary="">
<tr height="50">
<td valign="top" width="100%"><font style="color:#900000;font-weight:bold;
font-size:24px;font-face:verdana;">Inventory Management</font></td>
<td valign="top" align="right">#NAVIGATION_BAR#</td>
```

Figure 13.10: *After modifications.*

Using the information from this section and the section on Cascading Style Sheets, it should be possible to create a custom CSS class to use for the banners created above. In that case, the text would be replaced:

```
<font style="color:#CC0000;font-weight:bold;font-size:24px;font-
face:verdana;">
with
<font class="inventory">
```

Using the Templates You Have Created

Now it is time to create an application page that uses the two templates created in the previous sections. The page will be created in the Easy HTML DB Book application so it can be used for reference in the future.

1. Navigate to the Application home page.

2. Click on the Create Page button.

3. Choose Blank Page and click Next.

4. Page: 1130 and click Next.

5. For page name, enter Template Samples and click Next.

6. No Tabs and click Next.

7. Click Finish.

8. Click the Edit Page icon.

9. Click the Create Region icon.

10. Choose the HTML option and click Next.

11. For the page Title, enter Page Information and click Next.

12. For HTML Text Region Source, enter some text to be displayed in the region and click the Create Region button. Later the template will be changed to the *easyRegion* template.

    The text can look something like this:

    ```
    <p>This is a custom region template created for the
    Easy HTML DB Book. It uses a custom cascading style sheet
    to define the look of the region.</p>
    <p>The cascading style sheet file is named
    <b>easy_region.css</b>.</p>
    ```

13. On the Page Definition page, click on the Page Information link for the new region.

14. On the Edit Region screen, change the Template to easyRegion and click the Apply Changes button.

    At this step, the *easy_region.css* will not be linked into the current page. The next steps will take care of that as well as change the page template.

15. Back on the Page Definition page, click on the Edit Attributes button.

16. On the Edit Page screen:

    - Page Template: modify this to the Inventory Management template we created earlier.

    Enter the following text in the HTML Header to link in the easy_region.css style sheet.

```
<link rel="stylesheet" href="#WORKSPACE_IMAGES#easy_region.css"
type="text/css" />
```

- Click the Apply Changes button.

17. Run the page.

The page that was just created should look like Figure 13.11.

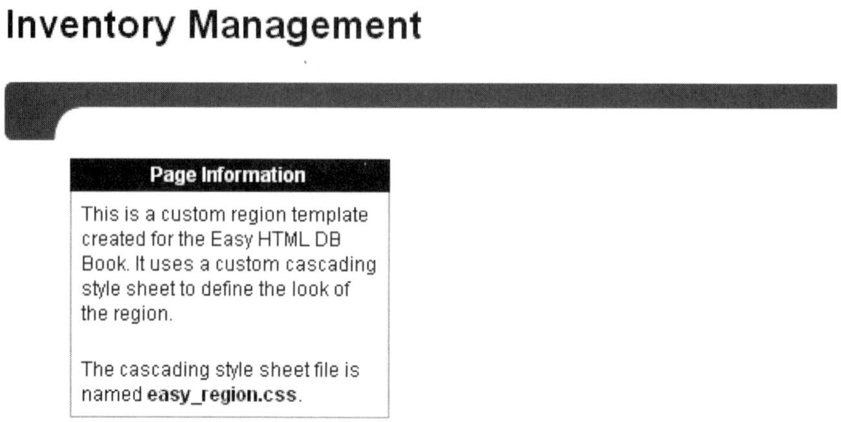

Inventory Management

Page Information

This is a custom region template
created for the Easy HTML DB
Book. It uses a custom cascading
style sheet to define the look of
the region.

The cascading style sheet file is
named **easy_region.css**.

Figure 13.11: *Using the CSS and Regions created in this chapter.*

Conclusion

Themes, templates, JavaScript, and CSS are what a developer uses to control
the overall look and feel of an application. The basics have been presented in
this chapter to get you started, but much can be accomplished with just a
little work using templates, JavaScript, and CSS. Templates are the
foundation of how a page component will look and may use CSS to help
influence the look of page components using a template. JavaScript is used
to add functionality to an application page.

This chapter has shown how to use CSS to override a property in the HTML
DB provided CSS files. It also included information on how to create a new
region template in a template and use a custom CSS in that template to
indicate how the new region should look when rendered. Furthermore, the
three different methods for including CSS were covered as was where to use
each of them. Details were presented on how and where to include custom

JavaScript. Another important skill that was covered is how to set the default templates for a theme.

The next chapter will introduce the steps for deploying an application. It will also cover how to make sure that when an application is deployed, it still looks and acts the same as when it was developed.

Application Deployment with HTMLDB

Introduction

At this point, much time and effort have been expended developing your application. Now, it is time to deploy it on the production server. With HTML DB, moving an application from development is easy and quick. Using the Export/Import utility within HTML DB, the application, as well as any uploaded files to support your application can be copied.

During the course of the book and the exercises in each of the chapters, an Easy HTML DB Book application has been created. In that application tables and an application have been created, and JavaScript and a Cascading Style Sheet (CSS) have been uploaded. Some user interface defaults have also been created for the DEMO_ORDERS table.

The following are the various tasks available for deployment of the application to production.

Development Server

- Generate the DDL to make sure the latest changes have been included

- Export the DDL file

- Export any necessary data, typically for the lookup tables

- Export the Application

- Export Cascading Style Sheets

- Export Images

- Export Static Files

- Export Themes

- Export User Interface Defaults (optional)

Production Server

- Create a tablespace on the production server

- Install HTMLDB on the production server.

- Create the Workspace to install into along with a user

- Import and run the DDL in the production server

- Import the Application

- Import the CSS, Images and Static Files

Depending on how much data is in the database, the process of deploying the application could take less than 20 minutes to complete. The first step of the process is exporting the DDL for the application schema.

Generating the DDL for the Application

HTML DB provides an easy way to export the Data Definition Language (DDL) from the application's parsing schema into a file. With this utility, database objects can easily be moved from the development server to the production server.

1. To export the DDL, navigate to the Generate DDL page via SQL Workshop → Utilities → Generate DDL.

2. The Schema Objects page will show a list of schemas available in which to create a DDL script. The example application will only have the EASYHDB schema. Click the Create Script button.

3. On the Schema page, choose the EASYHDB schema and click Next.

4. On the Object Type page:

   - Output: Select the Save As Script File option.

     The Display Inline option can be chosen the DDL is to be generated to get a feel for how the schema objects look.

   - Object Type: Choose the object types for which to create the DDL. The available choices are shown in Figure 14.1.

   - Click the Next button.

It is possible to generate the DDL at this point, and it will create all objects of the type chosen. The choice for this example is going to be reduced to a subset of the objects, so click Next.

Figure 14.1: *Generate DDL – Object type selection.*

The Object Name page will show a list of all the objects available for DDL generation. On the prior page, shown in Figure 14.1, all the options were chosen on purpose in order to show the objects available on the Object Name page.

5. On the Object Name page, select the items to generate DDL for and click the Generate DDL button.

6. On the Script page enter EasyHDB_DDL for the Script Name. Providing a description is optional. Then, click the Create Script button.

So far, the DDL generation has been run and the script has been saved to the Script Repository with the name EasyHDB_DDL. The DDL script will be created and stored in the Script Repository. From here, the script can be exported to a file on the operating system.

Exporting the DDL Script File

After generating the DDL file and saving it as a script file in the Script Repository, the file will have to be exported to an operating system file. When the DDL script creation was completed, the application would have navigated to the SQL Scripts page. If you are not there, simply Navigate to the SQL Scripts section in the SQL Workshop. Figure 14.2 shows the initial screen of the Script Repository.

	Edit	Owner	Name	Updated By	Last Updated ▼	Bytes	Results	Run
☐	🔖	EASYDEV	EasyHDB_DDL	-	4 minutes ago	18,949	0	🔲
☐	🔖	EASYDEV	easy_person	EASYDEV	4 hours ago	285	1	🔲

Figure 14.2: *Initial Screen of the Script Repository*

The right side of the SQL Scripts page will show a Tasks list for the Script Repository, as shown in Figure 14.3. The task on this screen is to Export the DDL script to an operating system file.

1. Start by clicking on the Export link.

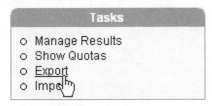

Figure 14.3: *Task list for the Script Repository*

After clicking on the Export link, the script to export will be selected. HTML DB provides a list from which to choose, as shown in Figure 14.4.

2. On the Scripts page depicted in Figure 14.4, check the checkbox next to the EasyHDB_DDL script and click the Add to Export button.

3. After clicking on the Add to Export button, a region on the right side of the SQL Scripts page will show the scripts selected for export, as shown in Figure 14.5. At this point, a name for the File Name can be entered, and the Export All button clicked.

4. On the File Download page, hit the Save button and save the file to the operating system.

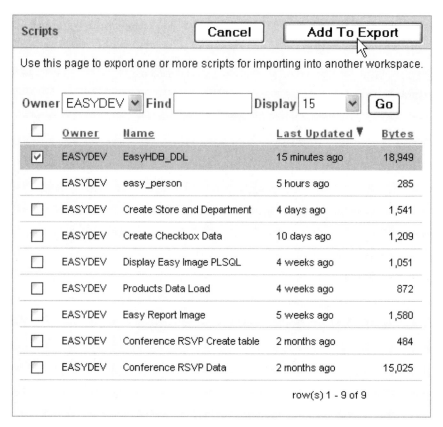

Figure 14.4: *Export SQL Scripts*

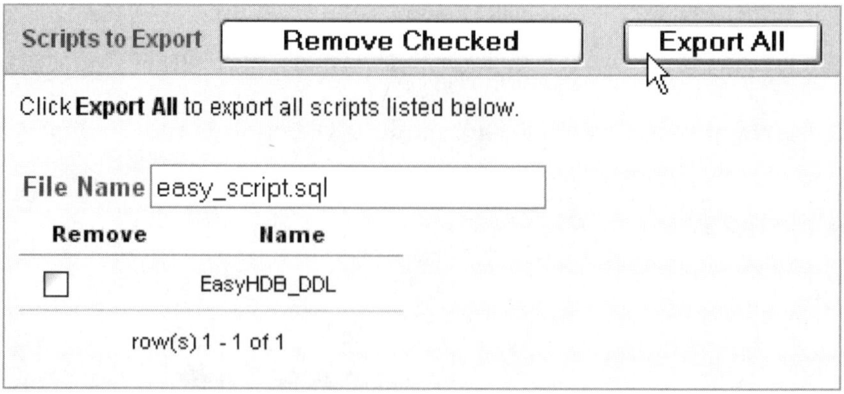

Figure 14.5: *Export List of scripts*

Exporting Data

Now that there is a file for the DDL, data can be exported from any tables that may be needed. This data is being exported so it can be loaded into our production HTML DB server. This function is another part of the SQL Workshop utilities. Navigate to the utility by using the buttons or menus to follow the path SQL Workshop → Utilities → Data Import/Export.

Within this section are three choices: Import; Export; and viewing the Import Repository. Although the Export function will be covered here now, the Import function will be used later to load files into the Import Repository.

1. To begin the export procedure, navigate to the Export To Text wizard via SQL Workshop → Utilities → Data Import/Export → Export → Export to Text.

2. On the Schema page, choose the schema and click Next. The example schema is EASYHDB.

3. On the Table Name page, choose the Table to export and click Next. The selected table name for this example is CONFERENCE_RSVP.

4. On the Columns page, select the columns to export and click Next. For this example, chose all columns.

5. On the Options page, information will be entered to identify how to format the date in the export file. When the options have been set, click the Export Data button.

    Figure 14.6 shows the options available for the formatting of the export file. A comma is a common separator as well as the "|" character. The Optionally Enclosed By field should be used if the data being exported includes characters the same as the delimiter. For example, if there is a name column that is storing data like "Wilson, Julie" there will be a problem on import because of the extra comma in the middle of the text. Enclosing the text with a double-quote makes it look like one piece of data when being imported.

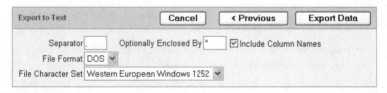

Figure 14.6: *Setting export file format options.*

6. The default file name being exported will be that of the table name plus the file extension. Click on the Save button and save the file.

In the example above, the data was exported to a comma separated value (CSV) file. It is also possible to choose to export the file to an XML format.

Exporting the Application

This is the main function that is needed to move the application to production, and it is an easy one! This function is performed from the application's home page.

1. Navigate to the Application home page.

2. Click on the Export / Import icon.

3. On the next page, choose the Export option and click Next.

   The next page is the Application Export page. The tabs across the top of the Export Application region, as shown in Figure 14.7, provide the navigation to all attributes of the application: Application; CSS; Images; Files; Themes; and User Interface Defaults.

4. On the Export Application page:

   - Application: Select the application being exported.

   - File Format: Select the file format to export to. As a personal preference, I always choose Unix even if I am on a Windows operating system. Either format will work.

   - Owner Override: To make a different schema the owner of this application, that choice can be made here.

   - Build Status Override: Choose the Build Status. Choosing Run Application Only will import the application so it can only be executed. The developers will not be able to see the application listed in the Application Builder home page.

   - As of: This is normally left blank. However, if it is possible that a page was deleted by accident during development, this option can be used to export the application as of five minutes ago, a time before the page was deleted, and then re-import the application to rescue the deleted page. After re-import, the page will be there again.

   - Click Export Application.

5. The File Download window will display with a default filename representing the application id. Click Save and save the file.

See? I told you it was easy...

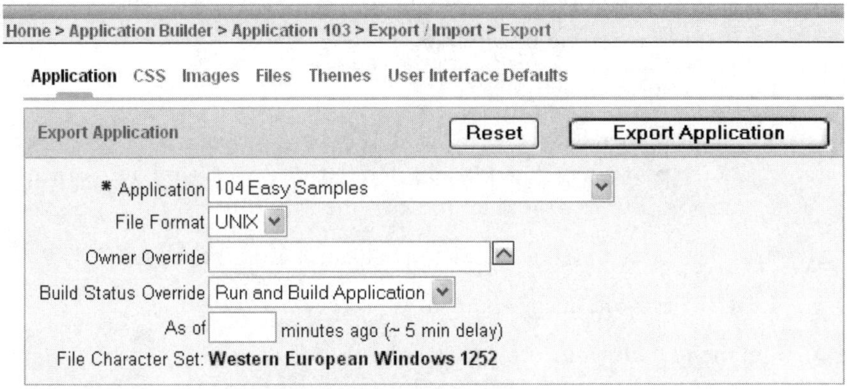

Figure 14.7: *Export page for applications.*

Exporting Cascading Style Sheets

As familiarity with CSS grows and they are added to applications, they will also need to be exported during the deployment of an application. In the examples in the book, a CSS named easy_region.css was created. The scenario below would be used to export that CSS file.

1. To export the CSS, navigate to the Export page as shown in Figure 14.7 and click on the CSS tab.

2. On the Export Cascading Style Sheets page:

   ▪ Stylesheets: Select the style sheet(s) for export.

   ▪ File Format: Make a selection. Again, I always choose Unix.

3. Click the Export Style Sheets button.

4. On the File Download page, click the Save button.

   One thing to note is the default filename for exporting style sheets is simply css.sql. It is a good habit to modify this filename so it has more meaning to the developer.

Exporting Images

If images, such as those used for the logo in an application, were loaded, they will need to be exported so they can be imported in the production system.

1. To export the Images, navigate to the Export page as shown in Figure 14.7 and click on the Images tab.

2. On the Export Images page:

   - Export Images in Application: There are two options. One choice is to export images loaded into the workspace, and the other is to export images loaded into one of the applications.

   - File Format: Make a selection. Again, I always choose UNIX.

3. Click the Export Images button.

4. On the File Download page click the Save button.

Exporting Static Files

If JavaScript was used in the application, as it was during the examples in the book, those files will have to be exported, too. Also, any other static files in the application will be exported here.

1. To export the Static Files (JavaScript), navigate to the Export page as shown in Figure 14.7 and click on the Files tab.

2. On the Export Static Files page:

   - Static Files: Select the static files to export.

   - File Format: Make a selection. Again, I always choose Unix.

3. Click the Export File(s) button.

4. On the File Download page click the Save button.

   One thing to note is the default filename for exporting static files is simply static_file.sql. It is a good habit to modify this filename so it has more meaning to the developer.

User Interface Defaults

The User Interface Defaults that have been setup for the application can be exported. It is not necessary to import user interface defaults into the production system. The application will run fine without them. However, that option is available. The real advantage of exporting user interface defaults is to transfer them to another workspace where development may be going on. The changes made to the user interface defaults involved the changes to the DEMO_ORDERS table in an earlier chapter.

1. To export the User Interface Defaults, navigate to the Export page as shown in Figure 14.7 and click on the User Interface Defaults tab.

2. On the Export User Interface Defaults page:

   ▪ Schema: Select the EASYHDB schema.

   ▪ File Format: Either option can be chosen, but again, I use Unix.

   ▪ Click the Export User Interface Defaults button.

3. A File Download window will display. Click the Save button and save the file. The default name for the file will be <schema>_hints.sql. For this example, the filename is easyhdb_hints.sql.

The previous sections outlined all the possible steps that might be needed to prepare an application to be installed in another HTML DB environment. The next sections describe how to import it.

Importing and Running the DDL script

Now that all the files are needed have been identified, it is time to import them. This example assumes that the tablespace has been created, HTML DB has been installed, and a workspace has been created.

With that done, the first step is to import the DDL script and execute it. This step is performed in two parts. The first part is uploading the DDL script, and the second part is running the script. Again, HTML DB makes all this easy!

1. Navigate to the SQL Script repository page: SQL Workshop → SQL Scripts. This page was shown in Figure 14.2.

2. To upload the easy_script.sql file, click on the Upload button.

---

3. On the Upload Script page, as shown in Figure 14.8:

   ▪ File: Enter the filename for the easy_script.sql file exported earlier.

   ▪ Script Name: Assuming you were in a different environment, the name shown in Figure 14.8 would be entered.

   ▪ Click the Upload button.

Upload Script		Cancel	Upload
* File	C:\temp\easy_script.sql		Browse...
Script Name	EasyHDB_DDL		
File Character Set	Western European Windows 1252 ▾		

Figure 14.8: *Import Script utility*

Now, the script needs to be executed. It is simple; just click on the traffic light icon under the Run column. HTML DB will give a confirmation screen, shown in Figure 14.9. Click on the Run button and the script will execute. If there are errors, they will be displayed. The script can then be edited and re-run.

Run Script		Cancel	Run

You have requested to run the following script. Please confirm your request.

Script Name	**EasyHDB_DDL**
Created	**on 01/28/2006 12:35:53 AM by EASYDEV**
Updated	**on 01/28/2006 02:21:16 AM by EASYDEV**
Number of Statements	**1**
Script Size in Bytes	**132**

Figure 14.9: *Run Script confirmation.*

Importing the Application

Since the database example has been built, the next step is to import the application.

1. Navigate to the Application Builder home page.

2. Click on the Import button.

3. On the Import page:

- Import file: Browse to the application export file being used to build the new application.

- File Type: Application/Page Export

- Click Next.

4. On the next page, click the Install button. This will not start the install yet. There is still one more step.

5. The next page, shown in Figure 14.10, is the final step before installing the application. On the Install Application page:

- Parse As Schema: Choose the parse as schema.

- Build Status: Choose the Build Status. Choosing Run Application Only will import the application so it can only be executed. The developers will not be able to see the application listed in the Application Builder home page.

- Install As Application: Make the appropriate selection.

- Click the Install Application button.

That is it for the installation of the application. The remaining sections of this chapter will outline how to install CSS, Images, JavaScript, Themes, and user Interface Defaults.

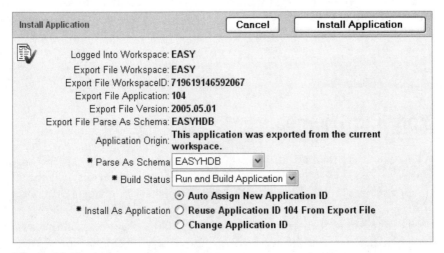

Figure 14.10: *Installing an application.*

Importing a Cascading Style Sheet

Navigate to the Shared Components for the application to which a Cascading Style Sheet will be imported:

- Click on the Cascading Style Sheets link.

- Click on the Create button.

- On the next page, Browse for the file containing the exported style sheet and click the Upload button.

Importing a Static File (JavaScript)

Navigate to the Shared Components for the application to which a Static File will be imported:

- Click on the Static Files link.

- Click on the Create button.

- On the Create Static File page:

  - Application: Choose either "No Application Associated" which will install the static file as workspace file, or choose the application to associate it with. If referencing the static files (JavaScript) using the #WORKSPACE_IMAGES# substitution string, install with "No Application Associated". If #APP_IMAGE# is being used, associate it with the application.

  - Filename: Browse for the file containing the exported static file.

  - Click Upload.

Exporting Themes

The exporting themes section has been moved to the end of the chapter because exporting themes is done for a different reason than all the other exports covered thus far in this chapter. That is because when an application is exported, the themes are also exported; therefore, it is not necessary to export and import the themes when deploying applications. The reason to export and import a theme is to move any customizations to other applications so all of a developer's applications could look the same.

---

1. To export the Blue and Tan theme, navigate to the Export page as shown in Figure 14.7 and click on the Themes tab.

2. On the Export Theme page:

   - Export Theme: Select the Blue and Tan theme.

   - File Format: Either choice can be made, but I always use Unix even if I am on a Windows operating system.

   - Click the Export Theme button.

3. A File Download window will display. Click the Save button and save the file. The default name for the file will be fxxx_theme_2.sql.

Importing a Theme

Navigate to the Shared Components for the application to which a theme is to be imported:

- Click on the Themes link.

- Click on the Create button.

- Choose the From Export option and click Next.

- On the Import page:

  - Import file: Browse for the file containing the exported theme.

  - File Type: Theme Export.

  - Click Next.

- On the next page, click Install.

- On the next page, verify the correct Install Into Application is selected and click the Install Theme button.

Conclusion

This chapter covered how to Export and Import application components to deploy applications. Exporting an application and its components include:

- Generating and Exporting the schema DDL

- Exporting the Data

- Exporting the Application metadata

- Exporting the CSS, if applicable

- Exporting images, if applicable

- Exporting Static Files including the JavaScript, if applicable

The importing of the application is performed in the same order as the export.

It is also possible to choose to export the User Interface Defaults and transfer them to another development environment. Finally, customized Themes can be exported and imported.

The next chapter will provide greater detail on administering the development environment.

HTMLDB
Administration II

Administering the Development Environment

Now that creating applications in HTML DB has been covered in detail, it is time to learn how to administer the development environment. The HTML DB Administrator is responsible for the HTML DB instance and has the power over the entire site. Some of the duties of the administrator are to manage the HTML DB environment, the workspaces, the users, and security. Only a few people should be given this privilege.

To manage HTML DB, the administrator will use the following URL to access the administrator area:

```
http://localhost:7777/pls/htmldb/htmldb_admin
```

The hostname and port are where the HTTP Server has been installed. For more information, see the chapter on Installing HTML DB. At the login page, you will use the special username, admin. The password will be the HTML DB administrator account password that was specified during the installation of HTML DB. Upon login, the following four icons will be displayed:

Manage Service   Manage Workspaces   Manage Applications   Monitor Activity

Figure 15.1: *Icons on the HTML DB Administration home page.*

These icons provide the button and on the right side of the icon, the drop down menu. As the icons imply, this is where the HTML DB services, workspaces, and applications can be managed. Also, the activity that has occurred within HTML DB can be monitored from here.

Manage Service

In this section of the Administration area, the administrator can manage various aspects of the environment of HTML DB. Any configuration changes made here are for the entire instance of HTML DB. Workspace specific settings can be accomplished through the Workspace Administration. This is covered in the Managing Workspaces section of this chapter. This Administrative section provides management for the following parts:

COMPONENT	DESCRIPTION
Environment Settings	These settings control the configuration of HTML DB which is applied to all Workspaces in an instance.
Site-Specific Tasks	Site-Specific tasks will appear in a Site-Specific Tasks list, shown in Figure 15.10, on the Workspace home and login pages. These links are specified by the Administrator.
Service Requests	This is where the Administrator will handle any requests for workspaces.
Change Requests	Like service requests, these are requests for changes to a workspace, such as more space or to add a new schema.
Logs	This area allows the Administrator to manage the size of the various logs that HTML DB provides.
Session State	The Administrator can manage the amount of space the session states are consuming.
Mail Queue	Management of the mail queue.

Environment Settings

The environment settings of HTML DB allow the Administrator to control various aspects of the HTML DB configuration. There are six configuration areas: Application Development; Self Service; Email; SQL Workshop; Monitoring; and Security.

Application Development

The Application Development section has two different settings to be configured. These are depicted in Figure 15.2.

- Allow PL/SQL Program Unit Editing: Turns off the editing capability in the Object Browser of the SQL Workshop. The administrator may want to keep control of the content of the procedures, packages and functions and not allow every developer of an application the ability to edit them

- Create demonstration objects in new workspaces: When HTML DB creates a new workspace, it will also create a demonstration application in the workspace if the Create demonstration objects in new workspaces option is set to YES. Setting this option to NO will prevent their creation. This would be set to NO for production environments.

Figure 15.2: Application Development Settings

Self Service

The Self Service section, shown in Figure 15.3, controls how the requests for workspaces are handled. If the Provisioning Status is set to MANUAL, the request link will not show on the login page for users to request a workspace. In this case, the administrator would create each workspace by hand. If set to REQUEST, the link will show on the login page and the request will go into the queue for approval. If approved, the Development Service URL will be sent in the email back to the user as the URL to use for login. If no URL is entered, one will be derived from the environment automatically.

Figure 15.3: *Self Service Settings*

Email

The Email section configures how HTML DB will interface with the SMTP email service. These settings will allow HTML DB to send email to the user when an email request has been made. The SMTP Host Address can be set to the local server or it can utilize another server. SMTP Host Port is set to the default for the SMTP server which is 25. Only change this setting if necessary. Lastly, the Administration Email Address is the address used to send email to the user. This is the FROM address.

Email	
SMTP Host Address	localhost
SMTP Host Port	25
Administration Email Address	admin@mycompany.com

Figure 15.4: *Email Settings*

SQL Workshop

The SQL Workshop section configures various aspects of the SQL Workshop.

- SQL Commands Maximum Inactivity in minutes: This sets the maximum time in minutes that a transaction can be inactive before it times out and issues a rollback. This is to prevent a locking problem to persist if a transaction is not committed in the SQL Workshop.

- SQL Scripts Maximum Script Output Size in bytes: This sets the maximum amount of bytes of output that a script can produce. The output from a script will not be rendered until it has completed. If there is a run-away script or plain SELECT statement producing a large amount of data, it may cause the page to take a long time to be rendered. This setting will limit the amount of information.

- SQL Scripts Maximum Workspace Output Size in Bytes: This setting limits that amount of output that any particular workspace can produce. This setting is designed to prevent network problems that may be caused by a workspace that is inefficient and placing a burden on the other workspaces.

- SQL Scripts Maximum Script size in bytes: This setting limits the script size which can be submitted through the SQL Workshop. The Administrator may want to limit this to prevent the user from consuming too much buffer space. Each SQL Script will consume buffer space in memory.

- Enable Transactional SQL Commands: Setting this value will allow users to submit many commands in a single database transaction: otherwise, the user must submit the commands singularly.

SQL Workshop

SQL Commands Maximum Inactivity in minutes	60
SQL Scripts Maximum Script Output Size in bytes	200000
SQL Scripts Maximum Workspace Output Size in bytes	2000000
SQL Scripts Maximum Script Size in bytes	500000
Enable Transactional SQL Commands	Yes

Figure 15.5: *SQL Workshop Settings*

Monitoring

Monitoring enables or disables database monitoring through HTML DB. In the SQL Workshop, HTML DB gives the user a method of accessing a variety of reports about the activity, storage, and configuration of the database instance. The user must have a valid database login with DBA or SELECT_CATALOG_ROLE privileges.

Monitoring

Enable Database Monitoring	Yes

Figure 15.6: *Monitoring Setting*

Security

Security is one of the more important areas to set. Here, the Administrator can disable the ability for anybody to log in as the Administrator, including the administrator! This is to prevent users from getting into the Administrator areas and compromising user logins or causing other damage.

- **Disable Administrator Login**: After setting this option to YES and logging out, no user will be able to login as an Administrator. The only way to allow access to the Administrative areas is to login through SQL*Plus as the HTML DB schema owner, FLOWS_020000, and execute the following script:

```
begin
   wwv_flow_api.set_security_group_id(p_security_group_id=>10);
   wwv_flow_platform.set_preference(
   p_preference_name => 'DISABLE_ADMIN_LOGIN',
   p_preference_value => 'N' );
end;
```

```
/
commit
/
```

- **Disable Workspace Login**: Disables or enables the login to the HTML DB INTERNAL workspace. The HTML DB development environment is written in HTML DB. Those applications are kept within a workspace entitled HTML DB. Without this option, users can login into the HTML DB workspace and view the actual pages which are used in the development environment. Of course this kind of access can be dangerous if it is gained by anyone having gained a little knowledge about HTML DB. That person could cause many problems. The Disable Workspace Login setting can prevent this. It will not allow logins to any workspace using the URL as shown below. Attempting to do so will produce a 404 error.

```
http://localhost:7777/pls/htmldb/htmldb_login
```

- **Restrict Access by IP Address**: Lastly, access to the HTML DB instance can be restricted to certain IP addresses by filling in the Restrict Access by IP Address field. Enter a comma delimited set of values which can access. Wild cards can be used to specify the IP addresses. For example, 192.168.0.12, 192.168.0.* or 192.168.* are valid entries. Do not use numbers after the wild card. For example, 192.*.0.2 is not a valid entry.

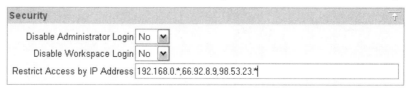

Figure 15.7: *Security Settings*

Site Specific Tasks

Anyone going through HTML DB has probably noticed the task list that appears on the right side of the development pages. The task list provides additional help to the developer during development. An example of a task list appears on the Application Builder page and is shown in Figure 15.8.

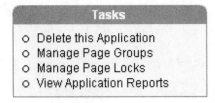

Figure 15.8: *Application Builder Task List*

In the Site Specific Tasks, a list of site-specific links can be created. By specification, these links can appear on the Workspace Login or Home page. It is also possible to manage whether or not the link appears on the list. Figure 15.9 shows the entry screen. The example is adding a link to Oracle's HTML DB Studio website which can be a great resource for the developer.

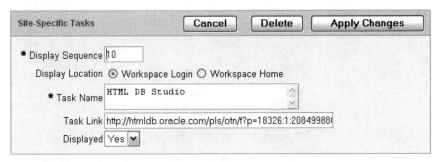

Figure 15.9: *Example of a Site Specific Task List entry*

1. Click on the Manage Site Specific Tasks

2. Fill in the Site Specific Tasks list with the information

   ▪ Display Sequence to order where the link will be placed.

   ▪ Specify the Display Location, Workspace Login or Workspace home page.

   ▪ Enter the Task Name which will appear on the list.

   ▪ Enter the link to the site. This can be a external or internal link using the f?p notation.

   ▪ Specify if the link is Displayed or not.

3. Click on Apply Changes.

On the Workspace Login or Home page, a new list of links for the developer will appear. If the links are removed, where there is no link in the list, the list will not appear. Figure 15.10 shows the new Workspace Login page with the new task list. Figure 15.11 displays the entry in the administrators' page.

Figure 15.10: *Example of a New Site Specific Task List*

Name	Sequence	Displayed On Page ▲	Task Link	Display
HTML DB Studio	10	Workspace Login	http://htmldb.oracle.com/pls/otn/f? p=18326:1:2084998804482312684::NO:::	Yes
			row(s) 1 - 1 of 1	

Figure 15.11: *Specific Task List entry in Administrator screen*

Managing Service and Change Requests

One of the duties of an HTML DB administrator is to provide a new workspace, schema, and storage for a new project. An Administrator can either create these manually or automatically through the workspace request system. HTML DB must be in the Request mode for the workspace request system to function. The workspace request system allows a user to request the workspace, schema, and storage. Information on the manual and automatic creation of workspaces is contained elsewhere in this chapter.

When a requested is made, it will be put into a pending status and placed in the request queue for the administrator as shown in Figure 15.12.

Figure 15.12: *Pending Service Request*

The administrator can now act upon the request in the manner that they wish. The request queue allows the administrator to modify the request by clicking on the edit icon, delete the request, email the requestor for more clarification, or accept/decline the request. An appropriate email will be sent to the user if the Administrator accepts or declines the request.

Users can also submit change requests to have additional space added to a workspace or to have a new schema created for a workspace. This queue is managed much the same way as the Service requests. The Administrator can accept or decline the request.

Managing HTML DB Logs

HTML DB captures information in logs as the system is being used and the applications are being developed. The clean up of these logs can be controlled by the administrator. The logs kept by the system are:

- **SQL Workshop logs**:

  - **Script File execution log entries**: These entries are kept whenever a script file is run to record the success or failure of the execution.

  - **SQL Command Processor history entries**: Each command executed in the SQL Command Processor is recorded for a user. These commands can be retrieved by the user, if necessary, for easy editing.

- **Page View Activity Logs**: HTML DB records page views for all pages in the system. These logs can be reviewed through reports for analysis to find the most common pages used or for some other purpose. HTML DB maintains two activity logs, one current and one non-current. Every 14 days, a log switch occurs where the non-current log is truncated and becomes the current log.

- **Developer Activity Logs**: Developer activity logs record the changes made on a page during development. These logs can be used to see what change has been made, who made the change, and when the change occurred.

- **External Click Counting Log**: This log records any clicks on URLs to external sites.

- **Mail Log**: Each successful email that is sent by HTML DB through the email API is recorded in this log.

All logs can be truncated manually by the Administrator. Entries over a month old will be cleaned out of the SQL Workshop logs, Developer Activity Logs, and the External Click Counting Log automatically. The time period can also be adjusted by the administrator from one to 31 days. The Mail Log is not automatically cleaned out. This must be done manually.

Managing Session State

In HTML DB, a session is defined for each user that logs into the system. The session information is tracked and stored before and after each page is submitted. The information stored is the session number, when the session was created, the workspace for the session, who is the user, and most importantly the value of all the variables used in that session. The information is referred to as the Session State. Figure 15.13 displays an example of a session state.

The session state can be used to track down problems or possible security violations. Session state is normally purged from the system every 24 hours. The Administrator also has the option of deleting these sessions manually through this interface. Automatic deletion of the session states also can be adjusted from 10 seconds all the way up to one year.

The Administrator can also gather statistics concerning the sessions, the entries for all the session states, and the average number of entries per session.

| Session Number | 12604882591123231198 | [∧] [Go] |

Session Number	**12604882591123231198**
Created By	**HTMLDB_PUBLIC_USER**
Created On	**12 minutes ago**
Cookie (User)	**DFELT**
On New Instance Fired For	**:4350**
Security Checks Passed	**: 47302021031728224:**
Security Checks Failed	**:FLOW:ADMIN:**
Workspace	**1849003232797416**

Item Name	Session State Value	Session State Status	Application
COMPANY	TCIDEV	I	4350
F4350_P52_WEB_PASSWORD	-	I	4350
F4350_P56_USER_PASSWORD	-	I	4350
F4350_P56_WEB_PASSWORD	-	I	4350
F4350_P57_PW_CONFIRM	-	I	4350
F4350_P57_WEB_PASSWORD	-	I	4350
F4350_P58_CONFIRM_PASSWORD	-	I	4350
F4350_P58_PASSWORD	-	I	4350
F4550_P1_COMPANY	-	R	4550
F4550_P1_PASSWORD	-	R	4550
F4550_P1_USERNAME	-	R	4550
FB_FLOW_ID	-	I	4350
FB_FLOW_PAGE_ID	-	I	4350
P1_A1	520	I	4350
P1_A2	-	I	4350
P1_A3	-	I	4350
P1_N1	TCI Registrar General	I	4350
-	1:500:3:0	-	-
			row(s) 1 - 18 of 18

Figure 15.13: *Example Session State*

Managing the Mail Queue

When an email is sent through the HTML DB htmldb_mail.send API, the email is first placed in the mail queue for processing. The queue is processed every ten minutes and the email is sent. Sometimes emails have problems being sent and become stuck in the email queue, or possibly an errant email has been queued for delivery. The Mail Queue can be accessed through this interface to take the appropriate action on the email item. Usually the email is deleted.

The Administrator also has the option to push all emails. When pushed, the emails will be sent immediately and will not wait for the ten minute processing service to start.

Managing Workspaces

The second main function of the Administrators area is to manage the Workspaces which are used in the system. A workspace is an area where applications can be developed. Database schemas are associated with a workspace as well as users. Lastly, a workspace is assigned some storage space in the database in which to save data. The interface can manage each of the workspaces.

The Manage Workspaces area can be accessed by clicking on the Manage Workspaces icon shown in Figure 15.1.

Actions that can be performed here are explained in Table 15.1. Some of the actions are self-explanatory and will not be covered in detail.

ACTION	DESCRIPTION
Create Workspace	Used to create a new workspace.
Existing Workspaces	List and view all the workspaces in the system.
Workspace Details	View the details of a workspace.
Remove Workspaces	Removal of a workspace.
Manage Workspace to Schema Assignments	Management of the schemas which are assigned to a workspace.
Manage Developers and Users	Management of the developers and users of a workspace.
Import Workspace	Used to import a workspace file that has been generated by the Export Workspace function.
Export Workspace	Used to export the definition of the workspace as well as users in the workspace. It will not create database schemas or objects.

Table 15.1: *Actions performed in the Manage Workspaces area*

Creating a Workspace

This function is used to manually create a workspace. Also, the schema for the workspace can be defined as well an administrator for the workspace.

1. To create a workspace, click on the Create Workspace link.

2. On the Create Workspace page, fill in the name of the workspace. Optionally a description of the workspace can be given. Click on Next.

3. On the next page, the schema and storage requirements will be given. If a schema already exists to be used, choose YES to re-use an existing schema. For the Schema Name, supply the name for the existing schema to re-use or the name of the new schema. This will become an actual user in the database. Next, provide the password for that schema.

    The Space Quota for the workspace is also specified here. There are only four choices available: Small (2 MBs); Medium (5 MBs); Large (50 MBs); or Very Large (100 MBs). The amount can be augmented later, if needed.

4. The next page in the wizard is where the administrator for the workspace is given. This is a user who can administer the particular workspace through the developers interface. See the Managing Workspaces section later in this chapter.

5. This next page is the confirmation page where a summary of the choices are provided. Create the Workspace by clicking on the Create button.

The workspace, workspace administrator, and space will be created at this point.

Existing Workspaces

Previously created workspaces can be modified using the Existing Workspaces pages. When this area is entered, a report of the workspaces will be provided as shown in Figure 15.14.

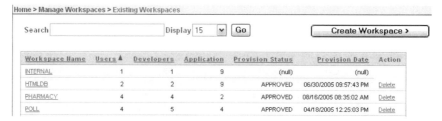

Workspace Name	Users ▲	Developers	Application	Provision Status	Provision Date	Action
INTERNAL	1	1	9	(null)	(null)	
HTMLDB	2	2	9	APPROVED	06/30/2005 09:57:43 PM	Delete
PHARMACY	4	4	2	APPROVED	08/16/2005 08:35:02 AM	Delete
POLL	4	5	4	APPROVED	04/18/2005 12:25:03 PM	Delete

Figure 15.14: *Existing Workspaces*

The INTERNAL workspace is the workspace used by the HTML DB environment.

To see the details on an existing workspace, simply click on its name. Figure 15.15 shows a partial screen for the PHARMACY workspace. This screen provides details such as:

- Name of the Workspace

- Schemas associated with the workspace

- Which Tablespace the schema is using

- Applications that exist in the workspace

- Developers created in the workspace

- Users created in the workspace

- Count of the objects in the schema

- Pending Change Requests

- User Activity

- Developer Activity

This detail page also provides links to manage the Workspace to Schema Assignments, Applications Developers, and Users.

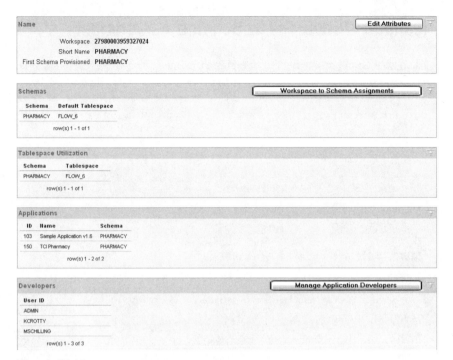

Figure 15.15: *Existing PHARMACY Workspace*

Removing a Workspace

Eventually there will come the time for a workspace to be removed because it is outdated or unused.

1. On the Manage Workspaces page, click on the Remove Workspace link.

2. Enter the name of the workspace or click on the up arrow to obtain a list. Click Next.

3. The next page will provide a checkbox to confirm the removal process. Also, there is a checkbox for removing any requests for the workspace. It is best to check both boxes to clean up everything.

4. The confirmation page will give the summary of the objects in the database that are associated with the workspace. The removal of the workspace will not remove the database objects. These must be done in the database itself.

Manage Workspace to Schema Assignments

Each workspace must have a schema associated with it. This schema is the Parsed As schema, which will be used in the applications. There can be more than one schema associated with a workspace. Each schema can be used by different applications in the workspace, but an application can have only one parsing schema

Workspace ▲	Schema
EASYHTMLDB	easydev
EASYHTMLDB	easyprod
EASYHTMLDB	easytrain

Figure 15.16: *Workspace with many schemas*

To associate a schema with a workspace or to create a new schema, click on the Create button.

1. Indicate if the schema will be a new schema or if an existing one is to be reused, and then click Next.

2. Use the up arrow to choose the workspace then click Next.

3. Provide the existing schema name or a new schema. This is an actual user schema in the database. Enter the password for the schema owner. Next, the default and temporary tablespaces are chosen by using the up arrows. Check with the Database Administrator to ensure the correct choices are made. Click Next.

4. The Confirmation page will appear with the summary of the choices made in the wizard. Click on Add Schema to create or re-use the schema.

Managing the Developers and Users

Inside HTML DB, a person can be one of three types of users: an Administrator; a Developer; or a User. A User is simply a person who has a login but no Developer or Administrator privileges. A user can only run the production web site. A developer can create and develop applications within a workspace. The Administrator will be able to use the Administrator functions within HTML DB.

When adding a new person to the system, the administrator will be presented the page shown in Figure 15.17. This is the same page used for managing users.

- **User Name**: This will be filled in with the login id for the person

- **Email Address**: This will be the email address of the user

- **Default Schema**: This is the schema associated with the workspace that the user will work with.

- **Workspace**: This is the workspace to which the user will have access.

- **First Name, Last Name and Description**: These are optional fields.

- **Password and Confirm Password**: These are the password for the login id.

- **Developers Privileges**: These are to indicate the users' privileges within the system. The user can be a developer or an administrator. If both are set to NO, the user will only have privileges to run an application.

Figure 15.17: *Creating or Editing a HTML DB user*

Exporting a Workspace

At some point, it may be desirable to export workspace information as a backup or even to move the information to another HTML DB instance. When exporting a workspace, the Workspace information, groups defined, and the users for that workspace will be exported. CAUTION: The applications and database objects are not exported. An application export and database export will have to be performed for those. Exporting an application is covered in the chapter on Application Deployment with HTML DB.

When exporting, the first page will ask for the Workspace name. This is shown in Figure 15.18. After filling in the name of the Workspace either by entering the name or using the up arrow icon, click on the Export Workspace button. Next, as shown in Figure 15.19, the file format to use for the exported file will have to be specified. The File Character set will be equal to the character set for the database. When the Save File button is clicked, a file will be downloaded to the local machine in ASCII text format.

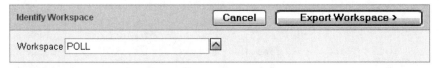

Figure 15.18: *Exporting a Workspace*

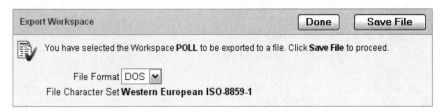

Figure 15.19: *Specifying the File Format for the Workspace export*

Importing a Workspace

At some point, it may be necessary or desirable to import a workspace and its information in order to create a new workspace. Actually creating the workspace is a two step process. The first step is to import the workspace export file into the import repository. The second step will be to actually install that workspace. When installing the workspace, it is possible to specify whether to use the existing schema, which is specified in the export file, or create a new schema.

1. Import the workspace export file. Use the browse button to search the operating system directories for the file.

Figure 15.20: *Specifying the workspace export file to import*

2. After the file is imported, click on the Install button.

Figure 15.21: *Confirmation that the file was imported.*

3. Next, either use an existing schema or specify a new one. If a new one is to be created, a password and space quota will have to be supplied.

Figure 15.22: *Creating a new schema in the database for the workspace*

4. The final page is the confirmation page. Check it over, and when ready, click on the Next button.

Manage Applications

This is the third section of the Administration menu. This section is primarily used to report on certain attributes of the applications. The Manage Workspaces area can be accessed by clicking on the Manage applications icon shown in Figure 15.1.

Application Attributes

The report shown in Figure 15.23 provides information on key attributes on all the applications in the HTML DB instance. The information it provides are:

- Workspace name
- Application ID number

- Parse As schema

- Application Name

- Last updated by whom

- Last updated date

- How many pages are in the application

- Language for the application

Workspace ▲	Application	Parse As	Application Name	Last Updated	Date	Pages	Language
HTMLDB	104	HTMLDB	Sample Application v1.6	ADMIN	7 months ago	21	en-us
HTMLDB	401	HTMLDB	4350 - HTML DB Development Service Home	ADMIN	5 months ago	77	en-us
HTMLDB	402	HTMLDB	4300 - HTML DB Data Workshop	ADMIN	5 months ago	32	en-us
HTMLDB	403	HTMLDB	4500 - HTML DB SQL Workshop	ADMIN	5 months ago	154	en-us
HTMLDB	404	HTMLDB	4000 - HTML DB Application Builder	KCROTTY	4 months ago	753	en-us
HTMLDB	405	HTMLDB	4050 - HTML DB Internal Administration	ADMIN	5 months ago	78	en-us
HTMLDB	407	HTMLDB	4411 - HTML DB System Messages	ADMIN	5 months ago	1	en-us
HTMLDB	408	HTMLDB	4550 - HTML DB Development Service Login	ADMIN	5 months ago	5	en-us
HTMLDB	409	HTMLDB	4700 - HTML DB New Service Signup	ADMIN	5 months ago	7	en-us
PHARMACY	103	PHARMACY	Sample Application v1.6	ADMIN	5 months ago	21	en-us
PHARMACY	150	PHARMACY	TCI Pharmacy	MSCHILLING	5 months ago	4	en-us
POLL	102	POLL	Sample Application v1.6	KTC	9 months ago	21	en-us
POLL	300	POLL	POLL	KTC	9 months ago	6	en-us
POLL	400	POLL	POLL	KTC	6 months ago	6	en-us
POLL	600	POLL	POLL_ADMIN	KTC	9 months ago	5	en-us

row(s) 1 - 15 of 31 ⊙

Figure 15.23: *Application Attributes Report*

Build Status

The build status of an application determines if the application can be further modified through the Application Builder. The build status of an application can be set to Run and Build Application or to Run Application Only. If the application is set to Run and Build Application, the application can be selected in the Application Builder. If set to Run Application Only, the application will not appear on the application list for select. Normally this is set when the application is in production and no changes are allowed. Figure 15.24 shows an example of the report.

Edit	Workspace	Application	Application Name	Parse As	Build Status
📝	PHARMACY	103	Sample Application v1.6	PHARMACY	Run and Build Application
📝	PHARMACY	150	TCI Pharmacy	PHARMACY	Run and Build Application
					1-2

Figure 15.24: *Build Status Report*

From the report, the administrator can modify the build status by editing the application.

Conclusion

As the administrator of an HTML DB environment, this chapter has shown many tools that are available to you. The administrator has the ability to manage many aspects of application development as well as monitor several attributes with the HTML DB environment. The administrative tasks covered in this chapter include:

- Managing the HTML DB environment

- Self service workspace provisioning and managing service and change requests

- Database monitoring

- Security for administrators, developers, and users as well as restricting access to a specific IP Address range.

- Custom site-specific tasks

- Session state management and purging

- Workspace management

- Exporting and importing a workspace

- Application reporting

The next chapter returns to the development aspects of HTML DB with detailed information on best practices and techniques.

Best Practices and Techniques

The best practices and techniques chapter is intended to help new development efforts be more efficient.

Publish and Subscribe

In larger HTML DB systems involving multiple applications, efficiency will be gained and maintenance will be reduced by using the publish and subscribe feature. It is common to create an application that acts as the container for these global publish and subscribe components. The global application is where all the components would be defined, and they would act as the source for any application that wanted to subscribe to them.

The following components can participate in publish and subscribe:

- Authentication Schemes
- Authorization Schemes
- Templates
- Lists of Values (LOV)
- Shortcuts

Publishing

When a component is subscribed to, it becomes the master. Upon making changes to the master, the developer would then go into the attributes page for the master component and publish the changes to the subscribing applications. This will update the component in all subscribing applications.

Refreshing the Subscriber

When a component is a subscriber to a master component, any changes to the master can be updated by navigating to the attributes page for the component and clicking the Refresh button.

Creative use of Substitution Strings

During development, it is advantageous to add images to the static files repository when dealing with CSS and JavaScript. It is also faster for development to add images to the repository than to be putting them on the file system, especially when doing remote development work.

The normal use of substitutions strings would be to reference the HTML DB supplied substitution strings. However, when adding images to the repository and later moving them to the file system, this also applies for static files *.js and *.css, it would be necessary to make changes all over the source code to change #APP_IMAGES# to #IMAGES_PREFIX#, for example.

To make this process more efficient, a user defined substitution string can be created as shown in Figure 16.1. This process was covered in an earlier chapter of this book.

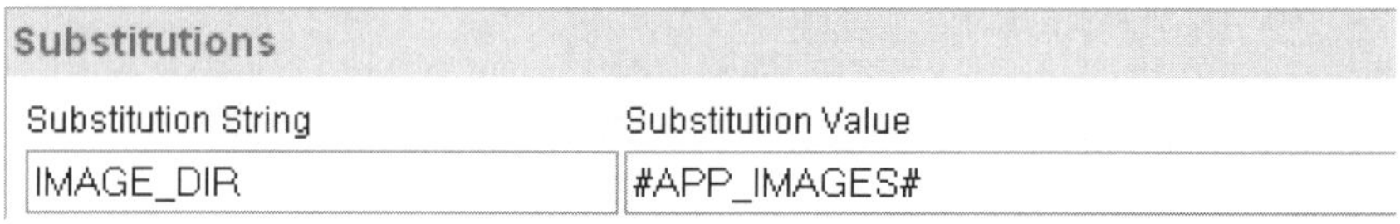

Substitutions	
Substitution String	Substitution Value
IMAGE_DIR	#APP_IMAGES#

Figure 16.1: *Custom user defined substitution string.*

To use the new substitution string, the code would be modified as shown in the examples below. Notice the change from using the ## to using the exact substitution notation of & and the period.

- Before

```
<link rel="stylesheet" href="#APP_IMAGES#.easy_region.css"
type="text/css" />
```

- After

```
<link rel="stylesheet" href="&IMAGE_DIR.easy_region.css"
type="text/css" />
```

It is also possible to create user defined substitution strings that are custom for the type of file they reference such as IMAGE_DIR, JAVA_DIR, and CSS_DIR.

Performance Considerations

Report Pagination

Reports yield the ability to provide a pagination scheme named Row Ranges X to Y of Z. It may not be a good idea to use this pagination scheme if there is heavy use on the system. The reason is that for HTML DB to inform the user of how many rows there are it has to build the result set completely. That can use database resources you may not want to give up.

Report Sorting

Similar to the statement on pagination, it is up to the developer to decide whether or not to provide users with the ability to sort the report by clicking on the column headings. This too can take up resources on the database, because in order to return with a sorted report, the database has to query all records in the query, sort them in memory, and return them as requested.

Page Zero

When putting together components to display on every page in an application, Page 0 should be used to display them. A good use for page 0 is for a table of contents list as seen on many web pages along the left side of the page. Another good use for it is a banner that would be displayed on every page in the application. If there are pages on which it is not desirable for page 0 objects to display, it can be prevented by using the conditional display attribute. Page 0 is explained further in an earlier chapter of this book.

User Interface Defaults

The User Interface Defaults feature allows default attributes to be setup for table columns. Then, when a report or form is built using the wizard, the page items placed on the application page will be built with the defaults setup previously. This can make page building extremely fast because there will be less customizing to change date formats, labels, widths, number formats, and other attributes available in the user interface defaults. User Interface Defaults is explained in greater detail in an earlier chapter of this book.

Opening Multiple Browsers for Development

When developing in HTML DB, it is easier to do development by opening multiple browsers. Code can be modified in one instance of the browser, and in the other browser, the running application page can be refreshed in order to see the changes. However, do not make copies of a browser by clicking on the File → New → Window menu. This will cause problems. Instead, open a new browser and login as a new session to HTML DB.

Using APP_ID and APP_PAGE_ID

When building page URL strings to navigate between pages in an application, it is more efficient to not hard code the APP_ID into the URL as shown:

```
f?p=103:1132:&SESSION.
```

It would be better to use the APP_ID substitution string. This way when the application is deployed, the URL will keep working regardless of the APP_ID.

```
f?p=:APP_ID:1132:&SESSION.
```

When building branches that redirect back to the current page after submitting the page, it can be better to not use the page ID directly in the branch. Instead, enter &APP_PAGE_ID. for the target page ID.

Application Page Reuse

When developing a large system in HTML DB, it is imperative to have the ability to invoke a page, or set of pages, within another application and return without losing the session state of the calling routine. Having several small applications makes deployment easier since each application could be enhanced individually and deployed to the user community. Since an application page from one application cannot simply be dynamically included for reusability, some custom navigation will have to be performed.

Having standard shared application pages can simplify building large HTML DB applications. For example, a large system may have a standard application page to lookup a person, such as an employee or customer. This application would be part of a General, or Global, application to be used by several other applications. The ability to re-use HTML DB code application pages across application is critical for many reasons:

- Reduces developer effort: The ability to create reusable components reduces coding overhead, and there is never any need to reinvent the wheel and re-write a common routine.

- Adds screen uniformity: Shared components reduce end user training and provide a recognizable standard for shared system functions.

- Simplifies maintenance: When a change to a shared component is made, the change will be immediately available to all calling components without any code changes.

The following example shows how to create a cross-application reusable subroutine page in HTML DB. This example interfaces a page in another application to access and return from a shared person lookup HTML DB page.

Step 1: Setup the Re-usable Application Page

The shared page needs to receive the application id, APP_ID, and application page, APP_PAGE_ID, into some hidden page items. These page item values will be used by the re-usable page to know where to navigate back.

In this case, there is an application with a report region of persons. On that application page, it is necessary to create two page level items to store the values of the calling application id, P200_FROM_APP_ID, and the calling page id, P200_FROM_PAGE. It is also necessary to provide a link in the report to navigate back to the calling application.

This has created two hidden page items:

- P200_FROM_APP_ID

- P200_FROM_PAGE

On the report region, the Full Name field, shown in Figure 16.2, must be converted into a link field.

Person Search

Full Name	Email
Vorse, Robert	RVorse@htmldbbook.com
Hill, Alan	Alan.Hill@htmldbbook.com
Azordegan, George	GAzo@htmldbbook.com
Jones, Albert	Albert@htmldbbook.com
Davis, Philip	PDavis@htmldbbook.com

Figure 16.2: *Report with a link column.*

From the Report Attributes page, click on the icon to the left of the FULL_NAME column as shown in Figure 16.3.

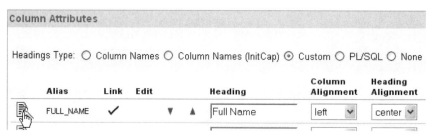

Figure 16.3: *Column definition showing the column is a link.*

On the Column Attributes page, scroll down to the column link section to modify the properties for the link. Figure 16.4 shows the following in the URL text:

- P200_FROM_APP_ID and P200_FROM_PAGE are being used to navigate back to the calling application.

- The same session id is used by implementing &SESSION. It is important to navigate using the same session. Otherwise, all the session state setup thus far will be lost.

- The application item, global variable, will be set to the value of the PERSON_ID column.

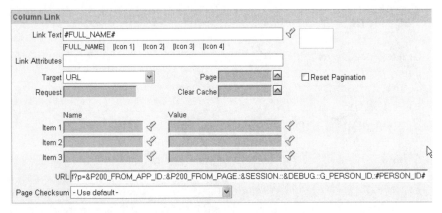

Figure 16.4: *Setting the Column Link attributes.*

Step 2: Setup the Calling Application

There needs to be a page item for the returned values from the reusable application page. To make this process simple, create an application level item by the name of G_PERSON_ID. The application item will be used by page process later.

Step 3: Setup the Calling Application Page

There are few things that have to be created to provide navigation to the Global application page and keep track of the fact this has been done:

- **Page Item**: To hold a value indicating a specific function has been initiated.

- **Button**: To submit the page with the request FIND_PERSON

- **Branch**: To navigate to the global application and set the appropriate page items.

- **Computation**: To set a page item, that can also be an application item to the function being performed.

- **Page Rendering Processes**: To populate the page with data when the application returns.

Page Item

Create a page item to hold a string value indicating the function that has been initiated. For the demo, a page item named P100_SEARCH has been created.

Button and Branch

A button named FIND_PERSON has been created. Then, a branch was created to navigate to the global application page to search for a person. The Action for the branch is shown in Figure 16.5. The conditional processing for the branch is set to execute when the FIND_PERSON button is pressed as shown in Figure 16.6. This shows navigation to APP 500: PAGE 200. This is the application id and page id of the reusable page. The P200_FROM_APP_ID and P200_FROM_PAGE page items are being set so the reusable page knows where to navigate back to when a person's name is selected.

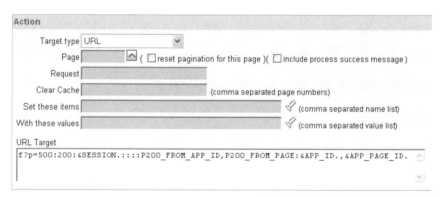

Figure 16.5: *Setting the URL Target for a branch.*

Figure 16.6: *Setting the button the branch will respond to.*

Computation

The computations job is to set a page item to indicate that a Find Person function has been initiated. This value will be used by the processes when the page returns from doing the search. This is done by creating an After Submit computation for the P100_SEARCH page item. The page item will be set to a value of Find Person. Figure 16.7 shows the Source and Conditions for the computation.

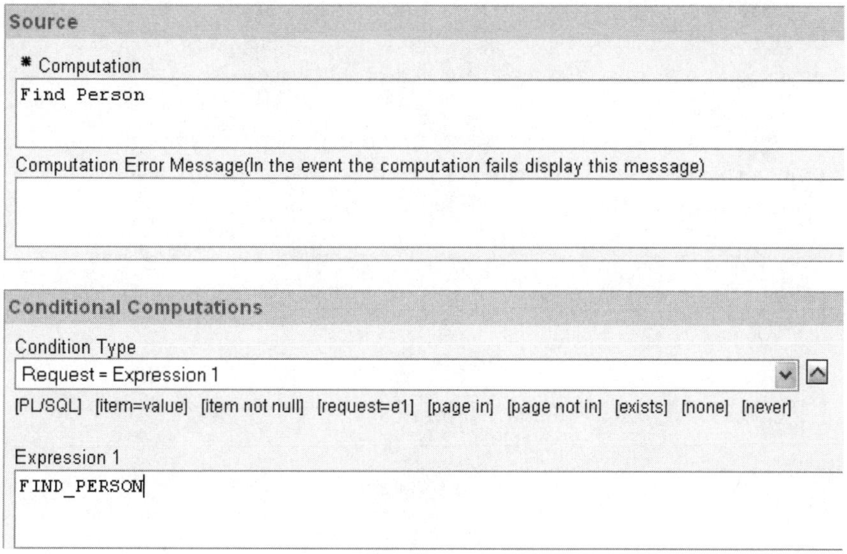

Figure 16.7: *Source and Conditional attributes for a computation.*

Page Rendering Process

So far, a button and a branch to navigate to the reusable application page have been created. The page item, P100_SEARCH, has been set to a value of Find Person. At this point, we have navigated to the reusable page and are awaiting its return. When the page returns, it will set the application item G_PERSON_ID to the person_id found while searching.

Now, the value in G_PERSON_ID will be used to populate the person data page items.

When finished, there should be two Before Regions processes, as shown in Figure 16.8.

Processes

Before Regions
- 10: Set Person Id
- 30: Populate

Figure 16.8: *Two processes to handle the page population.*

The Set Person Id process source is shown in Figure 16.9. This process must be executed before the Populate process because the Populate process depends on the value set in the Set Person Id process.

The Set Person Id process is checking the P100_SEARCH page item. At this point, it will be set to Find Person and set the P100_PERSON_ID to the value returned by the reusable application page.

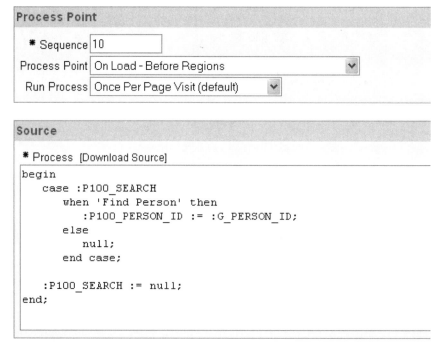

Process Point

* Sequence	10
Process Point	On Load - Before Regions
Run Process	Once Per Page Visit (default)

Source

* Process [Download Source]

```
begin
   case :P100_SEARCH
      when 'Find Person' then
         :P100_PERSON_ID := :G_PERSON_ID;
      else
         null;
      end case;

   :P100_SEARCH := null;
end;
```

Figure 16.9: *Process to set the P100_PERSON_ID item when returning.*

The Populate process is also a Before Regions process, but it has a higher sequence than the Set Person Id process. Thus, HTML DB will execute the Populate process after the Set Person Id process.

The Populate process, shown in Figure 16.10, takes the key value in the P100_PERSON_ID page item and uses it to query the person data from the database.

Source

* Process [Download Source]

```
if :P100_PERSON_ID is not null then
   select p.first_name, p.middle_name,
          p.last_name, p.date_of_birth,
          p.per_sex

   into    :P100_FIRST_NAME, :P100_MIDDLE_NAME,
           :P100_LAST_NAME, :P100_DATE_OF_BIRTH,
           :P100_SEX
   from    person p
   where   p.person_id = :P100_PERSON_ID;
end if;
```

Figure 16.10: *Process to populate the page.*

This same process could be used to populate several page items on a single page. An example would be page items for an employee and page items for the person's manager. Providing another button to search for the manager and the other page components discussed, the same application page could be reused to search for the manager.

Setting the Sizes of Page Components

Regions

To set the height and width of a region to a specified width, set the following attributes in the region. Use this to set all regions to the same width if desired:

- Region Header

```
< table height="400" width="400"><tr><td>
```

- Region Footer

```
</td></tr></table>
```

Select Lists

To set the width of a select list, enter the following <style> tag code. The caution is that if the text goes beyond the width it will not be visible to the user. For HTML Form Element Attributes:

```
style="width:100;"
```

Tabular Form Field

There is no way to set a maximum length of text to allow for a tabular form column by using the available properties in HTML DB. To set the maximum length of the text that can be entered into a tabular form column, edit the column attributes for the tabular form column. Then make the following changes.

- Tabular Form Element → Element Attributes

```
onFocus="javascript:this.maxLength=20;"
```

To force UPPERCASE characters only on a tabular form column, edit the column attributes for the tabular form column. Then make the following changes:

- Tabular Form Element → Element Attributes

```
style="text-transform:uppercase;"
```

To influence the width of a tabular form column set the following:

- Tabular Form Element -> Element Attributes

```
style="width:200;"
```

Viewing the HTLM DB Source Code

Trial and error is the best way to learn new aspects of any program. The goal of this section is to illustrate how it is possible to teach oneself how to do something that has not been covered or documented in the book.

An earlier chapter covered Application Deployment with Oracle HTML DB. This is where how to export and import applications was covered. Well … guess what? HTML DB is itself an exported application; nine of them, actually. Therefore, the HTML DB application files are used to create new HTML DB applications. It is not possible to run them due to security restrictions, but it is possible to look at the code to see how the developers of HTML DB did things. This is a great way to learn how HTML DB was intended to be used.

Loading the HTML DB application files

When testing a new skill or trying something new, it is wise to create a new workspace into which these applications can be imported. That way, the workspace can be dropped later if problems arise. Also, make sure there is enough space in the HTMLDB20 tablespace. If a practice tablespace was created as suggested in an earlier chapter, expand the size to 200MB. A statement like the following can be used:

```
alter database datafile 'C:\oradata\hdb20\htmldb20_01.dbf' resize
204864m;
```

 CAUTION: When attempting this, it is important to pay close attention to Removing the Application Alias from each of the applications.

Ok, now that the customary disclaimers are out of the way, load the applications. The following process assumes that a new workspace has already been created. For explanations, the parsing schema will be named as HDBAPPS.

An earlier chapter covered the download of the installation files for HTML DB. If the steps in that chapter were followed, there will be nine files in the C:\htmldb_book\htmldb\builder directory.

1. Navigate to the Application Builder home page and click on the Import button.

2. On the Import page:

   ▪ Import file: C:\htmldb_book\htmldb\builder\f4000.sql.

   ▪ File Type: Application/Page Export.

   ▪ File Character Set: Leave the default

- Click Next.

3. On the next page, click the Install button.

4. On the Install Application page:

    - Parse As Schema: HDBAPPS, unless the user's schema has a different name, in which case that schema should be used.

    - Build Status: Run and Build Application.

    - Install As Application: Change Application ID.

    - New Application: 400.

        If possible, enter the same application ID's shown in Figure 16.11. Otherwise choose what is available.

5. Click the Install Application button.

6. On the Application Installed page, click on the Edit Application Attributes link.

7. On the Application Attributes page:

    - For the Name, add the number of the file loaded to the front of the name. For example, file f4000.sql was loaded, so change the Name field and add 4000. The name should then be 4000 – HTML DB Application Builder. This will make it easier to associate with the file used to load the application in the future.

    - Application Alias: Clear this field so it is NULL. This is very important.

    - Click the Apply Changes button.

For this example, the author has loaded all the HTML DB applications in the environment and shown the Application Builder home page in Figure 16.11.

Continue loading the applications in the C:\htmldb_book\htmldb\builder directory. If they are not all loaded at this time, they can be loaded at a later time. The next exercise, however, will show why the HTML DB application should probably be loaded.

Application ▲	Name	Updated	Page Count	Updated By	Run
101	Sample Application v2.0	2 months ago	21	admin	
400	4000 - HTML DB Application Builder	5 weeks ago	801	admin	
401	4050 - HTML DB Internal Administration	2 months ago	80	admin	
402	4300 - HTML DB Data Workshop	2 months ago	33	admin	
403	4350 - HTML DB Development Service Home	2 months ago	70	admin	
404	4411 - HTML DB System Messages	2 months ago	1	admin	
405	4500 - HTML DB SQL Workshop	2 months ago	307	admin	
406	4550 - HTML DB Development Service Login	2 months ago	6	admin	
407	4700 - HTML DB New Service Signup	2 months ago	8	admin	
409	4155 - Scheme Authentication Login	2 months ago	5	admin	
				row(s) 1 - 10 of 10	

Figure 16.11: *HTML DB Applications loaded into a workspace.*

Learning from the HTML DB Applications

Ok, so now the HTLM DB applications have been loaded, but no one is quite sure what to do with them.

The best way to explain is to describe a scenario I used while trying to learn HTML DB. Figure 16.12 shows the mouse pointer over the Conditions link. Clicking on that link will scroll the page to the conditions region. Well, I wanted to know how they did that.

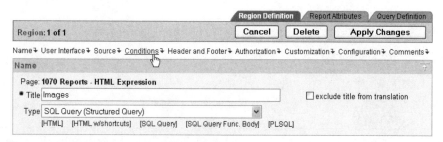

Figure 16.12: *Learning how HTML DB does it.*

Step 1

When editing a region as shown in Figure 16.12, take note of the URL in the browser. Look for the APP_ID and PAGE_ID arguments. The URL shown below says this is application 4000, page 4651:

```
http://localhost:7777/pls/hdb20/f?p=4000:4651:6482256901421161860
```

Step 2

Navigate to the application created earlier. Figure 16.11 shows that HTML DB application ID 4000 is the HTML DB Application Builder application. Click on the link to edit the application.

On the Application home page, enter the page ID from above into the Page field and click the Go button as shown in Figure 16.13.

Figure 16.13: *Navigating to page 4651.*

Step 3

Edit the 4651 application page by clicking on the Edit Region link as shown in Figure 16.14.

Figure 16.14: *Editing the Edit Region page.*

Figure 16.15 shows the regions on page 4651. There is a region named Page Anchors. This is the region that rendered the links at the top of Figure 16.12. It is an HTML DB List. Click on the Page Anchors list to view the region definition.

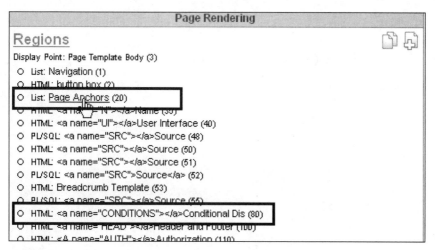

Figure 16.15: *Regions on page 4651 of HTML DB Application Builder.*

The region definition page shows that the list has URL targets that point to bookmarks as shown in Figure 16.16. This shows how HTML DB is providing the navigation to a bookmark but we still have to discover how the bookmark was defined.

Step 4

Navigate back to the page definition page for page 4651. Click on the Conditional Display link to view the region definition. This is the second region outlined in Figure 16.15. Figure 16.16 shows that the Title of the Conditional Display was embedded in an anchor tag with the NAME property set to CONDITIONS. The name property in the region title, as shown in Figure 16.17, is the same as the URL Target set in the page anchors list in Figure 16.16.

Therefore, clicking on the Conditions link at the top of a regions definition page navigates to the #CONDITIONS bookmark as indicated in the title of the Conditional Display region.

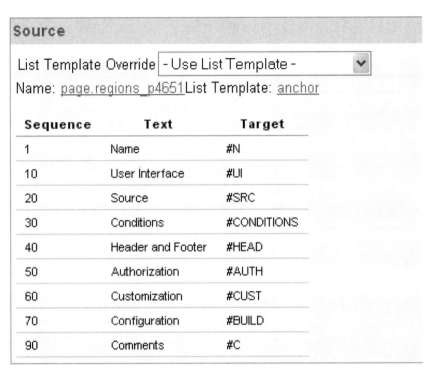

Figure 16.16: *Source definitions for the Page Anchors region.*

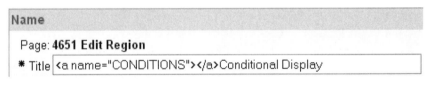

Figure 16.17: *Setting a bookmark in a region title.*

This exercise has shown how the HTML DB source code can be used to learn how to perform a development task. The key is to identify in the HTML DB development environment something you would like to duplicate on your own application pages.

Conclusion

This chapter covered Best Practices and Techniques. The techniques presented here are from experiences the authors have had working together on a project. Best Practices have also been from our experiences, but they are also from other developers and articles we have read while learning HTML DB. Another topic covered was Publish and Subscribe. As you start building larger systems that are actually several applications working together, this feature will save lots of time on maintenance.

Finally, we showed how to use the HTML DB applications themselves to learn further. Using this method allows new developers see exactly how the original developers of HTML DB used their own product to build screens used while developing applications.

The next chapter will cover debugging. Some of the best programmers I have ever worked with were skilled in the area of debugging applications.

Debugging

Is this still the first read-through, or has the book been dusted off because there is a problem to be solved? In my experience, the debugging chapter is an afterthought. It usually only gets read when there is a problem. After all, no developer that comes to mind writes buggy code, so why would anyone read this stuff anyway?

Reading this chapter means one of two things: either SQL errors have popped up in some code; or there was a need for something to read on the PBL. That's right … every new book needs a new Three Letter Acronym (TLA). Our contribution to the world of TLAs is PBL: Porcelain Bowl Library. Yep, most good programmers do it! They read while taking care of business. So, there might as well be a fitting name for the place where some of our most effective reading is done. That ought to make you think twice next time you are borrowing someone else's book.

In either case, this chapter is about what to do about SQL errors, or other bugs, in an application.

Displaying Debug Information

To display debug information, click on the Debug link in the developer toolbar. The Debug argument in the URL can also be used. It is the 5th argument, as shown here:

```
http://localhost:7777/pls/hdb20/f?p=103:2300:10221629323751869385::YES
```

Looking at the output from a session in debug mode reveals several pieces of information. The following debug information is from the same page used in Figure 12.8 in this text. From the debug output, the following becomes apparent:

- There is some PL/SQL running in the BEFORE_HEADER processing point.

- In the AFTER_HEADER computation point, there is a static computation setting the session state for page item P2300_REGION_1.

- The AFTER_HEADER processing point has another PL/SQL procedure running.

- The elapsed time since the page rendering began can be seen. The 0.02 and 0.04 are how many seconds it took to get to this point in the page rendering process.

```
0.02: Fetch session header information
0.02: ...fetch page attributes: f103, p2300
0.02: Fetch session state from database
0.02: Branch point: BEFORE_HEADER
0.02: Fetch application meta data
0.02: Computation point: BEFORE_HEADER
0.02: Processing point: BEFORE_HEADER
0.02: ...PLSQL (BEFORE_HEADER) begin htp.p( 'BeforeHeader Process
Point' ); end;
BeforeHeader Process Point
0.02: Show page template header

0.02: Computation point: AFTER_HEADER
0.02: ...performing static computation
0.02: ...P2300_REGION_1 session state saving same value: "Must be
set with Before Header or After Header."
0.02: ...performing static computation
0.02: ...P2300_AFTER_HEADER session state saving same value:
"Must be set with Before Header or After Header."
0.02: Processing point: AFTER_HEADER
0.02: ...PLSQL (AFTER_HEADER) begin htp.p( 'AfterHeader Process
Point' ); end;
AfterHeader Process Point
0.04: Region: After Header
```

Troubleshooting a Performance Problem

To intentionally cause a performance problem to illustrate the troubleshooting process, I created another Before Region process on the page from Figure 12.8. The added code is guaranteed to show up in the debug output as a performance problem. The code is shown below. All it does is query a data dictionary view, but it will help the explanation.

```
declare
   n_count number;
begin
   select count(*) into n_count from all_objects;
end;
```

Running the same page is now going to take longer than it did previously. It should be noticeable. When any page takes noticeably longer, it should be run in debug mode. Debug mode on this example page will reveal the following output:

```
0.02: Computation point: BEFORE_BOX_BODY
0.02: ...performing static computation
0.02: ...P2300_TEMPLATE_BODY_1 session state saving same value: "Can
be set with any Points from above."
0.02: Processing point: BEFORE_BOX_BODY
0.02: ...PLSQL (BEFORE_BOX_BODY) declare n_count number; begin
select count(*) into n_count from all_objects; end;
2.99: ...PLSQL (BEFORE_BOX_BODY) begin htp.p( 'BeforeRegions Process
Point' ); end;
BeforeRegions Process Point
2.99: Region: Template Body 1
```

The page was loading fine until it hit that nasty PL/SQL statement. It had taken only 0.02 seconds to reach that statement. The next statement did not execute until 2.99 seconds. This shows the PL/SQL statement took 2.97 seconds. This information will help the developer take corrective action.

Troubleshooting SQL Errors

An earlier chapter mentioned that the semi-colon should not be included in the region source for a report. Well, on any given day, one could forget and include the semi-colon. The following sections show how to troubleshoot that and other SQL problems.

The following scenario involves working with the report built in the Conference RSVP application in an earlier chapter of this book. To create a problem, all I did was to add the semi-colon to the region source. Since the report is attempting to add an ORDER BY clause onto the SQL statement, it will cause an ORA-00911: invalid character error. What to do when that happens? Put the page in debug mode, of course.

Figure 17.1 shows that the select statement failed. Further examination of the SQL statement reveals there is a semi-colon located before the ORDER BY clause. The SQL statement can be modified, and the problem will be corrected.

Figure 17.1: *Displaying debug mode for troubleshooting.*

More About Troubleshooting

Is it not frustrating to work on an application page that was working fine, just to have it fail after one little change? Well, luckily there is a mechanism in HTML DB that shows the History of a page. This can help narrow down the change that caused the problem. To view the history of a page, navigate to the page definition screen, change the View to History, and click the GO button. This will reveal recent changes to the application page. It is not perfect, but sometimes it is the best place to start.

Isolating the Region with the Error

Sometimes it is difficult to determine which region is having an issue. Even more difficult can be determining which page process is causing a SQL error. To track down problems like this, it is common to set conditional display or conditional processing to a condition type of NEVER. This can either be done one-by-one or several at a time until the page runs correctly. At least then it is possible know where to focus debugging efforts.

SQL Trace

This is the ability for HTML DB to produce a trace file. Trace files can help identify where performance problems exist. Whenever a new or inexperienced developer is facing a performance problem, this feature can be used to produce a trace file, which can be shared with a DBA for analysis. For those experienced with the tracing sessions and using tkprof, it should be a relief to know it is very easy in HTML DB to produce a trace file. It is as simple as appending the proper information to the URL. The syntax to add to the end of the URL is shown below in bold (&p_trace=YES).

```
f?p=102:3:7646151020298818363::NO::P3_ID:28&p_trace=YES
```

The trace file will be written to the location identified by the Oracle parameter user_dump_dest. The trace file produced can be converted to a readable format using the tkprof program, which is provided by Oracle, and provides results similar to the following:

```
SELECT "ID","LAST_NAME","FIRST_NAME","EMAIL","PHONE",TO_CHAR("RSVP_DATE",
  'MM/DD/YYYY'),"COMPANY","DONATION","PAYMENT"
FROM
 "EASYHDB"."CONFERENCE_RSVP" WHERE "ID" = :B1
```

call	count	cpu	elapsed	disk	query	current	rows
Parse	1	0.00	0.00	0	0	0	0
Execute	1	0.01	0.00	0	0	0	0
Fetch	1	0.00	0.00	0	2	0	1
total	3	0.01	0.00	0	2	0	1

WWV_FLOW.DEBUG

The wwv_flow.debug can be used to display text information in an application page when the Debug argument of the command link is set to YES. This is a very valuable way for checking the session state of a page item during different processing points. Using the WWV_FLOW_DEBUG procedure in the PL/SQL from above reveals the following:

```
declare
  n_count number;
```

```
begin
   select count(*) into n_count from all_objects;
   wwv_flow.debug( '<b>Finished with really bad query.</b>' );
end;
```

On the application, it will be displayed when the page is rendered in debug mode.

Where this procedure can be extremely valuable is in a stored procedure within the database. There are times when a developer would want to know what the stored procedure is doing as well as having the ability to display it in an application is a great feature. A question posted on the HTML DB forum asked about being able to display the SQL statement being executed onto the application page. This can be done by including code similar to what follows in the stored procedure.

WWV_FLOW.SHOW_ERROR_MESSAGE

The WWV_FLOW.SHOW_ERROR_MESSAGE procedure will redirect the flow of the application to the error page and display the information provided in the arguments. This is intended for use in Page Processing processes or stored procedures being called during page processing, not page rendering. A sample procedure call is shown here.

```
wwv_flow.show_error_message (
   p_message   => 'The customer you were searching for does not
exist.',
   p_footer    => '<b>Customer not found.</b>',
   p_query     => 'select dummy from dual;' );
```

The results will be displayed on an error page as shown in Figure 17.2.

Customer not found.

Error The customer you were searching for does not exist.

<u>OK</u>

Figure 17.2: *Using SHOW_ERROR_MESSAGE.*

The value sent in the p_query argument from above is displayed inline as a comment in the HTML source for the page. Viewing the source in the browser, View → Source menu, reveals the SQL statement. It also shows the last query that executed from HTML DB giving a better idea of where to look for the problem.

```
<!--Application:"103" Page:"2701" User:"EASYDEV" -->
<!--request: "SUBMIT"-->
<!--command:select dummy from dual;-->
<!--lastQuery (1st 1000 chars):begin begin
   test_debug;
end;
 end;-->
```

Conclusion

Although debugging is not a favorite topic among programmers, it is necessary at times to have some debugging skills. This chapter exposed several troubleshooting techniques. As far as debugging goes in HTML DB, methods for how to debug the page rendering and see valuable information such as that needed to find a performance problem have been covered. Techniques for finding SQL errors both on screen in the rendered page and in a trace file on the database server were also included. Finally, the WWV_FLOW package was used to display additional error text on screen while in DEBUG mode.

The next chapter covers the HTML DB Application Programming Interface (API) and provides some explanation on its uses.

HTML DB API

The Application Programming Interface (API) essentially allows developers to write the language used internally by HTML DB. There is a powerful world available to the programmer who can use the API. The following is not a complete coverage of the HTML DB API. There simply is not enough room in this text. However, this chapter will serve as an introduction to commonly used API procedures and functions. This should provide enough experience to go further by referencing the HTML DB documentation.

To download the HTML DB documentation, navigate a browser to the following URL and click on the Books tab. That page will provide a link to download the HTML DB User's Guide (2.0).

http://www.oracle.com/pls/db102

HTMLDB_UTIL

The HTMLDB_UTIL packages provide several procedures that can be used in HTML DB or in stored procedures within the database. The HTML DB development environment provides other methods of performing the same function as many of these functions. However, when developing stored procedures, the same functionality is available through the use of the HTMLDB_UTIL package.

clear_app_cache
(p_app_id in varchar2 default null);

This procedure will clear all session state for the application provided in the parameter.

Example:

```
begin
   clear_app_cache( :APP_ID );
end;
```

clear_page_cache(
p_page_id in number default null);

This procedure clears the session state in the current application for the page provided in the parameter.

Example:

```
begin
    clear_page_cache( :APP_PAGE_ID );
end;
```

clear_user_cache;

This procedure will clear the cache for the current user. It will also remove all preferences for the user. The added benefit of this procedure is it will clear the cache for all applications in which the user has session state. The down fall is it clears the preferences. CAUTION: Doing this for your development login will reset any preferences that have been set, such as the View being set to Icon or Details for the page definition and other attribute pages.

Example:

```
begin
    clear_user_cache;
end;
```

get_current_user_id return number;

This returns the ID number of the currently logged in user.

Example:

```
declare
    n_id number;
begin
    n_id := get_current_user_id;
end;
```

get_email(p_username in varchar2) return varchar2;

This returns the email stored in the database for the provided username. This procedure can be used with the HTMLDB_MAIL package for sending mail.

Example:

```
declare
    s_email varchar2(255);
begin
    s_email := get_email( 'EASYDEV' );
end;
```

get_last_name(p_username in varchar2) return varchar2;

This returns the Last Name of the username specified. There is also a get_first_name function to return the user's First Name.

Example:

```
declare
    s_lname varchar2(255);
begin
    s_lname := get_last_name( 'EASYDEV' );
end;
```

get_username(p_userid) return varchar2;

This returns the username of the user ID provided.

Example:

```
declare
    s_username varchar2(255);
begin
    s_username := get_username( get_current_user_id );
end;
```

get_numeric_session_state(p_item in varchar2) return number;

This returns the value of session state converted to a number. HTML DB provides a shorthand function to the same thing, named NV.

Example:

```
declare
   n_salary number;
begin
   n_salary := get_numeric_session_state(:P100_SALARY);
   n_salary := nv(:P100_SALARY);  -- this does the same
end;
```

get_preference(
p_preference in varchar2 default null,
p_user in varchar2 default v('USER'))
return varchar2;

This returns the value of a preference for the user provided.

Example:

```
declare
   s_sort_pref varchar(255);
begin
   s_sort_pref := get_preference('SORT_PREF',:APP_USER);
end;
```

get_session_state(p_item in varchar2) return varchar2;

This returns the value of an item in session state. HTML DB provides a shorthand function to do the same thing, named V.

Example:

```
declare
   s_last_name varchar2(255);
begin
   s_last_name := get_session_state( :P100_LAST_NAME );
   s_last_name := nv( :P100_LAST_NAME ); --does the same
end;
```

remove_preference(
p_preference in varchar2 default null,
p_user in varchar2 default v('USER'));

This removes a stored preference for the username provided.

Example:

```
begin
   remove_preference( 'SORT_PREF', V( 'USER' ) );
end;
```

remove_sort_preference(p_user in varchar2 default v('USER'));

This removes the sorting preferences stored for the user. The sorting preferences keep track of how a user sorted a report in a prior visit to the web page. This is a way for HTML DB to sort the report the same way the next time the user visits the web page.

Example:

```
begin
   remove_sort_preference( V( 'USER' ) );
end;
```

set_preference(
p_preference in varchar2 default null,
p_value in varchar2 default null,
p_user in varchar2 default null);

This procedure will store a value for the user in persistent session state. The persistent session state is called a preference. The next time the user visits the application, the preference can be restored.

Example:

```
begin
   set_preference( 'SORT_PREF',
      'LNAME:FNAME', V( 'USER' ) );
end;
```

set_session_state(
p_name in varchar2 default null,
p_value in varchar2 default null);

This procedure will set the session state for an item. This is valuable because it allows the session state of page items to be set from within a stored procedure.

Example:

```
begin
   set_session_state(:P100_CUSTOMER_ID,n_customer_id);
end;
```

string_to_table(
p_string in varchar2,
p_separator in varchar2 default ':')
return htmldb_application_global.vc_arr2;

This converts a delimited string into a PL/SQL array. This function is primarily used when working with checkboxes, multi-select lists and radio buttons. Examples are shown in detail in another chapter of this book.

table_to_string(
p_table in htmldb_application_global.vc_arr2,
p_string in varchar2 default ':')
return varchar2;

This function is the partner to string_to_table. It will convert an array into a delimited string. When selecting data from a database table, this function can be used to set the session state for a checkboxes, multi-select lists and radio buttons. Examples are shown in detail in another chapter of this book.

url_encode(p_url in varchar2) return varchar2;

This converts special characters to hexadecimal value.

Example:

```
declare
   s_url varchar2(255);
begin
   s_url := url_encode(
      'http://localhost/search?hl=en&lr=&q=htmldb' );
end;
```

HTMLDB_CUSTOM_AUTH

application_page_item_exists(
p_page_item in varchar2)
return boolean;

Sometimes there may be a stored procedure or PL/SQL, such as an application level process, that works for several application pages. This function gives the ability to check for the existence of a page item.

Example:

```
begin
    if htmldb_custom_auth.application_page_item_exists(
        'P100_CUSTOMER_ID' ) then
        -- Do something.
end;
```

get_session_id return number;

This returns the users session id. It can be used within stored procedures. For example, if audit records are being inserted in the database, this function can be used to get the session id.

Example:

```
declare
    n_sid number;
begin
    n_sid := htmldb_custom_auth.get_session_id;
end;
```

get_username return varchar2;

This returns the authenticated username. If the application page is public, the return value will be NOBODY.

Example:

```
declare
    s_username varchar2(255);
begin
    s_username := htmldb_custom_auth.get_username(
        get_username );
end;
```

login(
p_uname in varchar2,
p_password in varchar2,
p_session_id in varchar2,

p_app_page in varchar2,
p_entry_point in varchar2,
p_preserve_case in boolean);

This procedure performs authentication and session registration. It is commonly referred to as the Login API.

Parameters:

- p_uname: User's Login name.

- p_password: Password in clear text.

- p_session_id: Session ID of the current session.

- p_app_page: Application ID and page ID of where to navigate to after login. Format APP_ID:APP_PAGE_ID (colon delimited).

- p_entry_point: Used internal by HTML DB only.

- p_preserve_case: If TRUE, do not change case of p_uname to uppercase.

Example:

```
begin
    -- Only use V( ) when referencing APP_SESSION
    login( 'MCUNNING', 'easybook',
        V('APP_SESSION'), :APP_ID || ':1' );
end;
```

HTMLDB_MAIL

The ability to send email from HTML DB is provided by the HTMLDB_MAIL package. This package uses the UTL_SMTP package in Oracle.

send(
p_to in varchar2,
p_from in varchar2,
p_body in [varchar2 | clob],
p_body_html in [varchar2 | clob] default null,
p_subj in varchar2 default null,
p_cc in varchar2 default null,
p_bcc in varchar2 default null);

The send procedure is used to send email. The two columns, p_body and p_body_html will accept either a data type of varchar2 or clob. However, they must match each other. If a varchar2 is used in one, the other must be NULL or a varchar2. The same holds true for a clob. They need to match or be NULL.

Example:

```
declare
    s_pager easy_person.pager%type;
begin
    select pager
    into   s_pager
    from   easy_person
    where  id = :P1080_ID;

    htmldb_mail.send(
       p_to => s_pager,
       p_from => 'easyhtmldb@rampant.cc',
       p_body => :P1080_TEXTMSG,
       p_subj => 'Text message from HTML DB' );
    htmldb_mail.push_queue( 'localhost', 25 );
end;
```

htmldb_mail.push_queue(
p_smtp_hostname in varchar2 default,
p_smtp_portno in number default);

When using the htmldb_mail.send procedure to send emails, a mail queue is used. Mail is sent from the queue at ten minute intervals. This procedure can be used to force the mail in the queue to be sent immediately. An example of that is shown in the example code for the htmldb_mail.send procedure.

HTMLDB_ITEM

The HTMLDB_ITEM package can be used to create your own page items. The normal way, of course, is to create them on the application page using the wizards. However, if the need ever arises to create them in a web application dynamically at runtime, this is how it is done.

The most common use for the HTMLDB_ITEM package is in a report or tabular form. The most common of all the procedures is the checkbox procedure. This was used extensively in the information on Checkboxes. A few of the HTMLDB_ITEM procedures are outlined below. With the examples provided, users should have enough information to go the HTML DB documentation and be able to use the rest of the dynamic page item procedures.

checkbox(
    p_idx in number,
    p_value in varchar2 default,
    p_attributes in varchar2 default,
    p_checked_values in varchar2 default,
    p_checked_values_delimiter in varchar2 default)
    return varchar2;

This procedure can be used to dynamically create checkboxes on a web page during rendering. This procedure is covered in detail in an earlier chapter.

Parameters:

- p_idx: This indicates the ID number of the global htmldb_application variable. The range of values is one to 50. A ten will product a page item with the name f10. It can then be referenced with htmldb_application.g_f10.

- p_value: This is the value of the check box. This is the return value that will be in the g_f10 array if the checkbox is checked when the page is submitted.

- p_attributes: HTML tags can be added here.

- p_checked_values: These are the default values to be checked. A valid value here is 4:5:2:4

- p_checked_values_delimiter: This is the character used as the delimiter for the p_checked_values parameter.

Example:

```
-- This code is a sample of what would be used to
-- create a checkbox in an HTML DB report.
select
   class_id, class_name,
   htmldb_item.checkbox( 10, class_id,
      decode( available_flag, 'Y', 'CHECKED', NULL) )
      AS available_flag
from  ...
```

hidden(
p_idx in number,
p_value in varchar2 default)
return varchar2;

This procedure can be used to create a hidden page item at runtime.

Parameters:

- p_idx: This indicates the ID number of the global htmldb_application variable. The range of values is one to 50. A ten will product a page item with the name f10. It can then be referenced with htmldb_application.g_f10.

- p_value: This is the value to set or the hidden field.

Example:

```
select
   class_id, class_name,
   htmldb_item.checkbox( 10, class_id,
```

select_list_from_lov(
p_idx in number,
p_value in varchar2 default,
p_lov in varchar2,
p_attributes in varchar2 default,
p_show_null in varchar2 default,
p_null_value in varchar2 default,
p_null_text in varchar2 default,
p_item_id in varchar2 default,
p_item_label in varchar2 default)
return varchar2;

This procedure can be used to dynamically build a select list on a web page. The procedure accepts the name of a defined LOV and displays its contents in an LOV. The parameters should be familiar, as they are attributes of the select list when they are created using the wizards.

Parameters:

- p_idx: This indicates the ID number of the global htmldb_application variable.

- p_value: This is the current value. When the select list is rendered, this is the default selected item.

- p_lov: This is the text name of a defined LOV.

- p_attributes: These are the extra HTML parameters to be added.

- p_show_null: This will add an extra item to the select list as a NULL selection. Acceptable values are YES and NO.

- p_null_value: This is the value of the NULL select list item. This is the value set in session state if the NULL item is selected. p_show_null must be set to YES.

- p_null_text: This is the value displayed for the NULL select list item. p_show_null must be set to YES for the NULL text to display in the list.

- p_item_id: This is the value to render in the HTML <input> tag for the ID attribute.

- p_item_label: This is the text to display for the label of the select list.

Example:

```
select first_name, last_name,
       htmldb_item.select_list_from_lov( 1, trade_id,
          'TRADES', null, 'YES',
          '-1', '- Select Trade -'  ) trade
from   union_member
where  member_id = :P110_MEMBER_ID;
```

select_list_from_lov_xl(
   p_idx in number,
   p_value in varchar2 default,
   p_lov in varchar2,
   p_attributes in varchar2 default,
   p_show_null in varchar2 default,
   p_null_value in varchar2 default,
   p_null_text in varchar2 default,
   p_item_id in varchar2 default,
   p_item_label in varchar2 default)
   return varchar2;

The select_list_from_lov_xl procedure is the same as the select_list_from_lov except this procedure will populate a select list that contains more than 32K of data. Attempting to use the select_list_from_lov with data larger than 32K, the following error will result:

```
ORA-06502: PL/SQL: numeric or value error: character string buffer
too small
```

The select_list_from_lov_xl procedure can be used to remedy the error.

select_list_from_query
```
        htmldb_item.select_list_from_query(
        p_idx in number,
        p_value in varchar2 default,
        p_query in varchar2,
        p_attributes in varchar2 default,
        p_show_null in varchar2 default,
        p_null_value in varchar2 default,
        p_null_text in varchar2 default,
        p_item_id in varchar2 default,
        p_item_label in varchar2 default,
        p_show_extra in varchar2 default )
        return varchar2;
```

The select_list_from_query procedure will dynamically render a select list on the web page. A query for the select list to use for the data can be provided.

Parameters:

- Except for p_query, the parameters of the select_list_from_query are the same as the select_list_from_lov above.

- p_query: Enter the query to use for the population of the select list. The query must return two values: one for the display data; and one for the return value. Also, the query must not contain the customary semi-colon on the end or an error will occur.

Example:

```
select first_name, last_name,
       htmldb_item.select_list_from_lov( 1, trade_id,
           'select desc, id from union_trade order by 1',
```

```
        null, 'YES', '-1', '- Select Trade -'  ) trade
from    union_member
where   member_id = :P110_MEMBER_ID;
```

select_list_from_query_xl
htmldb_item.select_list_from_query(
p_idx in number,
p_value in varchar2 default,
p_query in varchar2,
p_attributes in varchar2 default,
p_show_null in varchar2 default,
p_null_value in varchar2 default,
p_null_text in varchar2 default,
p_item_id in varchar2 default,
p_item_label in varchar2 default,
p_show_extra in varchar2 default)
return varchar2;

The select_list_from_query_xl procedure is the same as the select_list_from_query except this procedure will populate a select list that contains more than 32K of data. Using the select_list_from_query with data larger than 32K will result in the following error:

```
ORA-06502: PL/SQL: numeric or value error: character string buffer
too small
```

The select_list_from_query_xl procedure can be used to remedy the error.

HTMLDB_APPLICATION

The HTMLDB_APPLICATION package exposes several global variables used internally by the HTML DB engine.

- g_user: This is the ID of the currently logged in user.

- g_flow_id: This is the ID of the currently running application.

- g_flow_step_id: This is the page ID for the currently running application page.

- g_flow_owner: This is the parsing schema for the current application.

- g_request: This is the most recent REQUEST. Requests are set by buttons in HTML DB.

The HTMLDB_APPLICATION package also exposes a global array which references values from certain page items. The HTMLDB_ITEM package can be used to create items on an application page. This means the developer creates them programmatically during page rendering instead of creating the page item with a wizard. When items are created like this, they are provided a numeric value. HTML DB then references the page item in an array. Up to 50 items can be created using the HTMLDB_ITEM package and still be allowed to reference them using HTMLDB_APPLICATION package. An example of this was provided during the checkbox explanation in an earlier chapter of this book. There, the htmldb_item.checkbox procedure was used to add checkboxes to a report. The arrays in the htmldb_application package were then used to reference the checkbox during page processing.

For the checkboxes shown in Figure 10.3, the HTML code that was rendered by using the htmldb_item.checkbox procedure looks like the following:

```
<input type="checkbox" name="f10" value="1" CHECKED />
<input type="checkbox" name="f10" value="2" CHECKED />
<input type="checkbox" name="f10" value="3" />
<input type="checkbox" name="f10" value="4" CHECKED />
<input type="checkbox" name="f10" value="5" />
```

When the page is submitted, only the checkboxes which are checked will appear in the arrays of the htmldb_application package. For the example above, there will be three array elements in the array named g_f10. Programmatically, it is possible to loop through the array in a page processing process and update the data in the database. The following code shows an example of how the code to loop through the htmldb_application.g_f10 array would look:

```
begin
  for i in 1..htmldb_application.g_f10.count loop
    update class
    set    available_flag = 'Y'
    where  class_id = htmldb_application.g_f10(i);
  end loop;
end;
```

While looping through the array and using the sample checkboxes from above, the values one, two, and four would appear in the array.

HTMLDB_COLLECTION

Collections were covered in an earlier chapter, but only a couple of procedures were shown there. The following section provides a larger list of many of the procedures commonly used while managing collections.

create_collection(p_collection_name in varchar2);

This procedure is used to create a new collection. If the collection exists, the delete_collection must be used first.

create_or_truncate_collection(p_collection_name in varchar2);

This procedure is used to delete all the data in the collection and leave the collection available.

create_collection_from_query(
p_collection_name in varchar2,
p_query in varchar2,
p_generate_md5);

This can be used to create a new collection and populate it with the results from the query provided. The p_generate_md5 parameter will produce a checksum value that can be used to check if data has changed.

delete_collection (p_collection_name in varchar2);

This procedure deletes the specified collection and all data in the collection.

delete_all_collections;

If multiple collections are in used, they can all be deleted with this procedure.

collection_exists (p_collection_name in varchar2) return boolean;

This procedure returns a Boolean if the collection exists. It can be used to check if a collection exists before calling create_collection. If it does exist, the delete_collection procedure should be used to delete it first.

add_member(p_collection_name in varchar2,

p_c001 in varchar2 defualt null,

...

p_c050 in varchar2 default null,
p_clob001 in clob default empty_clob( ),
p_generate_md5 n varchar2 default 'NO') return number;

This is used to add a new member to the collection.

This procedure returns the count of members in the collection.

collection_member_count(p_collection_name in varchar2);

This returns the count of members in the collection.

OWA_COOKIE

The Oracle Web Agent (OWA) packages are not part of the HTML DB installation, but they do warrant some coverage since HTML DB uses them. They are further documented in Oracle document B10802. The name of the document is PL/SQL Packages and Types Reference. It is a huge document and a valuable asset to which developers and programmers should have ready access. The document can be found by using the link at the top of the chapter.

The OWA_COOKIE package deals with browser cookies. It will write to a cookie and read from a cookie stored on the client machine. If no date is specified, the cookie only exists during the client's session.

Types used with the OWA_COOKIE package

```
type vc_arr is table of varchar2(4000)
index by binary_integer.

type cookie is record (
name varchar2(4000),
vals vc_arr,
num_vals integer);
```

owa_cookie.send(
name in varchar2,
value in varchar2,
expires in date default null,

path in varchar2 default null,
domain in varchar2 default null,
secure in varchar2 default null);

This creates a cookie on the client browser machine. The expires date should be specified or the cookie only exists during the life of the session.

Example:
```
begin
   owa_util.mime_header('text/html', FALSE);
   owa_cookie.send(
      name=>'EASY_COOKIE',
      value=>lower(:P2100_COOKIE_SOURCE),
      expires => sysdate + 365);

   -- Set the cookie and redirect to another page
   owa_util.redirect_url(
'f?p=&APP_ID.:2101:&SESSION.' );
exception
   when others then
      null;
end;
```

get(name in varchar2) return cookie;

This will return a type of cookie as explained earlier. It receives the name of the cookie to return.

Example:
```
declare
    v varchar2(255) := null;
    c owa_cookie.cookie;
begin
   c := owa_cookie.get('LOGIN_USERNAME_COOKIE');
   :P2100_COOKIE_TARGET := c.vals(1);
exception
   when others then
      null;
end;
```

owa_cookie.remove(
name in varchar2,
val in varchar2,
path in varchar2 default null);

This procedure forces the cookie to expire, which essentially removes its availability to be used. It does this by setting the expiration date to 01-JAN-1990.

Example:
```
begin
    owa_cookie.remove(
        name => 'EASY_COOKIE',
        value => NULL);
end;
```

print_cgi_env

This prints all CGI environment variable's available to the CGI Gateway. This procedure can be placed directly in a PL/SQL region to display the values of all the CGI variables. Put the following code in the PL/SQL region:

```
print_cgi_env;
```

OWA_UTIL

print_cgi_env

This prints all CGI environment variables available to the CGI Gateway. This procedure can be placed directly in PL/SQL region to display the values of all the CGI variables.

get_cgi_env(param_name in varchar2) return varchar2;

This returns the value of a single CGI environment variable.

Example:
```
owa_util.get_cgi_env( 'HTTP_HOST' );
```

Conclusion

This chapter provided a brief overview of some of the more common API procedures and functions used for building HTML DB applications. Some of these helpful procedures and functions, like the htmldb_item.checkbox function, were used in examples in previous chapters. As you gain experience with HTML DB, you will find yourself using the HTML DB API to extend the functionality of your applications.

Index

H

About Kent Crotty

Kent Crotty is an Oracle Certified DBA and a graduate of the University of Maryland with a Bachelors Degree in Computer Science. He is an IT professional with over 15 years of experience in a variety of roles ranging from Programmer/Analyst (developer) to Systems and Database Administrator. Kent is instrumental in developing complex Oracle systems architectures and specializes on web-based Oracle applications.

Kent lives in Raleigh, NC with his 3 dogs. He enjoys many different hobbies especially designing and building stunt kites. You can see him out in the grass fields on any windy day flying his kites. His next endeavor is to become certified in scuba-diving.

About Michael Cunningham

Michael Cunningham is a Database Administrator for an insurance company in Northern California. His responsibilities include database monitoring, performance tuning, disaster recover management, and some UNIX administration. He has more than 12 year of IT experience of which 10 was spent as a software engineering and the last two and a half years as an Oracle Certified database administrator.

Michael is proud to have served in the United States Marine Corps from 1983-1987 where he specialized in Electronic Countermeasures. Currently he is trying his thumb at growing his own grapes and hopes to make his own barrel (yep, just one) of wine in 2006. If Michael isn't at home you will find him traveling in his RV with his family or pulling small trees from the bottom of a lake with his fishing hook.